In Pursuit
of Principle
and Profit

ALSO BY ALAN REDER

*Investing from the Heart: The Guide to Socially Responsible
Investing and Money Management* (with Jack A. Brill)

In Pursuit of Principle and Profit

BUSINESS SUCCESS
THROUGH
SOCIAL RESPONSIBILITY

Alan Reder

A Jeremy P. Tarcher/Putnam Book
published by
G. P. Putnam's Sons
New York

A Jeremy P. Tarcher/Putnam Book
Published by G. P. Putnam's Sons
Publishers Since 1838
200 Madison Avenue
New York, NY 10016

Published simultaneously in Canada

Library of Congress Cataloging-in-Publication Data

Reder, Alan.
In pursuit of principle and profit : business success through
social responsibility / Alan Reder.
p.   cm.
"A Jeremy P. Tarcher/Putnam book."
Includes bibliographical references.
ISBN 0-87477-781-X (hard : alk. paper)
1. Social responsibility of business. 2. Business ethics.
3. Success in business.   I. Title.
HD60.R444   1994   94-11916 CIP
658.4'08—dc20

Design by Irving Perkins Associates, Inc.

Printed in the United States of America
1   2   3   4   5   6   7   8   9   10

This book is printed on recycled paper.

To the memory of my parents, Herb and Edith Reder.
This book is your child too, born in your hearts.

Contents

— ❧ —

phase of the research. Marjorie Kelly and Deborah Bihler provided a subscription to their magnificent magazine, *Business Ethics*, an inestimable resource of material on this subject. Fritjof Capra and his staff supplied a useful reference on environmental auditing.

Passion is as crucial to good publishing as it is to good writing. The fervor and personal enthusiasm that publisher Jeremy Tarcher and editor Connie Zweig shared for the subject matter of this project became part of its spirit. An especially gifted editor, Connie taught me valuable lessons about my craft with her incisive comments and corrections.

Many executives, managers, communications directors, consultants, nonmanagerial employees, and others shared their insights and experiences in interviews and provided valuable information, including: Elliot Hoffman of Just Desserts; Gary Hirshberg and Lynn Turner of Stonyfield Farm Yogurt; Gun Denhart, Gretchen Fields, and Stephanie Weiss of Hanna Andersson; Julie Lewis and Bruce McGregor of Deja Shoe; Suzanne Apple, Mark Eisen, Don McKenna, and Jerry Shields of Home Depot; Betty Schoenbaechler, Virginia Stone-Mackin, Edith Banta, Susan Howard, Vickie Dorsey, Mike Eremchuk, Angelia Burrell, Tina Ragin, Ron Garrett, Julie Turner, Lynn Drury, and Martha Larsh of NationsBank; Jim Kelly of Rejuvenation Lamp & Fixture; Errol Louis and Mark Griffith of Central Brooklyn Federal Credit Union; Bud Beebe, Robert Wichert, and Dace Udris of the Sacramento Municipal Utility District; Frank Navran of Navran Associates; Lisa Conte, Shari Annes, and Trish Flaster of Shaman Pharmaceuticals; Joanne Skinner of Nolo Press; Brent Stull of Kreonite, Inc.; Steve Manning of The Nature Company; Mel Bankoff, Rick On, and Pat Fagan of Emerald Valley Kitchen; Ron Spector of A Thread of Hope; Vivian Jenkins Nelson of INTER-RACE; Michael Levett of Businesses for Social Responsibility; B. J. Stiles of the National Leadership Coalition on AIDS; Lee Berry of Project PRIDE, American Red Cross; Larry Arney of Habitat for Humanity, Atlanta; Robert Frey of Cin-Made Corporation; and Joyce Shearer of Tabra, Inc.

Bill Ashworth's perspective on environmental economics greatly expanded my own. Our conversations over bagels and coffee at the Key of C in Ashland, Oregon, also introduced me to some of the best bagels in the West, and I ought to know. Bill supplied valuable reference material as well. I hope he's as anxious to read this book as I am to read his new one, *The Economy of Nature*.

Hyiah Reder, Sherman Severin, Bryan Frink, and Kevin Buck reviewed the manuscript and gave me valuable feedback. Bryan's input, in fact, helped me find a more focused book within the original draft.

Diane Franklin, good luck to both of us.

And again, thank you all.

PART I

The Practical Side of Business Responsibility: An Introduction

CHAPTER 1

Social Responsibility: The Double Bottom Line

IN AN OLD JACK BENNY ROUTINE, a mugger stops the frugal comic and demands, "Your money or your life!" For several long moments, Benny says nothing. The mugger snaps, "Well?" Benny answers, "Don't rush me, I'm thinking, I'm thinking!"

We often accuse business leaders of having a similarly misplaced sense of priorities, but they can't be entirely blamed when money—specifically, profit—is the lifeblood of their game. A company won't long survive if it doesn't ultimately take in at least somewhat more than it pays out.

Of course, a business's profitability depends upon it attaining any number of subgoals. Conventional management wisdom tells us that a company's ultimate success results from such attributes as

- The creation of products and services that are wanted and needed in the marketplace
- Employees who are skilled and knowledgeable, particularly with the demands of today's global, high-technology economy; who are loyal, because high work-force turnover is both disruptive and exceptionally costly; and who, at minimum, do not undermine the company's goals with below-par workmanship and customer service
- A management team that understands how to inspire both that

work force to perform competently and customers to purchase the company's output

That's just for starters. Executives know that companies that rise above the competition often distinguish themselves in other ways.

· Their employees are unusually productive and efficient, caring for the company as if it were their own; or
· Employees at all levels contribute creatively to the business, offering practical, innovative, money-making or money-saving ideas; or
· Management is uncommonly sensitive and responsive to changes in today's almost continually transforming marketplace; or
· Customers actually delight in buying the company's products and services and love to talk them up to other potential customers

Notice that social responsibility hasn't been mentioned yet. Placing it this high on a goals list probably wouldn't occur to the average manager, even one motivated to "do the right thing" whenever possible. However, as you will see, social responsibility helps ensure that virtually every quality of a successful company will emerge over time, and thus greatly increases a company's chances of long-term success.

Of course, it's much easier to pontificate about social responsibility in business than to get specific about what it means. Speaking at a 1993 conference I attended in Atlanta, Kirk Hanson, Stanford University Graduate School of Business lecturer and first president of The Business Enterprise Trust, an organization that honors exemplary business behavior, noted: "I don't think we [in the socially responsible business movement] have been able yet to articulate the overall vision of what business responsibility is. When people go to look for that overall vision, they sometimes think it's the 1960s agenda. Maybe it's the political agenda of a particular administration. Sometimes, they think it's whatever's on Ralph's [Nader, another conference presenter] mind that day and what his particular programmatic concerns are."

Kirk's right. My friends and acquaintances in the socially responsible business community include some individuals who are as distrustful of government regulation and big government in general as any Fortune 500 Republican, although they would likely break with their conservative counterparts on most issues involving business's obligations to society. I belong to the Social Venture Network (SVN), a leading national organization of socially conscious business leaders (the group, in fact, that Hanson was addressing), but I don't know of any poll that's ever been taken of members' social attitudes. Besides, many of these folks are so iconoclastic and creative in their thinking that I don't think a poll could capture them.

Therefore, much of what I will label "socially responsible" below and in the following chapters has not been submitted to a vote by any policy committee. But this label does reflect to a large extent the public behavior and explicit mission statements of many of these companies. Accounting for inevitable differences between organizations, it also reflects criteria that the socially responsible investment community, in which I traffic as well, uses to screen stocks and other investments for their clientele. Assume that unless otherwise credited, further articulation of these categories is my own.

An all-encompassing notion, social responsibility refers to both the way a company conducts its internal operations, including the way it treats its work force, and its impact on the world around it. Most socially responsible business and investment leaders endeavor to further the following agenda of ethical policies and practices:

- Reducing to the greatest degree possible the damage a company causes the environment
- Contributing in every conceivable way to environmental preservation, through resource conservation and energy efficiency, through environmentally conscious purchases and product design, through publicly auditing its environmental performance, and so on
- Not doing business in repressive regimes such as South Africa was prior to the ending of apartheid and such as Burma is today
- For companies doing defense contracting, not lobbying for the sale of weaponry to unstable regimes, otherwise resisting the classic military-industrial complex temptations, and converting to peacetime industries to the greatest degree possible in a post–Cold War world
- Aggressively hiring and promoting women and minorities, including to the company's upper management positions and board of directors
- Providing employees with a safe, clean, healthy work environment

- Helping employees care for their children and dependent elderly family members through such arrangements as dependent care assistance and flexible time
- Protecting employees from sexual harassment
- Fairly compensating employees for their labors and not undermining employees' right to organize
- Providing permanent, domestic jobs to the greatest degree possible
- Not exploiting campaign finance and lobbying laws for narrow corporate ends
- Obeying all laws and regulations affecting the company's industry
- Conducting international business in a nonexploitive manner and a manner consistent with the company's stateside policies and practices
- Humanely treating animals, including not testing products on them when appropriate alternatives exist
- Allowing employees to share the wealth they help generate through stock ownership, incentive pay, or other means
- Encouraging employees at all levels to contribute ideas and participate in critical company decision-making
- Giving something back, in the form of charity or voluntary community involvement, to the community and society in which the company does business
- Purchasing in the most socially conscientious manner possible, including contracting with minority- and women-owned companies and applying environmental standards to vendor relationships
- Designing high-quality, durable products that are safe for the consumer and make a beneficial impact on society
- Marketing products or services only in socially appropriate manners (i.e., not exploiting ethnic and gender stereotypes, not exploiting vulnerable markets such as children or Third World populations, and so on)

This still partial list ignores many specific points explored later in this book. Nevertheless, it does demonstrate the range of activities encompassed by the term "social responsibility," a wide range indeed because social responsibility implies conscientious attention to every conceivable social impact of a company's activities. Most items on the list run absolutely counter to conservative economist Milton Friedman's oft-quoted line that "the business of business is business." They run counter as well to the protests of many corporate leaders that environmental restrictions, family-leave legislation, safety regulations, giving employees stock in the company and a voice in decisions, and such impair a company's ability to compete.

However, the chorus of protesters has grown less robust as its numbers shrink. Many managers and company owners who first implemented socially responsible policies and practices simply as a matter of principle have reaped rewards in the form of improved employee allegiance, productivity, and work quality; management insight and creativity; and customer loyalty. As Arnold Hiatt, former chairman of Stride Rite Corporation and leading spokesman for the "enlightened self-interest" approach to social responsibility, told *Newsweek*:

> We look at public service as an investment. We believe the well-being of a company cannot be separated from the well-being of the community. If we're not providing the community with access to day care and eldercare, if we're not providing proper funding for education, then we're not investing properly in our business. . . . [As for the costs], take our family-leave policy. It costs us next to nothing. And yet the statement it makes to employees is powerful. It says to them that we care. And when employees know you care about them, they tend to be more productive. It's the same with our day care. To me, it's a no-brainer.

The burgeoning socially responsible investment field has also maintained that good company behavior makes for good business. The best evidence to support their claim has been the steady performance of socially responsible mutual funds and stock portfolios. Many of the socially responsible mutual funds have outperformed the average funds in their investment category over the long term. In single years, some have led the nation. Despite the inevitable runts, the field overall demonstrates that social investors need not concede any profits to invest in socially responsible companies. One implication is that picking stocks by applying both ethical and financial criteria identifies a high percentage of well-run companies.

The above are just a few items in a growing list of evidence suggesting that many companies that are doing well today are doing so in large part because of their socially responsible policies and practices.

Their success also implies that those companies that have not implemented socially responsible practices might well improve their performance by taking that step.

An Idea Whose Time Is Overdue

However economists and executives regard the socially responsible business approach, time is running out on unprincipled business behavior because of the pace of social change and environmental decay. Whether or not global warming turns out to be scientific fact, the climate, as far as business is concerned, has changed forever. Consider that

- Women and minorities now constitute most entrants into the labor force.
- Minorities are becoming such a huge proportion of the general population that the very term "minority" may be meaningless by the middle of next century.
- Human activity has already exceeded the planet's carrying capacity, according to several leading environmental experts.
- The extinction of many valuable resources, American old-growth timber and Third World rainforest hardwoods among them, is now within sight, and scarcity of potable water has already begun to occur in several nations including the U.S.
- Increasingly significant numbers of consumers are applying social criteria to their purchasing decisions.
- The federal government, saddled with $4 trillion in debt, and the strapped governments of many states find themselves incapable of addressing major social problems, at least in ways requiring large infusions of dollars. This leaves corporate America with the uncomfortable challenge of maintaining earnings in a decaying social milieu unless it finds a way to help reverse the decline.
- Many of today's dominant industries—forestry, chemical-based agriculture, petroleum, beef cattle–raising, passenger vehicle manufacture, to name just a few—are based on socially untenable premises and processes. In other words, their supposed economic viability has been figured without taking into consideration environmental and other societal costs, costs that society will soon determine it can no longer afford. In fact, the besieged

forestry industry is already experiencing the effects of such resistance. Speeding the approach of their obsolescence is the fact that each of the industries mentioned could be replaced or retired today with environmentally appropriate alternatives. In fact, the forestry industry has quietly pursued a transition to non-timber paper fibers and alternative wood products such as manufactured lumber even as it loudly campaigns to chain-saw the rest of America's trees.

I will examine each of these trends in detail in upcoming chapters, including future-friendly products and services.

Making a Difference Socially and Otherwise

The Body Shop and Ben & Jerry's Homemade stories have been related almost as often as tales of young Abe Lincoln reading by candlelight. These outstanding business citizens remain, despite the occasional contrary impression conveyed by cynical reporters, pre-eminent examples of "values-driven businesses," or in less formal terms, what Ben & Jerry's calls "caring capitalists." Virtual legends on the basis of incendiary growth alone, these companies not only make few social compromises, relative to mainstream firms anyway, but devote considerable energy and resources to aggressive social initiatives.

Stonyfield Farm Yogurt's story, although not nearly as widely known, is hardly less inspiring. Co-founders Samuel Kaymen and Gary Hirshberg started the New Hampshire–based business in 1983 not to become international yogurt moguls but to fund educational efforts in sustainable agriculture and other appropriate rural technologies. Hanging on with their fingernails to the romance of a farm-based enterprise, Kaymen, his wife, Louise, and Hirshberg milked the cows at the Kaymens' hilltop farm in Wilton, in addition to making and delivering the yogurt, financing the business, and running a nonprofit farm school.

However, the yogurt was so good that demand began to crowd out the romance. In 1984, they let the herd go and started buying milk from local farmers. By 1988, they had outgrown the picturesque farm entirely, and moved the operation to a custom-designed yogurt works in nearby Londonderry.

If exceptional quality had gotten them this far, a broader approach to social responsibility was about to carry them to the top strata of their industry. In 1989, Stonyfield Farm began to invest more heavily "in our people, in our facilities, in basically making the place happier," CEO Hirshberg told me when we spoke in early 1994. "We also poured more money into our cause-related efforts on behalf of family farms and sustainable agriculture. And that's when we turned the corner." Stonyfield started growing at a clip of 50 percent per year, a pace it had maintained for five years running as of this writing in January 1994.

"We're far and away the fastest growing yogurt company in the country if not the world," Gary said. "That fifty percent is top-line growth, but we're also showing fantastic bottom-line results. I think that our success is a result of a whole bunch of things that we're doing and you couldn't pull away any of them and achieve the same levels."

Since every Stonyfield socially responsible policy or practice seems to have played its part in the company's explosive growth, let's dissect the combination. Social responsibility, of course, starts at home with how you treat your employees. In at least one area—career advancement—few treat them better than Stonyfield. In 1993, *Inc.* magazine named Stonyfield as one of the best small companies to work for in America for its commitment to internally post all new job opportunities and hire from within whenever possible. As of this writing, nineteen of twenty-two Stonyfield managers were promoted from within the organization, including production manager Ed Souza, a former limousine driver who started as a yogurt checker five years before.

You don't have to be a supervisor at Stonyfield to share in the goodies. Thanks to the leadership's dedication to open communication, employees at all levels have the opportunity to contribute ideas, on everything from planning and management to plant design, and to hear in detail what's going on with the company financially. The latter particularly intrigues them because the company pays incentives, in the form of cash bonuses and stock options, ranging from between 18 and 23 percent of pretax profits. Employees can also determine their own benefit package, through participation in a benefits committee that surveys the staff on their preferences.

Terrific employee relations don't by themselves define a socially responsible company, and they don't define Stonyfield. Conceivably, a company might lavish stock, high pay, and lovely work conditions on its work force only to make employees feel ashamed of their jobs because of a venally conceived product or environmental practice. Instead, this company's slogan to its customers, "We make you feel good inside," could apply to the way employees feel about their employer, as well as the product their labor produces. Stonyfield Farm's yogurt is not an entirely organic product because making it so would price it far beyond what even health purists have shown they're willing to pay. But it is as wholesome and chemical-free as it can be in current market conditions, which is why you'll find it in so many health food store refrigerators.

One of America's most charitably minded outfits, Stonyfield donated over 7 percent of profits to civic, charitable, and arts organizations in fiscal year 1993. For fiscal year 1994, the company has committed over 5 percent of revenues to advance the cause of sustainable agriculture, and 14 percent of net profits to environmental causes overall, including the premium they pay to buy milk from local farmers using sustainable methods.

Stonyfield's public citizenship doesn't end with the relatively simple act of writing checks. Hirshberg, a trustee of the Audubon Society of New Hampshire, helped found Audubon Associates, an organization of business leaders that meets on environmental issues. The company also works with other corporate sponsors to support New Hampshire arts and humanities and is an active member of three organizations—the Social Venture Network, Businesses for Social Responsibility, and New England Businesses for Social Responsibility—dedicated to advancing socially responsible business practices here and around the world.

Environmentally, Stonyfield has completed an energy audit of its production facility for the purpose of upgrading it to a demonstration-quality energy efficient plant; has hired an environmental auditor to help the company reduce all of its other environmental impacts; and is organizing other food manufacturers using similar plastic packaging to create a recycling infrastructure for its yogurt containers.

On behalf of the health of its customers and survival of its small dairy suppliers, Stonyfield has also campaigned against federal approval of bovine growth hormone (BGH). The hormone, which requires an increased use of antibiotics for dairy herds, may lead to contamination of the milk supply. It could also drive numerous family farms out of business by creating a milk surplus, thus further concentrating America's food supply in the hands of large, environmentally

destructive agribusiness. Among myriad other environmental initiatives, Stonyfield has also dedicated a yogurt flavor, Guava Papaya, to
the preservation of Amazon rainforest and the indigenous cultures
living there.

As Hirshberg presented the numbers to me, the company dedi-
cates some 30 percent of profits to its social mission and obviously
considerable human energy besides. That's not the usual formula for
success, especially for a still relatively small business. But it works for
Stonyfield. As Gary put it, "Our happy employees make better yogurt
and make customers feel better. So there's no question to me or to
anybody here—you could ask anyone in the company—that morale
here is very high and really contributes to our success." One unmistakable sign of that high morale: almost nonexistent turnover,
about one employee per year, Gary estimates, although he acknowledges that pressure has increased with the pace of growth.

Skeptics will undoubtedly point to the marketing advantages of
Stonyfield's highly visible community initiatives. Indeed, like The
Body Shop, Stonyfield does no advertising, while benefiting from
frequent free, positive press coverage. But Hirshberg stresses that the
economic benefits of the company's social stance help further its
mission: "I think a litmus test of all socially responsible practices is
that they be win-win. They've got to be more profitable. Otherwise,
they're not going to pass the test of time."

Stonyfield's example would boast little more than curiosity value if
it were unique. But it is not. A growing number of successful American businesses define themselves as idealistically as does Stonyfield
and then proceed to walk their talk. Many, such as Patagonia, Esprit,
Aveda, South Shore Bank, and Tom's of Maine, have begun to take
their places beside Ben & Jerry's and The Body Shop in the iconogra-
phy of conscientious companies.

And just beneath this tier of high-ideals businesses are a number of
successful major American corporations who, while defining their
social goals more modestly, still seek to balance their profit-making
charge with their social roles as influential organizational citizens.
Pitney Bowes, for one, seems to have found no conflict between large
market shares and profits, on the one hand, and ethical management,
on the other. The company not only hires a high percentage of women
and minorities but promotes them as well. Its 23,669 U.S. employees
include 8,722 women and 6,425 minority workers. Among the 2,746
regarded as upper management, there are 714 women and 354 minor-

ity employees. This equal opportunity attitude extends into Pitney Bowes' purchasing activities: It purchased 13.8 million in products and services from minority-owned firms in 1993.

Among work and family policies instituted before the 1993 family leave legislation, the company offers primary caregivers 90 days of unpaid leave beyond typical leave, runs a childcare resources and referral program, and allows flexible time to be negotiated between employees and supervisors. On the environmental front, three full-time staff—the director of Corporate Safety and Environmental Affairs, the manager of Corporate Environmental Engineering, and the corporate hygienist—monitor the company's environmental performance, including its waste minimization program. The company has put itself on the line with a publicly announced goal of zero discharge of hazardous pollutants by 1996.

Today, corporate campaign contributions have virtually crowded the interests of individual citizen voters, not to mention the general public interest, off the political stage. Pitney Bowes can't by itself change the equation but, on principle, its executives refuse to play. The company gives no money to PACs and its corporate credo bans the backing of political candidates.

Pitney Bowes is no more alone in its league than Stonyfield is on its turf. In addition to several corporate citizens with strong all-around ethical records such as Levi Strauss, Southwest Airlines, Federal Express, Donnelly Corporation, and Fel-Pro, several major corporation have demonstrated, in particular aspects of their operations, the economic attributes of socially responsible practices even if the company as a whole can't be held up as exemplary. For example, Reebok, with its human rights code for overseas business relationships, argues for a new social compact in the global economy.

Social Responsibility: A Process, Not a Position

Earlier in this chapter, I rendered a preliminary laundry list of socially responsible business behaviors. But Gary Hirshberg, for one, is under no illusion that social responsibility describes any special moral high ground: "We've realized that there isn't any black and white out there when it comes to being socially responsible or environmentally responsible. There's just a whole lot of gray. My idealism is still very much alive but the ultimate irony of a Stonyfield is that maybe less resources would be consumed if we didn't exist. We confront this dilemma daily."

In fact, the enormity of the environmental challenge to even conscientious companies keeps most of the socially responsible business leaders I know fairly humble. It might be philosophically tidy to define socially responsible business behavior as behavior that does not harm society, but that doesn't hold up in practical terms. Nearly all manufacturing, for example, involves some piggish level of energy use and probably other forms of waste and pollution as well. Even environmental organizations have to swallow hard over the trees they devour when they do mass mailings about, say, forest preservation. *Sierra* magazine analyzed its own product in late 1993 and discovered to its horror that, among other disturbing impacts, publishing the magazine resulted in the leveling of old-growth forest.

It's also impossible to describe behavior that doesn't harm society without first limiting how you define society. Business affects many constituencies: employees, customers, stockholders, the local community where it operates, local businesses in that community, society at large (including future generations), the company's industry, and the business community at large. Behavior that benefits one constituency may well harm another one. So, socially responsible decision-making is a process, not a choice between obvious rights and wrongs, or as Gary describes it, "The real issue is commitment, intent, and then progress toward achieving your intent." Socially responsible businesses are those that make it their business to engage themselves in that process—unrelentingly.

Toward a Social Bottom Line

The mythology of American business grew out of the pioneering drive that established this nation—the self-made success story, the tough-minded manager who will accept nothing less than the achievement of a stated goal, the ingenuity of great inventors like Edison, Bell, and the Wright brothers. I find it at once ironic and, to say the least, contradictory for some business and government leaders first to trumpet their roots in our "can-do" business history, and then to shriek that economics and environmental preservation or economics and fair labor practices can't possibly be reconciled.

We find what we seek. More specifically, we predetermine our answers by the questions we ask. In the social arena, many of our existing problems seem to defy solutions because instead of asking ourselves the fundamental and unfettered question of how to solve them, we try to get away cheaply by asking what minor surgeries we can perform on the status quo.

For example, faced with smog-choked cities, clean-air mandates, and the prospect of outright bans of automotive traffic in some international cities, European and Japanese automakers are racing each other to develop the first environmentally viable passenger vehicle. The corporation that wins the race will be the one that asks the right question: How can we power an acceptably performing automobile without polluting at all?

America's automakers, seldom comfortable with fundamental research and development that would distract them from short-term goals, have entered the contest with one foot on the gas pedal and the other on the brake. Although faced with the prospect of severe clean-air mandates at home, they've approached the challenge by formulating the least challenging self-query possible: How can we preserve the infrastructure supporting our current meal ticket? They announced their answer in late 1993: Instead of emphasizing zero-emissions vehicles, they would modify existing technology to drop emissions by 70 percent within a decade. In addition, they would use this commitment to persuade states to adopt permissive clean-air standards that allow for their new vehicles.

Ultimately, this strategy is doomed to environmental failure because an increase in cars on the road or in miles driven per trip can overwhelm any pollution saved by tweaking the technology, just as happened with catalytic converters. By framing their search for an environmentally improved car in this unimaginative and socially unresponsive manner, our automakers have all but guaranteed that one of their competitors, not them, *will* solve the problem and patent it. Perhaps that competitor will be Mazda, which *has* asked the basic question and is now developing a hydrogen-powered Miata. If they are successful, they could well own the automobile future because the only by-product of hydrogen combustion is water.

The analogy—that fundamental questions asked unflinchingly can solve seemingly complex human problems—applies to management issues, too. For example, many executives wonder how they can get employees to act like partners in the company. Packagers Cin-Made Corporation (Cincinnati) and engine rebuilders Springfield Remanufacturing (Springfield, Missouri) asked the question without qualifying it and got the obvious answer—*make* employees partners through stock ownership plans or other financial incentives, teach them the things that partners need to know, and give them a say in company decisions. The new partners in turn produced spectacular results for the executives who empowered them.

Another question that many frustrated managers ask is, "Just what *do* employees want these days?" But few ask it of the employees themselves. At Stonyfield, management took the more direct route, and it's been a key to the company's outstanding performance. "We've had seven or eight benefits that we've implemented that have been what the employees asked for," Stonyfield's Gary Hirshberg notes. "That's been a big factor in our high morale, that employees say 'We want this' and they get it six months later. That's pretty rare in business, I think, but it's the alternative to our approach that doesn't make sense to me."

Business responsibility in general begins with such basic questions as: "How do we make a difference socially and still survive as a business?" and "How do we minimize our impact on the environment and still make a profit?" instead of the usual "How do we maximize profits this quarter and to hell with the fallout?" In the following pages, we'll meet many executives like Gary Hirshberg and see many companies like Stonyfield that appear to do everything wrong—diverting enormous portions of company resources and energy into social initiatives, investing in workers for the long haul, and ruling out all business opportunities predicated on social exploitation—because they're asking different sorts of questions. But they're still making money hand over fist—and proving, as *Business Ethics* magazine editor Marjorie Kelly puts it, "that the profit motive is not inherently wicked, but is rather a powerful engine that can be harnessed for virtually any purpose—including a socially responsible one."

The business advantages of orienting a company toward social responsibility hardly stop with creating more loyal and productive line employees and more devoted customers. In *Newsweek*, Stride Rite's Arnold Hiatt noted how social responsibility also leads to a more sensitive management corps: "If you develop a certain acuity in listening to consumers, you also learn to listen well to your employees and to the community."

Hiatt's remarks speak to one of the essential, natural connections between social responsibility and profits. The company attuned to the needs of its customers, work force, and community also grows more in touch with shifts in the marketplace, culture, and its own internal functioning. Becoming more sensitive enables the company to do what all winning competitors do—that is, respond faster. This, not at all coincidentally, is also the literal definition of responsibility: response-ability, the ability to respond.

PART II

—— ❧ ——

Social Responsibility Between Company Walls

⁂

CHAPTER 2

Beyond Fairness: Diversity and Demographics

WE CALL THEM "GOOD OLD BOY NETWORKS" — insiders' loops of Caucasian men who play golf and cards together, drink together, share the same insiders' jokes, and ultimately hire and promote each other. Good old boys dominate nearly every significant American business, at least at management levels. And that fact hardly bodes well for those companies, now and in the future, because white males are a rapidly shrinking proportion of the population, particularly the working population. White men filled less than a third of the 10.7 million jobs created between 1985 and 1990, *Business Week* has noted, and they'll fill far fewer still in the decades ahead— only 10 percent of the new jobs added in the next ten years, the Labor Department projects.

Clearly, most of the new talent, including management talent, is either female, people of color, or both. Few businesses can maintain their competitive edge without changing their hiring and promoting habits to draw from those talent pools. And no business can retain that talent or motivate it unless management ensures that female and minority employees have every opportunity to advance and prosper that white males traditionally have enjoyed.

From a marketing standpoint as well, companies that cut minorities and women out of the decision-making loop may inadvertently be cutting themselves out of the competitive loop. After all, which companies are best able to reach the rapidly expanding minority markets? Which companies will best be able to take advantage of the growing buying power of women? Obviously, those companies whose decision-makers know those markets best.

Of course, a company's hiring and promotion practices don't always say much about its overall ethics. As Council on Economic Priorities founder Alice Tepper Marlin pointed out at a 1993 Social Venture Network conference, Philip Morris's only ethically strong programs, promoting minorities and women, target the same populations it works hardest to addict to its deadly product.

Ideally, businesses would provide equal opportunities to women and minorities solely out of the desire to play fair. In fact, the most progressive equal opportunity employers, such as Ben & Jerry's Homemade or Patagonia, demonstrate a commitment to equitable treatment that makes even the obvious monetary advantages seem beside the point. But while we may bemoan the fact that more businesses do not act out of such saintly concerns, we should celebrate the fact that, when it comes to equal opportunity, the purely pragmatic considerations mentioned above will compel smart companies to act in a manner that also serves a larger purpose.

Of course, running an equal opportunity shop requires far more cultural reform than simply adjusting the gender and ethnicity numbers or applying the same rules to everyone. Women, for example, not only bear children but, in most families, also bear the primary responsibility for their children's care. Add to this fact the increasing numbers of women who are entering the work force, plus the increasing numbers of single mothers and single fathers, and it's easy to see that employees' conflicts between work and family issues unavoidably concern their employers as well.

Companies new to fairness initiatives also will discover that the good old boy networks don't go into retreat just because there are a few more women or people of color on the floor. It's one thing for a company to hire more women and minorities. It's quite another for management to ensure that the subtle workings of its white, male culture don't subvert its efforts to level the playing field. White men can't jump? Don't tell that to a black worker who watches a less able Caucasian male leap past him/her in promotions and salary.

Of course, the dominant culture's prejudices also put at a disadvantage older workers, people with disabilities, and immigrants. And gays can't even count on the legal prohibitions against discrimination that give the aforementioned groups some measure of recourse. Each of these populations constitutes an important share of today's eligible work force. Each will play a bigger part in the American work force of the future.

Diversity Means Equal Opportunity Plus

Today, we speak of "diversity" rather than "equal opportunity" when we refer to gender- and culture-fair workplaces. The difference in nomenclature isn't just a "politically correct" artifice. "Equal opportunity" evokes images of the 1960s, but the civil rights movement's bitterly won achievement, integration, has since proven to be an insufficient goal. Minorities and women have indeed made their way through the personnel office obstacle course in ever-increasing numbers, only to hit invisible barriers outside its doors.

Those barriers, subtle as they were to discern, exposed the futility of the idea of assimilation and led to the more contemporary notion of "diversity-fairness." The newer term means embracing diverse cultures, not just forcing the diverse hires to blend in, because if blending in is what the company demands, then minorities and women are at a nearly insurmountable disadvantage in a good old boys' world. Promotions, like most other rewards in life, are rarely conferred on the basis of merit alone. Playing golf in your superior's foursome never hurts. Neither does sharing in whatever sexist or ethnically prejudiced banter might originate in the executive suite. For minorities and women to have the same access to the promotional ladder as the good old boys, the company's culture must bend—backwards, it will sometimes seem—and change to allow for cultural differences.

Woman-Fair Workplaces

While life may be lonely at the top for a male executive, it's near solitary confinement for females. Of *Business Week* magazine's top thousand companies in 1992, exactly one was run by a woman. Women are entering the work force in ever-increasing numbers. In

1992, they made up about 46 percent of the civilian labor force according to the U.S. Bureau of Labor Statistics. But once in, they don't get promoted at anywhere near the pace of males, particularly white males. Nor do they get paid nearly as well, even for comparable work and qualifications.

The following numbers tell the story: In 1968, according to *Business Week*, women held 15 percent of all management positions. Yet, while normal progress should have landed a similar percentage in senior management positions today, only about 3 percent have made it that far. True, the overall percentage of women managers has increased to 41 percent, the same publication notes, and half of the corporate entry-level management corps is now female, compared to 15 percent in 1979. But women get stuck somewhere on the upward climb. In 1972, they held only 1 percent of senior management positions. Two decades of "breakthroughs" later, they hold but 3 percent today. That's what is meant by the "glass ceiling."

Holding up the glass ceilings in today's workplaces are glass walls. Before an employee can advance vertically in most companies, he/she must gather experiences and credentials in key areas such as production, marketing, and sales. However, because of unintentional stereotyping in male-run companies, women tend to be steered away from these critical positions and into auxiliary functions such as human resources, finance, law, public relations, and so on.

Catalyst, a New York–based nonprofit research organization that studies women's issues in the workplace, investigated the "glass walls" phenomena by interviewing senior and middle managers from large corporations. The results, published in early 1992, illuminated the typical biases at play when male-run companies shunt women away from "line" jobs. Among the rationales offered by the study's subjects: women are hired into support positions because they are thought to be good support providers; men feel uncomfortable dealing with women in nonstereotypical, authoritative positions; and men fear that women will be unable to balance career and family. Sixty percent of the human resources managers interviewed said that putting women in line jobs was "risky."

Women get shortchanged at the pay window, as well. In fact, after making incremental gains in the late 1980s, women actually lost ground to men in 1991, earning 70 cents for every dollar earned by a man, down from 72 cents the previous year. During the economic slump of 1992, the gap narrowed substantially—women earning 75 cents on the male dollar—but only because men's wages fell faster than women's, noted in a *Working Woman* magazine story.

Because such studies don't always compare apples to apples, some researchers have compared the earning power of men and women with similar credentials. For example, an academic study by professors from Loyola and Northwestern universities followed the career progress of a thousand midlevel managers at twenty corporations. All subjects shared comparable education, career-orientation, and job functions. Over the five years of the study, the women's salary raises trailed the men's by 11 percent. Summing up, co-author Linda K. Stroh stated, "The women had done all the same things, and yet their progress was less and they earned less. The women were not only disadvantaged but discriminated against."

"Discrimination"—a nasty charge, to be sure, but one that's hard to refute. Even Lynn Martin, Secretary of Labor in the heavily pro-business Bush administration, alluded to it when analyzing her department's report of its "Glass Ceiling Initiative." Most of the report focused on pilot studies of nine corporations. The companies ranged in size from fewer than eight thousand employees to more than three hundred thousand, and varied widely in products and services offered. "But they had one thing in common," Martin wrote in an op-ed commentary. "They didn't make [advancement opportunities] as available to minorities and women."

The discrimination uncovered by the Labor Department project was not necessarily overt. Good old boy networks usually function more *reflexively* than *reflectively*, as the study demonstrated. Again, Martin: "Word of mouth, employee networking and mentoring were used by a number of companies to select senior management. . . . Many companies used executive search firms, but they usually forgot to remind the firms that they wanted a slate of candidates that included qualified individuals from all segments of society. . . . Most of the companies also failed to integrate equal employment responsibilities throughout the corporate structure." Nor, she added, did the companies studied monitor their advancement procedures for fairness.

GENDER-FRIENDLINESS

Lynn Martin did not mention one other significant factor that makes it tough for women to advance in most companies: The cultures of those companies, having evolved under male leadership, simply do not accommodate the special needs of women. For instance, most women will become pregnant at some time during their working life, yet few American companies offer much support for working parents.

Nor do many companies consider women's needs when planning daily calendars. Many companies expect their managerial personnel to work after-hours or attend hastily called late-hours meetings. Such scheduling fails to consider the demands on a working parent, especially one with young children and rigid day-care arrangements. Some companies schedule meetings in the early morning when a parent may well experience unforeseen problems getting children off to school or day care, and then don't forgive when the employee shows up late as a result. Women also face greater safety concerns than men, particularly in dim parking lots and rough neighborhoods after dark. As columnist Ellen Goodman has asked, how many qualified women avoid seeking management positions because they know the company will do little to protect them from late-hours dangers?

When women do make the grade in a male-dominated company, they often do so at the sacrifice of their own essence. National Minority Supplier Development Council president Harriet Michel, speaking at a 1993 Social Venture Network conference workshop, "Women in Power," said: "I was the executive director of the New York Foundation from 1970 to 1977. [We held our board meetings] in these very elegant Wall Street boardrooms and they would come around and offer cigars and brandy to everybody but me. So I decided the hell with it, I would smoke a cigar, too. I thought that was the way to be taken seriously. I cut my hair off because I thought having long hair in the 1960s and '70s made some sort of negative statement about me in the workplace. I wore severe clothes and very little makeup. What I've come to find out, of course, is that's all just crap. I've lived long enough to understand that the best way that we as women can influence the institutions in which we find ourselves is just be ourselves, be women."

Unfortunately, few women have reached sufficient executive heights to experience Michel's hard-earned sense of freedom. In a 1992 *Business Week* poll of female executives, 59 percent said the rate of progress for women had slowed down, stopped altogether, or worsened. Seventy percent reported that a male-dominated culture was an obstacle in their company.

THE FINANCIAL UPSIDE OF GENDER FAIRNESS

Doing the right thing vis-à-vis female employees also means doing the smart thing. As a *Business Week* editorial noted, "No company will be able to compete in an increasingly competitive world by willfully ignoring half its talent." And talent is just half the picture—insight into women's purchasing preferences is the other. Not only do more women work today, but more women head households, which means that more women make significant buying decisions outside the stereotypical confines of the supermarket and shopping mall. The companies best positioned to tap these markets are those with women in key decision-making roles in marketing, production, sales, and the boardroom.

Take auto sales, for instance. As of 1991, women were buying 49 percent of all new cars sold in the U.S., according to Ford Motor Company statistics, up from 36 percent just a decade earlier. While automakers increasingly consult women's advisory committees on design changes, marketing, and advertising, few employ women in positions with real decision-making power, which has led to some major blunders. For example, designers, an almost exclusively male profession in Detroit, burdened several years' worth of minivans with truck beds that were too high for most women carrying armloads of packages, even though the vehicles were planned with the family-oriented car buyer in mind. The designers finally corrected the problem, but only after inconvenienced female customers complained, notes an Associated Press story. Women designers might well have anticipated the oversight and solved it on the initial drawing board.

Gender-biased marketing faux pas also have plagued the industry. Advertisers often have assumed that women care far more about an automobile's looks than its performance, and have otherwise played to gender stereotypes. Surveys do reveal differences between men's and women's preferences. Women are more safety conscious, for one thing: when asked to list top-priority options, they most often name airbags and antilock brakes. However, the same surveys show that women care no less about performance and mileage than do men. "*Ms.* readers were so grateful for a routine Honda ad featuring rack and pinion steering, for instance, that they sent fan mail," wrote the magazine's founder Gloria Steinem in 1991.

Advisory committees have helped automakers avoid repeating past sins. Still, such committees only make suggestions: they don't vision or implement. Considering that women now compose about half the car-buying market, a female auto executive who knows how to reach other women can make a huge difference for her employer. Witness Jan Thompson's impact on Mazda. Thompson, marketing vice president for the Mazda division of Mazda Motor of America, Inc., is the highest-ranking woman in American auto sales. Industry experts credit much of Mazda's suddenly solid performance during the early 1990s auto slump to Thompson's contributions. In 1991, *Business Week* notes, the general market dropped 12 percent, Mazda only 2 percent. In 1992, Mazda showed a small sales increase, against an industry whose sales remained flat.

Thompson succeeded at Mazda not so much by circumventing the good old boys as infiltrating them. According to *Business Week's* Larry Armstrong, Thompson can match car talk (and expletives) with any male in the company. She has also spent long hours playing golf and hanging out with the boys. (She has since prodded the company into sponsoring the Mazda Golf Clinics for Executive Women, which teaches the game as a business networking device.) But her marketing approach drew on more conventional feminine instincts. Blatantly pursuing the undertapped female buyer, she junked "the Mazda way" campaign and its man's-man voice, James Garner, in 1988, in favor of a more sensitive, personal appeal. The next year, Mazda introduced its sporty Miata roadster and a new theme for all its ads, "It just feels right." The buying public's spectacular acceptance of both led a company sales turnaround.

Overlooking capable women like Thompson costs a company in other ways, too, especially if they get sued for it. In January 1992, a court awarded American Airlines employee Barbara Sogg $7 million in a discrimination suit. According to *Business Week*, she had charged that the company declined to promote her as general manager of operations at La Guardia Airport in favor of a younger, less-experienced man. A state judge later reduced the award to $3.8 million, which, as of this writing, American is appealing.

In late 1993, Lucky Stores agreed to pay up to $107 million to settle claims from thousands of women employees, past and present, after a federal judge ruled that the company had discriminated against them. As reported by the Associated Press, the judge found that while women composed only about half of newly hired personnel in its Northern California stores in the late 1980s, they were 84 percent of the employees in two departments, deli-bakery and merchandise, which paid less than others and offered little chance of promotion. The company argued unsuccessfully that women tended to prefer those jobs and daytime work in general.

New motherhood, a thankless enough job at home, has been a downright liability to mothers at some workplaces, but that too is changing with newer judicial rulings under the Pregnancy Discrimination Act (PDA) passed by Congress in 1978. Up to eighty thousand American workers lose their jobs each year after becoming pregnant. While many women employees lack recourse because of PDA exemptions (for example, the law exempts employers without sick leave policies, a loophole through which many small companies pass), others have won courtroom victories that expand the act's scope. For instance, in 1991, an Illinois federal court ruled that auto parts outfit Warshawsky & Company's sick leave policy discriminated against pregnant women by excluding all first-year employees. The reasoning, as reported in *Business Ethics* magazine: Since only women can get pregnant, they were eleven times as likely as the firm's males to be discharged in their first year of work. Forty states and numerous city and county ordinances also protect pregnant workers from discriminatory actions by their employers.

Minority-Fair Workplaces

During the early 1990s, disagreeable and widely publicized incidents involving Denny's and Shoney's restaurant chains awakened memories of a time some thirty years before that many Americans thought had passed forever. Black customers in several Denny's locations around the country, including a group of federal agents in Annapolis, Maryland, preparing for a visit by President Clinton, accused management of slighting them by not seating or serving them nearly as promptly as white patrons (the agents' charge), assessing "cover charges" before seating them, and not honoring its free birthday meal policy with them. Meanwhile, Shoney's settled a massive lawsuit in 1993 for promoting a culture of bias throughout the organization.

These alleged injustices, if true, *were* throwbacks, but more in their blatancy than their ultimate effect. Despite numerous outstanding exceptions, business as a whole has been slow to both make amends for past injustices and recognize its pragmatic stake in fairness toward minorities.

Making a workplace minority-fair justifies itself for the same short-term financial reasons that purging the company of its gender biases does. Reason Number One: the talent pool—as the numbers of white males entering the work force shrink, the numbers of minority job entrants are rapidly expanding. Reason Number Two: markets—minorities also make up a rapidly increasing percentage of the overall population (28 percent as of this writing, perhaps near 50 percent by 2050, the Census Bureau estimates). Business needs the input of minority decision-makers to reach these buyers, which are growing, however fitfully, in both cumulative and per capita purchasing power.

Business's responsibility to be fair to minorities also overlaps with its long-term pragmatic interests. The economic troubles of African-Americans, Hispanics, and Native Americans trouble the overall economy as well. (Rarely even figured into the minority equation, Native American families on reservations receive only about one third the income of white families, as compared to Hispanic families making about two thirds of white family income and blacks a little less than that.) Because American business is no innocent bystander to those troubles, it can play a big part in helping alleviate them. Besides, its stake in minority talent and markets only grows greater as time passes and minority populations expand.

A short refresher course in the recent socioeconomic history of African-Americans, the most studied minority, illustrates business's dual role. The mainstream American economy mostly excluded African-Americans until the federal government implemented the 1964 Civil Rights Act, which banned employment discrimination and mandated fair hiring practices to help African-Americans catch up. President Lyndon Johnson, whose lead would be followed by subsequent administrations (until Ronald Reagan) fortified the act with a series of directives designed to make the rhetorical goal of equal opportunity a reality.

Affirmative action, as the strategy was called, stirred up considerable white resistance. White-run companies resented Washington's bureaucratic invasion of their personnel offices. Less consciously, of course, they resented being forced to confront their hiring biases. And white employees and job applicants resented what they viewed as preferential treatment for African-Americans, rarely considering the preferential handling that whites previously and, despite affirmative action, still largely enjoyed in the overall job market.

Nevertheless, affirmative action became entrenched in most larger companies and many smaller ones, formalized in written policies and often overseen by a manager whose sole function was to coordinate it. The results, at least in overall job hiring, were as intended. In 1966, African-Americans, then about 10.5 percent of the U.S. population, composed only about 8 percent of the work force (as measured by their share of jobs in companies with a hundred or more employees). By 1989, their share of those jobs had risen past 12 percent, about the same as their expanded proportion of the population, and their median annual earnings had climbed as well.

But these statistics concealed as much as they revealed. Though African-Americans were getting through the front door of many companies that would have been closed to them in the past, few got much farther. As of 1991, less than 24 percent of the African-American work force held managerial, professional, or administrative jobs, compared to 59.5 percent of whites, according to Labor Department statistics. African-Americans were gaining, *Business Week* observed—they held 5 percent of the managerial positions in the U.S. by 1990, a fivefold increase from 1966 and a 30 percent increase from 1978. But their representation in management still considerably lagged their overall percentage of the population. Only a sprinkling of those positions were in upper management; many were in the same dead-end, "glass wall" departments such as human resources and public relations to which women managers were consigned.

As for annual earnings, African-American women made most of the gains; African-American men don't earn much more today than they did twenty years ago. In addition, like women in general, the narrowing earnings gap between whites and African-Americans is partly due to white males earning less than they did in 1969, and white females only marginally more.

As *Business Week* noted in a 1991 feature, African-Americans' progress has slowed considerably, both because of the hostile Reagan and Bush administrations and structural economic changes that affect minorities disproportionately. Led by Reagan and then Bush from the White House's bully pulpit, the Republican Party cried "quota" at every public opportunity to seduce blue-collar, backlashing Democrats over to their side. Backing rhetoric with action, both administrations sought to undermine voluntary and court-ordered affirmative action, despite its general acceptance by both their conservative Supreme Court and businesses most affected by the laws. Many companies, lacking moral commitment to affirmative action in the first place, noted the administrations' attitude, communicated in racial code words and symbols, and relaxed their own efforts. As of the end of 1992, the *Wall Street Journal* reported, African-Americans and Hispanics held only 3 percent of Fortune 1000 board seats, a percentage that had not changed in the previous five years.

This poisonous atmosphere persists post-Bush. In June 1993, conservative Republicans and pundits squealed "quota queen" when President Bill Clinton nominated progressive law professor Lani Guinier as Assistant Attorney General for Civil Rights, causing cowed Democrats on the Senate Judiciary Committee, and ultimately a racially sensitive but politically cautious President, to abandon her nomination with hardly a whimper.

Unable even to depend on what, in other times, would be a friendly White House, African-Americans are also being battered by changes rumbling through America's economic structure. Domestic manufacturing jobs used to be the urban African-American's ticket to economic security. The jobs paid well and often required few skills, an unbeatable combination for those from impoverished neighborhoods and inner-city schools. But those jobs have been disappearing overseas for some time now (8 million jobs from 1979 to mid-1992, noted *Business Week*), along with other good jobs for the less-skilled in light manufacturing industries such as apparel. And the pace will pick up as global competition intensifies and international trade agreements are hammered out.

Advancing technology has devoured vast numbers of other jobs. In fact, the low interest rates of the early 1990s and hefty increases in benefit—particularly health care—costs spurred many companies to replace people with machinery much sooner than they might have otherwise. The only "promising" job market for the lesser-skilled is in the service sector, where many jobs pay miserably and offer few, if any, benefits. The pervasive image of the former $17 per hour autoworker flipping burgers for minimum wage and no "bennies" is not exactly raising hopes in the inner city or inspiring youth to stop dealing drugs.

Obviously, these trends hurt whites, too. A *Business Week* writer observed that from 1973 to 1989, annual incomes of low-skilled whites in their twenties fell 14 percent (after adjusting for inflation). But African-Americans suffered more, much more. Over the same period, the annual income of African-American men in their twenties plummeted 24 percent, including 50 percent for high school dropouts!

Finally, of course, minorities suffer from prejudice, which in many quarters persists undiluted from the pre–civil rights era. According to a poll cited in *Business Week,* fewer than one white in ten reports being victimized by reverse discrimination, unmasking the bias behind the backlash. But the most damaging prejudice is that at the top, where a company's commitment to fairness begins. Says Vivian Jenkins, president and CEO of the cross-cultural consulting organization INTER-RACE: "One problem is that many companies headed by the older generation are insensitive to racial prejudice. They think that the civil rights and women's movements made their gains and now nothing more needs to be done." Without identifying the person or company, she mentioned the head of one major insurance carrier who asked, "Is there a need for black insurance agents? Do blacks buy insurance?"

THE BOTTOM LINE OF AFFIRMATIVE ACTION

Business leaders as a whole comprehend that most new hires in the coming years will continue to be women and minorities. Let's look more closely at the other major pragmatic consideration driving the smart company's fairness to minorities—the expanding minority marketplaces. As of the early 1990s, minority markets already were purchasing more than any foreign country in our trading circle. Although major marketing campaigns already target minorities, by the year 2050, according to census bureau projections, 47 percent of Americans may be nonwhite, upping the stakes considerably. The African-American population alone earned $278 billion in 1991, according to U.S. Census Bureau data.

Smart marketing decisions begin with understanding the chosen markets. Yet men and women find each other's behaviors baffling enough; toss in cultural differences and comprehension shrivels to near nothingness. In very general terms, Asian-Americans do not see the world the same way as African-Americans, who view life through a different set of cultural lenses than do Hispanics. Cultural values also vary with subgroups. To cite just one obvious example, the term "Asian-American" applies equally to people of Korean, Filipino, Chinese, Japanese, Vietnamese, and other clearly distinct heritages.

Values and behaviors change with generations as well. First-generation Japanese-American women tend to be far less assertive than non-Asians, but not so with third-generation Japanese-Americans.

No group of white decision-makers can hope to sort cultural factors into strategic marketing decisions as effectively as can a decision-making group that is more representative of the whole population. Smart companies know this. What they don't always know is what to do about it—specifically, how to nurture the careers of nonwhites in a white culture.

Smart companies also realize that prejudicial business behavior gets pricey when contested in the courtroom. In January 1993, Shoney, Inc., settled a racial discrimination class-action suit for $105 million, the largest award of its type ever against a private employer. As reported in *Business Week*, the charges covered the gamut of discriminatory practices: limiting the number of African-Americans hired at some restaurants; hiring all-black staffs in black communities but the reverse in white neighborhoods; hiring African-Americans only into the lowest-paying, nonmanagerial, and nonprofessional positions. Coincident with its legal troubles, the $1 billion, 1,800-restaurant company's fortunes slid in 1992 and 1993. Business analysts blamed the decline on, among other things, old ads and a stale menu. Musty hiring and promotion attitudes were not mentioned. It would be most unfair to assume that Shoney's settled for reasons other than putting the matter to rest. Nevertheless, the debacle is yet one more illustration that forward-thinking companies tend to be far less vulnerable to the troubles that have eaten away at the Shoney empire.

THE QUOTA QUESTION

Prominent critics have so relentlessly labeled affirmative action efforts as "quotas" that the public should be excused for thinking the two terms synonymous. In fact, government affirmative action directives prohibit quotas. Nevertheless, quotas creep into the system both because of the inevitable workings of government bureaucracy and because of the less than committed manner in which many companies conduct their programs. The federal government will generally require companies that contract with it to outline an annual affirmative action plan, which can include specific goals and timetables for increasing the diversity of the work force. When companies settle discrimination suits, they often consent to numerical targets as part of the deal. As a *Business Week* writer described the dilemma, "In effect, quotas are prohibited and required at the same time."

More perniciously, some companies that lack any altruistic commitment to affirmative action will deliberately "quota-fy" the program to guarantee minimal compliance. For example, the system does not penalize companies for operating their affirmative action program as a revolving door—that is, hiring a set percentage of, say, African-Americans into designated jobs, and simply replacing them with others from their "category" whenever some leave.

Do such token, uninterested efforts mean that affirmative action has been a failure? Hardly. Despite its many imperfections, affirmative action has greatly increased minority participation in the economy, benefiting both business and society at large. In those companies where racism and sexism still pervade the atmosphere, affirmative action, including numerical goals and timetables, may prod them to reform. In more sensitively run but not fully diverse companies, affirmative action guidelines set a minimal standard by which they can measure their progress. Besides, corporate America by and large supports affirmative action, despite conservative politicians' manipulation of the issue in business's name. In fact, some of our biggest companies, such as AT&T, Xerox, IBM, Polaroid, and Johnson & Johnson, are among its most vigorous proponents.

Numerical measures always will play a part in remedying current and past discrimination. How else would we measure? But forward-looking executives know that redoubling their efforts to hire and promote minorities and women is also wise business strategy. When they examine the numbers pertaining to labor and consumer markets, the affirmative action numbers become moot.

COMPETITION AMONG MINORITIES

The fight among minorities for hiring priority sometimes rivals in ferocity the overall fight for fair employment. Is there such a thing as a "more deserving" minority? The government won't make such a politically touchy determination. Do preferences for one minority disadvantage others? Without question, in companies that play the game by the numbers. And as minority populations expand, the competition will likely grow nastier.

In a profound irony, African-Americans have become the most

"advantaged" minority in terms of the remedies offered by majority society. For a variety of reasons including collective white guilt over the legacy of slavery and segregation, African-Americans have become the most studied minority and their issues have come to dominate public debate. As such, they're also the minority that's often first served. Even the progressive organizations that track corporate behavior for socially responsible investors and consumers tend to rate a company's minority-fairness solely by its treatment of African-Americans.

Yet the Hispanic and Asian populations, the other two large minority groups in the work force, each face unique problems in the work world that a company may ignore even as it extends itself for its African-American employees. For instance, some companies are unwilling to accommodate non–English-speaking Hispanics even when those accommodations, such as bilingual manuals and signs, could easily be made. Hispanics also suffer, with African-Americans, from negative racial stereotypes. As such, they often find doors closed to all but menial jobs. Stereotypes actually favor Asian-Americans to a degree. They tend to be thought of as well-educated and industrious. But they're also thought of as meek, so while they are more likely than other minorities to be hired into white-collar jobs, they rarely advance to management.

Because affirmative action also covers business's hiring and promotion records with women, including America's 48 million white women, the competition becomes stiffer all the way around. No minority is getting a fair shake from American business, but non–African-American minorities probably have a harder time than any in getting someone to act in their behalf.

Of course, nobody ever said managing diversity was easy. To give every minority its due can be a delicate balancing act in even the most conscientious companies. However, when done well, managing diversity becomes an enriching experience that both expands the personal perspectives of those involved and teaches a company much more about the diverse world in which it does business.

MINORITY FRANCHISING

Not surprisingly, minorities are no better represented in the ranks of franchise ownership than they are in other forms of company management. Minorities operate only about 9.5 percent of American franchises, according to preliminary results in a 1992 Arthur Anderson & Co. study of 366 franchises in sixty different businesses. In the auto industry, as of early 1993, Ford led the pack with just 4.8 percent of its 5,144 dealerships minority-owned, according to *Business Week*. Chrysler and General Motors trailed with 2.7 and 2.1 percent, respectively.

Prospective minority owners, of course, face numerous technical disadvantages: inability to obtain financing and, typically, a lack of background. Open-minded corporations know the opportunity hidden in those deficits: a vastly underutilized talent pool, access to markets in minority neighborhoods and, certainly, a new market for the franchises themselves if properly supported. Mature companies, in particular, realize that inner cities are an important frontier and minority owners have the best chance of success with a largely minority clientele.

A few chains have seized the initiative and reached out to minority prospects with special programs. KFC Corporation, for example, works through local banks to guarantee fifteen to twenty loans annually for minority operators. The company also reduces liquidity requirements (as of this writing, from $170,000 to between $65,000 and $70,000). With only 170 of its 5,000 units minority-owned (by only 64 franchisees), KFC closed franchise sales to all but minorities in 1992. Ford, another company making amends, lends most of its $3 million to $6 million dealership fee to minority applicants and pays them $40,000 annually during their two-year training period.

While KFC's and Ford's efforts are laudable, minorities owned 40 percent of three thousand franchised 7-Eleven stores as of mid-1992 without any special money program by parent company Southland Corporation (Dallas). The relatively low $93,465 investment certainly helps, but so do the company's conscientious recruiting efforts. For example, Southland now targets minorities leaving the military, a particularly good source of managerial talent, the company believes.

Businesses looking for long-term returns on their equality efforts should note that, from a social standpoint, franchise ownership makes a particularly potent contribution to minority communities. Franchises create jobs (albeit often poorly compensated service jobs). They also return successful role models to disadvantaged communities, which are largely bereft of them now because affluent minorities, like other upwardly mobile Americans, have headed for the suburbs as soon as they could afford them.

Other Disadvantaged Groups: Older Workers, Disabled Workers, Gays, and Immigrants

For the above demographic reasons, business is looking anew at populations that, like women and minorities, have been denied full opportunities to contribute. In doing so, employers often discover that putting their hiring and promotion prejudices aside enriches the company culture. Some disadvantaged populations, such as older workers, also bring special attributes to work that can upgrade a company's performance. Nevertheless, to the extent that a population has been excluded from a work force, inviting it in raises new issues. The following section reviews the attributes and special needs of several such populations.

OLDER WORKERS

As America's work force grows increasingly nonwhite, it also grows grayer. Over the last two decades of this century, the numbers of the middle-age group of American workers, those from 25 to 54 years of age, are expected to double to 101 million, while the younger group shrinks, according to U.S. Labor Department projections. And these folks are virtual babes in swaddling clothes compared to the ready pool of older job applicants.

One out of four retirees goes back to work, most compelled by financial need. Add to these numbers other older workers laid off because of their expensive salaries and benefits, and older widows and divorcees applying for work for the first time. Yet many, perhaps most, companies are reluctant to hire workers they think are slower to learn and will increase their health-related costs.

It's true that older workers cost about 15 percent more for health care than average employees, according to an American Association of Retired Persons (AARP) study. However, because older employees have fewer dependents than younger workers, they compare favorably to young workers with families. And when older workers reach age 65, benefits often cease to be a factor: a Small Business Administration study revealed that most older workers are retirees with health and pension plans.

Besides, they offset any health care disadvantage in myriad ways.

For example, Days Inns of America (Parsippany, New Jersey), which since 1986 has recruited older persons as reservation agents, has discovered that the older workers stay with their jobs an average of three years compared to one year for younger employees. Consultant/psychologist Robert Rosen, author of *The Healthy Company*, explains that, as polls indicate, most older workers simply want to be of service; they aren't looking to get ahead.

Older employees also bring to work such intangible assets as experience, good work habits, and emotional maturity. General Mills Restaurants (Minneapolis), which actively recruits older employees, has found that its senior workers make excellent role models for the younger employees. As for the fear that older employees don't learn quickly enough in the technological whirlwind that is the modern workplace, the Travelers Corporation (Hartford) has found that older workers mastered complicated software just as facilely as did younger staff. The twenty-person work force at Kuempel Chime Clock Works and Studio in Excelsior, Minnesota, most of whom are aged 62 to 84, includes many who came to the company with no prior experience in woodworking or clock repair, learning those skills on the job. Kuempel has hired primarily older workers, whom it considers the ideal employees, since its founding in 1916.

Without children at home to care for, older workers also adapt easily to irregular schedules. That's one reason that American Airlines has begun seeking out older applicants for its flight attendant positions. Another reason is that older workers tend to be more conscientious in the vital arena of customer service than perhaps any other group in the labor force.

Unfortunately, one reason that so many older applicants are available is that some employers callously dump their long-term employees, who cost more in salaries and benefits than newer workers, at the first opportunity, particularly in tough times. They do so at their considerable risk. As of this writing, food-processing corporation Ore-Ida (Boise) is being sued for $16 million by a group of twenty-eight employees who were laid off in a cost-cutting program. The suit alleges violations of the federal Age Discrimination in Employment Act of 1967 (which protects workers aged forty and older) and other federal antidiscrimination laws. A company may downsize to cut costs; however, it may not discriminate against any class of workers to do so. The company denies that older workers were singled out.

GAYS

The basic rights of gays and lesbians suffer more assaults, and receive less protection, than those of any other group in America:

· No federal law specifically protects gays and lesbians from discrimination, including workplace discrimination.

· The U.S. military specifically forbids homosexuals from entering its services, although closet gays have incontrovertibly served with distinction throughout U.S. military history.

· Only six states and about a hundred cities offer homosexuals statutory cover.

· Right-wing groups have sponsored anti-gay ballot initiatives in numerous states and municipalities. These measures, through deceptive language designed to seduce anti–affirmative action voters, typically seek to deny homosexuals fundamental protections, including antidiscriminatory employment protection. Such an initiative became law in Colorado in 1992, although the Colorado Supreme Court later ruled it unconstitutional.

The workplace bias of which gays complain is no paranoid fantasy. In a 1987 *Wall Street Journal,* 66 percent of the 351 senior executives questioned said they would hesitate to promote a gay employee to the management committee level; only 1 percent admitted to a similar bias about female staff. In 1991, Cracker Barrel Old Country Store, Inc., a Lebanon, Tennessee–based chain of more than a hundred restaurants in the southeastern states, adopted an explicit policy of terminating employees who did not exhibit "normal heterosexual values." As widely reported in *Business Week* and other publications, numerous employees lost their jobs with no obvious legal recourse, since none of the locations where Cracker Barrel operates prohibits discrimination based on sexual orientation.

Although their success varies with location and circumstances, gays have won a few legal tussles. The same year as the Cracker Barrel firings, *Business Week* reported, a court ruled that a former Shell Oil Company executive had been dismissed illegally for being gay and awarded the man $5.3 million. Shell appealed, claiming he was let go for other reasons. The parties settled the case during the appeal, with terms kept confidential.

In this vitriolic atmosphere, few companies have stood firmly beside their gay and lesbian employees before the rest of the work force, not to mention the culture at large. Notable exceptions among major corporations include U.S. West, Hewlett-Packard, U.S. Bancorp., Prudential Insurance, Honeywell, Unisys, Levi Strauss, Apple, and Xerox, all of which ban bias against homosexuals in their non-discriminatory employment policies. According to *Business Week,* as of late 1991, only 20 percent of companies "with strong equal-opportunity policies explicitly cite sexual preference."

Communications company U.S. West has been among the most aggressively fair-minded of the majors in several ways. It was the only company to purchase space in Oregon's 1992 voter's pamphlet to condemn anti-gay initiative, Measure 9. In 1986, a group of U.S. West employees banded together as the Employee Association for Gays and Lesbians (EAGLE). The organization now boasts ten chapters within U.S. West and advises the company, centered in Denver, on how to best eliminate workplace bias against homosexuals.

U.S. West is one of a handful of companies that realizes that even antidiscriminatory policies don't go far enough. Homosexuality is one of the culture's most contentious social issues, heated by hetero-sexuals' confusion and fears, religious prohibitions, and misinforma-tion spread by those who manipulate the issue for political and/or economic ends. In recent years, dread of HIV infection and AIDS, mischaracterized as a gay disease, has amplified homophobia to hys-terical proportions. U.S. West, along with Levi Strauss, AT&T, and Pacific Gas & Electric, have counteracted homophobia by addressing it within their diversity workshops.

Levi Strauss, along with Ben & Jerry's, has also asserted fairness toward gays and lesbians by extending benefits to employees' same-sex partners. (Some companies, including Levi Strauss and Ben & Jerry's, offer benefits to employees' unmarried heterosexual partners as well.) Numerous others may soon follow. In September 1991, Lotus Development announced that it would offer full spousal benefits to partners of gay and lesbian employees who file an "affidavit of spousal equivalency" (10 percent of Lotus employees are homosexual). Since then, hundreds of companies have contacted human resources vice president Russ Campanello to inquire about the policy's details. Of course, the company's fairness toward gays simply enhances its al-ready solid reputation as one of the country's best overall employers. Perhaps the software company understands better than most firms the meaning of "garbage in, garbage out."

DISABLED WORKERS

Kreonite, Inc., a Wichita, Kansas, darkroom equipment manufacturer, began utilizing disabled workers in 1973 when for strictly financial reasons it subcontracted some small parts manufacturing and assembly with a sheltered workshop in the local area. Management soon found it even more cost-effective to move the disabled workers in-house. Recalls plant manager Brent Stull, "We started growing from that point, learning from the people with disabilities about ourselves and about our organization, and we just evolved into a company that recognizes the ability in all people." As for the original two disabled hires: "One man has been here for twenty years and a woman has been here nineteen years."

Their performance told the company something. As of this writing, 15 percent of the 240-member work force are disabled employees. Notes Stull, "We try not to isolate the people with disabilities as a group but if you do isolate them, you recognize that their turnover, their attendance, their productivity, and their loyalty to the organization are just tremendous. They're much higher than people without disabilities."

Kreonite's experience with the disabled has even helped the company in unforeseen ways. For instance, working with people who were deaf and deaf/blind forced the company to become aware of how much vital company information was taken for granted rather than expressed. Kreonite is now much more committed to precise communications and policies.

Of course, Kreonite's example is exceptional. Many companies still struggle with basic prejudices about disabled workers, prejudices that can be expensive:

· The 43 million disabled Americans constitute yet another source of underutilized talent.

· It's usually far more cost-effective to make the appropriate accommodations for employees who become disabled than to prolong their disability benefits apathetically. The Washington Business Group on Health calculates that business and society earn a return of eight to ten dollars for every dollar spent on rehabilitating disabled people.

· The Americans with Disabilities Act (ADA) prohibits discrimination against the disabled in firing, refusing to hire, and failure to make "reasonable accommodations." "Reasonable" means accommodations that do not cause the employer undue financial hardship.

In *The Healthy Company*, Robert Rosen makes a clever distinction between disabled workers and "disabled jobs." Jobs become disabled when preconceived notions about disabled workers' abilities blind employers to simple accommodations they can make to enable those employees to perform. Such accommodations might include:

· Matching the employee to a job that fits his/her medical condition, and identifying positions within the company into which disabled job applicants can be hired and disabled employees can be returned if they cannot perform their old jobs

· Making disabled people feel welcome and included in all company activities (for instance, planning company social and recreational activities in which they can participate)

· Making technical, mechanical, and space adaptations appropriate to the disabled employee's restrictions

Regarding the latter, Stull says, "Most people stereotype when they think of accommodations required by ADA. The way I train my managers is that we are here to try to improve the process for everyone so that they can become better employees and more efficient. When we make a capital equipment purchase, we cost it out and plan it toward reasonable return on investment. That's the way I approach accommodations for people with disabilities. Cost the thing out, plan it out properly. You get a return on your investment and everybody wins."

IMMIGRANTS

When my wife and I relocated with our daughter to southern Oregon from Encinitas, California, we were warned to mask our roots, even though we brought an Oregon-like menagerie of horses, goats, and dogs with us. Oregonians hate Californians, our friends insisted, because they're deathly afraid the immigrants from "la-la land" will ruin their state. Sure enough, once we settled in our new home, we encountered those sentiments everywhere we turned. But we also discovered that nearly everyone mouthing them was a California transplant. I began to wonder if there was such a thing as a native

Oregonian until a neighbor, himself a refugee from Riverside, California, set me straight. "An Oregonian," he explained, "is an ex-Californian with more seniority than you."

Nationwide, many Americans—too many—harbor similar proprietary feelings about who got here first. How many of us have heritages of more than two or three generations in this land? Yet, according to a 1992 *Business Week*/Harris poll, 68 percent of Americans think immigration is "bad" for the country. The numbers measuring the impact of immigration tell a much different story: immigrants' contributions, recent as well as historic, to our economy have been overwhelmingly positive.

By the same token, the sentiments of two thirds of the population, even if misguided, cannot be lightly dismissed. Many Americans feel that immigration dilutes, rather than enriches, American culture, especially when immigrants insist on speaking in their native tongues, dressing in their native fashions, and maintaining other native traditions and beliefs. Much of the population also worries about the strain that immigration puts on social services, including financially starved schools, in this era of scant resources. And, of course, fears about immigrants competing in a shriveling job market have run rampant in the hard times of the early 1990s. The fact that, as of mid-1993, some 10 million immigrants have poured into the U.S. since 1980 only feeds the apprehensions. Forty-four percent of Los Angeles's adult population is foreign-born, as is 70 percent of Miami's, observes *Business Week*.

Many of these potential workers are highly skilled, however. On average, newcomers from India, the Philippines, China, and Korea have more education than Americans (Indians much more). Those from Vietnam, Europe, Jamaica, and Cuba are not far behind the American average. In industries where education is a premium attribute, such as computers, biotechnology, and software, this talent infusion plays a critical role; about a third of Silicon Valley's engineer corps is Asian-born. If you poke around, you'll hear story after story about a foreign-born employee bringing a fresh perspective to a problem or seeing an opportunity that a native might have missed.

The influence of immigrants on American high-technology companies will grow even more profound in the future, *Business Week* writers predict. Thirty-seven percent of science doctorates earned between 1981 and 1991 went to foreign-born students. In 1991, students born elsewhere received 51 percent of the computer science Ph.Ds.

Immigrants have made unusually prolific contributions to other sectors of the economy as well. Successful foreign-born entrepreneurs abound in many American cities. Equipped with obvious connections and a global sensibility, immigrant entrepreneurs have also played a big part in the recent U.S. export upsurge. And because they tend to be drawn to cities, immigrants are not only starting businesses, but also helping to revitalize declining neighborhoods, where they buy homes, pay taxes, and shop. In those same cities, lesser-skilled immigrants grab up the lower-paying positions, such as housekeeping and dishwashing, upon which businesses such as hotels and restaurants depend and for which few natives apply. They also fill jobs for which natives seem to have less cultural aptitude. For example, Tabra, a small San Francisco Bay Area jewelry manufacturer, finds foreign-born workers much more willing to stick with the persistent close work that jewelrymaking requires than are U.S.-born trainees.

Of course, many immigrants, particularly those with lesser skills and education, fail to find the steady employment they seek, swelling the ranks of the indigent. But the data shows that, on balance, immigrants contribute much more to the economy than they take from it. Illegals are ineligible for welfare, and many legal immigrants refuse to apply for it, believing it will hamper later applications for citizenship. Although current national data were not available at this writing, experts doubt that immigrants use social services at a much higher rate than native-born Americans, and may well use less. For instance, in 1992 in Los Angeles County, with immigrants comprising 30 percent of the population, only 16 percent of those on Aid to Families with Dependent Children, the primary federal program, were foreign-born.

Overall, as of mid-1992, *Business Week* writers noted, immigrants were receiving $5 billion annually in welfare but paying $90 billion in taxes, on $240 billion in wages, much of that pumped back into the economy as consumption. Nevertheless, these numbers do conceal an important, and unfortunate, fact: only a small percentage of the federal taxes that immigrants pay comes back to municipalities, which provide most of the social services and education to the newcomers. Until this inequity is corrected, backlash will continue to build in the big cities to which immigrants are drawn.

As the Tabra experience suggests, the concern that immigrants take jobs that would otherwise go to natives and drive wages down, may be misguided. A recent academic study of the wage decline of Americans with at least a high school education found that import competition and rising skill expectations for jobs, not immigrant competition, are to blame.

Add it all up and immigrants have been a pretty good deal for the U.S. economy. Unfortunately, they aren't always treated that way.

· Immigrants sometimes experience hiring discrimination because of their foreign accents or looks.

· Immigrants are not always promoted with the same enthusiasm with which they are hired, often because of prejudice about their managerial abilities.

· Some companies culturally discriminate against immigrants by requiring that they speak only English on the job. Such rules don't provoke much controversy when communication about safety or dealing with the public is a necessity. However, some companies forbid foreign languages anywhere on their premises, even during breaks or in other casual conversation.

Those affected have begun to fight back. The 1964 Civil Rights Act protects immigrants from discrimination on the basis of "physical, cultural, or linguistic characteristics" traceable to their homeland. Until the 1990s, however, few foreign-born workers filed complaints, and far fewer won judgments. But 14,394 national-origin charges were filed with the Equal Employment Opportunity Commission (EEOC) in 1992, up 30 percent from 1989. The language/accent issues have been particularly galvanizing. In January 1993, the Washington State Supreme Court upheld a $389,000 award given to English-speaking Cambodian-American Phanna K. Xieng, who had charged that his employer had denied him a promotion because of his accent. (The employer, a Washington bank, argued that his accent would interfere with his ability to placate upset customers, a situation he would encounter on the job he sought.) Immigrants also have won significant out-of-court settlements in the 1990s.

The English-only issue remains legally muddled. EEOC guidelines (which lack the force of law) permit language restrictions if the employer can prove them to be a "business necessity." As of this writing, courts have ruled against companies arguing that "business necessity" includes breaks, lunch, and other personal time. But no definitive case has been judged by the Supreme Court.

Of course, some companies that escape legal action for slighting their foreign-born employees pay in other ways. AT&T Bell Laboratories has watched its heavily (22 percent) Asian-American work force leave at twice the rate of white males, perhaps, a Chinese-American systems engineer suggested to a *Business Week* reporter, because they are promoted at a much slower pace than whites. Other losses are harder to measure. When a company's international employees become discouraged, how much does their productivity suffer? Do they withhold their talents in other areas—say, innovations and inventions? Some employers protest that their immigrant employees don't try hard enough to fit in—a pretty good sign that it's the company itself that needs to do the adapting.

Diversity-Fair Practices and Policies

Sexual harassment and family-fair policies, both crucial to any company that's serious about hiring and promoting women, are covered in detail in the next chapter, as are workplace HIV/AIDS programs. The following describes other ways of transforming a company culture into one that invites minorities and women to succeed. Most of these options are synergistic. That is, true diversity-fairness requires a combination of these approaches.

Diversity-Awareness Training.
A manager's naïveté or unexamined prejudices can quickly unravel a company's sincere efforts to diversify its work force. Preventive medicine begins with special trainings in which managers can confront their biases, learn the cross-cultural nuances of communicating with diverse employees, and understand the company's stake in making all its employees feel valued.

Tabra holds uniquely intimate diversity trainings for its managers and other staff that interact with its mostly foreign-born production workers. The sessions are informal affairs in which everyone talks about his or her native traditions and experiences, shares photographs from home, and so forth. "A lot of our people have had very difficult backgrounds," notes human resources manager Joyce Shearer about a work force that includes employees from Vietnam, Cambodia, Laos, Thailand, Samoa, China, Ethiopia, Taiwan, and El Salvador. "What came out of our last training were not only our differences but also our similarities with our families and children and so on." Tabra also teaches work-related English on company time to those employees for whom English is a second language, and endeavors to promote from within whenever possible.

At Corning (Corning, New York), managers are put through a two-day training to sensitize them to sexism and racism issues. Once they've graduated, their record on retaining and promoting women and minorities partially determines their own promotion eligibility.

Celebrating Diversity.

A company sends a strong signal of appreciation to its "nonmajority" employees when it, for instance, acknowledges such events as Black History Month; permits time off for such holidays as Martin Luther King Jr. Day, Rosh Hashanah, Cinco de Mayo, and other holidays important to some work force members; allows for ethnic clothing and hairstyles in the dress code; and finds other ways of honoring multiculturalism.

In 1992 and 1993, Shaman Pharmaceuticals, a San Francisco company that makes drugs from medicinal plants used by native peoples, celebrated Chinese New Year and Chinese Harvest Moon festivals, among other holidays. In addition, their Peruvian scientists entertained the staff with Latin music demonstrations.

Tabra celebrates diversity in near-Olympian fashion. In its production area, the company hangs large flags of each country represented by an employee. New employees are introduced to the entire company and their country of origin announced and applauded. Tabra also holds potluck luncheons featuring foods from all countries represented and celebrates holidays from each employee's country of origin.

Breaking Down Gender Roles.

BE&K, one of the nation's largest construction companies, has gone to special lengths to recruit and train women in a field far more male dominated than most. With raw strength no longer a prerequisite in this highly mechanized industry, the Birmingham, Alabama–based company has discovered that women perform some jobs better than do men—welding, for instance, which requires particularly dexterous handwork. The company plans to open a special women's welding center in Saginaw, Alabama, to attract women to the trade. But, in fact, BE&K has opened opportunities for women, through free training at its building sites, in virtually all building skills that don't require brute force.

Overall, BE&K's work force is 10 percent female, compared to a 2 percent industry average. Not surprisingly, *The 100 Best Companies to Work for in America* cites BE&K as one of the ten best companies for working women, and the leader in the construction field.

In at least one equal opportunity area, diversifying the executive suite, Stein & Co. has broken construction industry ground beyond even BE&K. Stein & Co.'s president is a woman, Julia Stasch, and her affirmative action efforts have won the Chicago outfit some megalithic contracts. Under the leadership of Stasch, hired as a secretary in 1976 and made president in 1990, Stein & Co. employs more minorities than do most Chicago builders, and also more women—6 percent, three times the industry average—than almost any builder in the nation.

Primarily because the company delivered on equal opportunity promises that other area builders made but didn't keep, the city of Chicago tabbed it to manage the construction of a $750 million light rail system and build a $675 million expansion of the McCormick Place convention center. As of early 1993, the company had completed $775 million worth of projects since 1990, the year Stasch took charge. Its track record with the city also allowed it to focus on managing public sector jobs while its competitors were struggling in a flagging industry.

While women often hold most posts in a bank, they usually take orders from men. Not so at First Federal Bank of California, however, where two thirds of the managers are women. That number includes eighteen of twenty-eight vice presidents and two of the top five officers. Forgive First Federal employees if they don't understand the term "glass ceiling": 41 percent of the bank's officers started in entry-level positions and a third of the managers are minorities.

Under chairman and CEO Bill Mortensen, First Federal is a notable employer in numerous other ways. The company offers generous cash and stock bonuses and pays much better salaries than most of its competition, according to Moskowitz and Levering. In *Forbes* magazine's 1991 rankings, First Federal led all other financial institutions in assets per employee, and was second in sales and profits per employee.

Special Development Programs.
Good old boy networks perpetuate themselves partly by passing insiders' tips on to junior members of their closed fraternity, and by senior managers huddling junior frat brothers under their wings.

Some companies attack the good old boy syndrome with alternative networks—company-appointed mentors and other career development aids for women and minorities that approximate the advantages that good old boys enjoy.

In some companies, alternative networks primarily function as peer-support groups because minorities and women can feel isolated in a white male–dominated company culture even when not dominated in terms of numbers. These ethnic- or gender-based networks also provide a forum for the airing of fairness concerns. In many cases, these groups meet with mentors and serve other career development functions as well.

As part of its settlement of a major discrimination suit in 1973, AT&T promised the federal government that it would hire and promote more minorities. Although the court order expired in 1979, AT&T's efforts did not. Among its initiatives, the company sponsors ethnic-based support groups, such as the Black Managers Group, some of which have branches at every AT&T worksite in the nation. Today, *Black Enterprise Magazine* recognizes AT&T as one of the "best of the best" places for blacks to work.

At Avon Products, Inc., headquarters in New York, ethnic-based organizations developed in the mid-1980s for strictly social purposes. Since then, however, the Black Professionals Association, Avon Hispanic Network, and Avon Asian Network have expanded their roles to include career development and the advocacy of fair recruiting practices. The groups meet separately each quarter, and then present their agendas to the CEO, president, and chairperson of Avon's Diversity Task Force.

Fairness Goals and Mandates.
Although numerical goals smack of quotas to many, a successful policy sometimes depends upon them. Some companies have elevated a talented woman or two to a high position only to have their token promotions undercut other efforts to hire and retain women. Managers of a Johnson & Johnson unit once queried a number of women managers who had recently left as to their reasons why. One of the loudest complaints: isolation.

Pitney Bowes requires that 35 percent of all new positions and promotions go to women and 15 percent to minorities, a policy it has had in place since 1985. Although Pitney Bowes ranks high by most measures of corporate social responsibility, bottom-line considerations drove its diversity policy revisions, particularly regarding women. "Women were putting in more time than men and more consistently beating their sales quotas," CEO George B. Harvey told *Business Week* in 1990. "If I'm going to get the best talent, I've got to look at the entire population." Pitney Bowes supports its mandates with generous family benefits, a Mentors program, Women and Minorities Resources groups, and a corporate ombudsman available to any employee who feels he or she has been unfairly treated.

NCR Corporation makes 25 percent of managers' compensation dependent on how well they help employees satisfy personal objectives, measured by employee surveys, including balancing work and family.

Antidiscrimination Policies.
Beyond numbers, media conglomerate Gannett declares its intentions on paper with a fairness statement that is one of the country's most comprehensive, prohibiting "discrimination or harassment because of sex, age, race, creed, color, religion, marital status, sexual orientation, national origin, disability, or veteran status."

Reform of Gender-Bias.
We refer to "glass" ceilings and walls because they are constructed from intangible cultural factors rather than written policies or standards. Good old boy business culture can be fraught with macho ideals and metaphors as conducive to gender-fairness as a stag party. Take, for example, the prototypical Type A manager who virtually lives for, and *at,* his job, considered a model employee in many companies. Or consider, as organizational consultant and California School of Professional Psychology president John O'Neill has observed, the football and military imagery favored in aggressive business talk. Confronted with managers who always put work before family or by executive exhortations about "taking no prisoners" or "kicking butt," a woman is likely to feel like she came in the wrong door.

Managers with hard-driving personal styles can undermine a company's work/family program by refusing to grant their charges' requests for flexible schedules and leaves even though the program allows for them. NationsBank, headquartered in Charlotte, North Carolina, puts all managers through special training to communicate that the company wants employees to use the "flextime" and leave policies as written.

Most of NationsBank's employees are women, however. Edgar Woolard faced a much deeper cultural challenge at Du Pont. Before he took charge as CEO in 1989, a small elite corps of white males ran the Wilmington, Delaware–based company as if it were their own private club. Woolard especially noted the regular executive retreats at the Eagle Lodge in Pennsylvania, where the boys would gather for golf, tennis, and, between games, strategic talk. Woolard abolished the retreats in his first year, replacing them with what he called the Corporate Leadership Conference, at which women and minorities and other nonexecutives were more than welcome. By the conference's second year, women and minorities made up some 75 percent of the attendees. While the transformation at Du Pont is far from complete (as of 1992, only one female out of seventy-five vice presidents), the numbers of women and nonwhites in professional and management positions are way up—double since 1980.

Fairness Follow-Through.
Some companies spend considerable time and money to recruit and train diverse new hires, and then watch that investment go down the drain because they don't understand how to retain them. If minorities or women feel isolated in their jobs, or alienated by a hostile culture, or slighted in pay and promotion decisions, they may not stay long no matter how bad the job climate outside. To protect its investment, a company must studiously track its diversity effort for pay and promotion equity and—friendliness.

For example, Corning's women and minorities used to leave at twice the rate of white men. In addition, the company was paying up to $5 million a year to replace them. In 1987, frustrated CEO Jamie Houghton put together two teams led by top executives to study the way the company distributed pay and promotions. Once the disturbing data were in, they sent the entire work force through diversity awareness trainings conducted by outside consultants, established the mentoring networks and managerial incentives covered above, and the work/family programs discussed in Chapter 3. The efforts paid off. The numbers of African-Americans and women reaching top management rose sharply. And attrition shrank—for women, from 16.2 percent in 1987 to 6.5 percent in 1993, and for African-Americans, from 15.3 percent in 1987 to 10.5 percent six years later.

Charitable and Community Initiatives.

Devoting a chunk of the company's charitable donations to minority causes, purchasing from minority- and women-owned businesses, sponsoring volunteer efforts in minority communities, and other such endeavors help make nonwhite and female hires feel acknowledged and appreciated. Conversely, ignoring these employee populations in the company's charitable, community relations, and purchasing programs sends an opposite message.

In addition to its other initiatives on behalf of minorities discussed above, Corning worked to increase minority employment in the city's stores. The company also convinced the local cable-TV outfit to carry the Black Entertainment Television channel.

CHAPTER 3

Work/Family, Sexual Harassment, and HIV/ AIDS Programs: The New Imperatives

IN THE PREVIOUS CHAPTER, we examined various issues related to a work force that, to borrow President Clinton's phrase, "looks like America." We also surveyed various approaches to diversity management. But I saved for their own chapter sexual harassment policies and programs for workers with family responsibilities because each deserves more than survey treatment. And for similar reasons, I cover below HIV/AIDS management, which is as much a diversity issue about fair treatment of disabled employees as it is a health and safety concern.

Work forces today include more women, more single male parents, and, tragically but inevitably, more HIV/AIDS–infected employees than ever before, and none of these trends shows any signs of reversing. However, the programs discussed below justify themselves in ways far beyond diversity-fairness, for employees aren't the only ones in jeopardy from the demands of caring for dependent family members, sexual harassment, and frightful diseases like AIDS.

The Case for Family-Fair Policies

When CEO Hugh McColl called for a task force to study work-and-family issues at banking company NCNB Corporation in 1986, it wasn't a mere academic exercise. Earlier in his career with the company, he had watched a single mother co-worker struggle to balance her work and family obligations, and had seen how both her worklife and her family at home suffered under the strain. That made him pretty uncomfortable—his three children had grown up while he was climbing the ranks at the company and he'd missed some important benchmarks in their lives. But it also made him realize that what was true for this woman must be true for many others. NCNB's work force was then 75 percent women.

The task force conducted an employee survey that confirmed his suspicions. "More than half the women and one in ten men had considered leaving the company because of their parental responsibilities. That was really the bottom line," Ginnie Mackin, a company vice president and director of work-and-family programs, told me.

With McColl's leadership, NCNB established a comprehensive work/family program that won it a "medalist" listing in Hal Morgan and Kerry Tucker's book *Companies That Care,* about family-friendly American companies. NCNB has since been subsumed by a new entity, NationsBank, the country's fourth largest banking institution. But McColl is still in the driver's seat, the corporation is still headquartered in North Carolina, and the work/family program is still state of the art.

McColl now says of the program, "We see our work and family programs as the cost of doing business, and at the end of the day, it doesn't cost us to take care of our employees. I think there is a correlation between an employee who takes family responsibilities seriously and one who takes responsibilities in the workplace seriously. We think the value of the program has paid for itself. We have certainly lowered our turnover rate and retained the people we wanted to retain. And I would dare say that since 1988, our work and family programs have been a competitive advantage in attracting talent outside of the bank."

In March 1993, I visited NationsBank's offices in Atlanta where, appropriate to their business presence, they occupy a 55-story spire that dominates the city's skyline. Employees at all levels of the company spoke about their experiences with various work/family policies. Communications officer Betty Schoenbaechler and Vickie Dorsey, an attorney in the bank's legal department, noted how SelectTime, a reduced-hours option for working parents, enabled them to both continue their careers and have more time for their young children.

Mike Eremchuk, a vice president in the insurance division, recalled the four weeks of paid paternity leave he had received after his wife gave birth to twins. ("That got us through the rough part," he said. The company considered Mike a primary caregiver because of the multiple births, even though his wife was not working at the time.) Tina Ragin fondly remembered the parental leave from which she had recently returned. Angelia Burrell expressed her gratitude for the regular subsidy she received, through ChildCare Plus, to help with childcare expenses. And Susan Howard related her appreciation for the Education Initiative program, which allows her two paid hours per week to volunteer at her child's school.

NationsBanks family/work program is designed to touch all the bases. It includes up to six months of unpaid but guaranteed parental leave; up to six weeks paid maternity leave (more in special cases); paid paternity leave for working fathers who are primary caregivers; childcare subsidies for lesser-paid employees; a dependent care pre-tax set-aside program; childcare resource and referral service; parenting seminars; and comparable benefits for adopting parents. It also includes interesting features such as the above-mentioned educational initiative. However, NationsBank's is not a leading-edge program. By design, *it is merely competitive,* good enough so that prospective employees won't find many better and so that current working parents are not likely to leave.

The NationsBank program emphasizes two other features that characterize successful work/family initiatives: employee responsibility and managerial support. Work/family programs are collaborative efforts, requiring employees to make every effort to minimize conflicts between family and work obligations. By the same token, the employer must make sure that all supervisory personnel understand and carry out the company's intent to help employees in balancing work and family concerns. NationsBank puts its managers through special training to teach them the administrative details of the program and to communicate that McColl wants employees' family needs accommodated whenever possible. McColl knows that the company that tells a distressed working parent "that's your problem" has badly miscalculated and will likely pay with lost productivity, high turnover, and a wounded ability to recruit good people.

THE GROWTH OF WORK/FAMILY PROGRAMS IN AMERICA

Although we may think of family-friendly workplaces as a snazzy new employee benefit, far sighted employers have been helping their employees balance work and family life since the Industrial Revolution nearly two hundred years ago. As factories and mills proliferated in the late 1700s, women began working outside their homes in significant numbers and the debate over what to do with the kids began. In 1825, Robert Owen, owner of a cotton mill in New Harmony, Indiana, built a school and preschool for his adult and child workers. Modeled after a school the English businessman had built at his mill complex in Scotland nine years earlier, the Indiana facility was likely the first employer-supported childcare center in American business history.

The founders of the first kindergartens, which began in Germany in the nineteenth century, also conceived of them as educational preschools for factory workers' children. By the early 1890s, numerous American cities had their own kindergartens, usually administered by settlement houses or charitable organizations but often sponsored by business consortiums.

However, the American public's ambivalence about women working, voiced over the decades by influential opinion leaders from President Theodore Roosevelt to Dr. Benjamin Spock, kept the brakes on the childcare movement despite the rising numbers of women joining the labor force and training for professions. Until quite recently, the number of companies attacking the work/family problem remained few and far between. IBM, Stride Rite, and Polaroid were among less than two hundred companies providing any form of work/family assistance in 1971. The numbers have swelled since, particularly from the mid-1980s forward. By 1988, thirty-five hundred companies provided some type of childcare assistance; by 1993, about fifty-six hundred. Inevitably, some of these companies do a better job of promoting their benefits to the media than they do encouraging their employees to use them, thus inflating the numbers. And the inflated figures still constitute a tiny percentage of the nation's six million employers. Nevertheless, the trend is clear.

THE UPSURGE IN WORK/FAMILY PROGRAMS: WHY NOW?

Why are so many American companies suddenly waking up to the needs of their working parents? Two reasons: demographics and the bottom line. The following facts are increasingly known, and understood, in the corporate world.

The Changing American Family.

The following statistics describe a revolution in American family life: The number of single-parent families has doubled since 1970. Single mothers head 8.7 million American families, and the fastest-growing family type in the U.S. is single-father headed (nearly 1.4 million in 1992, compared to less than 500,000 in 1970, *Business Week* notes). More than half of all working mothers return to their jobs before their infants' first birthdays, and 55 percent of women with children under three years of age work today, double the percentage in 1973, observes the same publication. In fact these days, married women with very young children are more likely than unmarried women to work.

In sum, the stereotypical image of Pop working full-time while Mom stays home to care for the kids and house describes domestic American reality about as accurately as a Norman Rockwell painting. Only 7 percent of American families fit this mold. In the modern home, Pop (if there happens to be one) helps out both with the kids and the chores. Often, that's because Mom also works most of the week and is just as dog-tired at the end of the work day as her husband.

Increasingly, however, men actively parent because they want to. Ironically, the gains women have made in shattering sexual stereotypes have freed men to acknowledge the nurturing side of their own natures. Thus, whether single or married, increasing numbers of both moms and dads face the harrying challenge of being both responsible employees and responsible parents.

And the unfortunate facts of contemporary socioeconomic reality will likely keep things that way. The cost of living has outstripped wage gains since about 1973. Because of that fact and other assaults on middle-class financial security, both partners in a middle-class couple often need to work just to maintain their standard of living (or slow the decline). Of course, working-class families always have lived with this reality, since one salary at their level often barely covers a single person's expenses, much less a family's. Meanwhile, corporate aggression against labor, global competition, and other structural developments continue to drive real compensation downward.

Changing Attitudes About Work.

According to a Dunhill Personnel Systems, Inc. (a Woodbury, New York–based personnel firm) poll, 52 percent of the three hundred baby boomers surveyed said that if they could change one thing about their lives, they would spend less time on their careers and more time on their families and personal lives. While this attitudinal shift is largely restricted to the middle class, it's still one to which corporate America is paying increasing attention because it is from this group of working Americans that most executives are recruited.

The shift also reflects the degree to which workplace changes have lagged behind social trends. For instance, few employers have allowed for the increased time pressures on their workers. It takes longer to commute to work on ever more crowded freeways, a factor that by itself can add hours to each work week. The bureaucratic demands on a household also have grown severalfold in most of our lifetimes. Preparing tax returns alone can take days even if one is only gathering data to hand over to a professional preparer. Plus, we're logging more hours on the clock. The average American now works a full month more each year than his/her counterpart did in 1970. The largest group of wage earners (hourly employees) have lost so much ground to inflation that in 1991, they had to work about two hundred extra hours a year just to maintain their financial level. Thus, it gets harder every year for most Americans to juggle family and career.

The Now and Future Work Force.

The composition of the American work force is transforming as dramatically as is the family: Between now and the year 2000, about two thirds of net new entrants into the work force are expected to be women, about three quarters of whom will become pregnant during their working years. In addition, economists and demographers forecast a labor shortage in the 1990s because of a post–baby boom population dip. This will cause businesses to make up the difference by recruiting more women and minorities, the categories from which most of the labor force growth has come in recent years.

The rapidly expanding service sector of the economy looks particularly to these groups, which are more accustomed to the low wages and minimal (or no) benefits that many service jobs offer. But, as numerous surveys show, these same low wage/benefit packages combined with the high cost of childcare—for which working women pay an average of 25 percent of their income, notes *Business Week*— make it impossible for many mothers, especially single mothers, to work. For similar reasons, other young potential recruits find the public assistance route more appealing as well.

Financial Benefits of Work/Family Programs: Short-Term.
In the mid-1980s, leaders from business, the childcare professions, government, the media, unions, and women's, religious, and community groups combined efforts to form the Child Care Action Campaign (CCAC). Corporate participants include, among others, American Express, Xerox, J. C. Penney, The Carnegie Corporation, Consolidated Edison Company of New York, Hoechst Celanese, Sara Lee, S. C. Johnson, and *The New York Times*. The coalition has extensively studied family/work issues, including their short- and long-term economic effects on business. Its policy paper, *Child Care: The Bottom Line*, summarizes the short-term effects as follows:

> Family concerns are just as likely to affect job performance and productivity as a host of other factors, including salary, benefits, and relationship to supervisor. Many working parents report that their worries about child care interfere with their job performance, either by causing them to spend unproductive time on the job, or to arrive late and leave early. Employers who support their employees' child care needs enjoy lower rates of absenteeism, tardiness, and stress, as well as lower recruiting costs and higher rates of retention.

Until recently, few researchers had attempted to measure an employer's costs of *not* addressing work/family issues. However, an early 1990s study by the Families and Work Institute, a nonprofit research group, showed that the average company spends 75 percent of a nonmanagerial employee's annual pay to hire and train a replacement, whereas filling in for an absent parent costs only 32 percent of annual salary. The costs of hiring and training replacement managers is considerably greater, 150 percent of annual salary. Of course, some talent is too valuable to lose under any circumstances. Thus, a company can save both cold cash and precious intangibles by instead shifting jobs and otherwise making the short-term accommodations to cover for a working parent on leave.

The Conference Board, a New York–based research group, has also documented lower turnover and absenteeism, and increased productivity, at family-friendly companies. Among companies that have researched the issues for themselves, Corning found in 1987 that women and minorities were leaving the company twice as fast as white males. The data stunned the company, which undertook an immediate overhaul of its culture, including extending its family leave, starting a part-time scheduling program, and contracting with Work/Family Directions to offer a national childcare resource and referral service to its employees. In 1992, Corning broke ground on a new $1.2 million childcare center. Company studies now indicate that employees who take advantage of its work/family benefits are also more likely to respond to the company's quality-improvement initiatives.

Du Pont surveyed its employees in 1988 and discovered that 25 percent of males and 50 percent of females had contemplated quitting to find a company with more flexible scheduling. Like Corning, the company took immediate preventive action. By 1992, twelve thousand to seventeen thousand employees were working either part-time or flexible hours. Du Pont also expanded its work/family efforts, becoming a national leader in this area.

Notably, Du Pont and Corning were good employers before upgrading their work/family initiatives. But they undertook research and acted on the results to become even better. They were also forthright in publicizing their research results. Companies that ignore the message that these two family-conscious corporations send do so at their significant peril.

Of course, being compassionate employers only partly addresses business responsibility. Corning's once solid public image all but collapsed after Dow Corning's breast-implant scandal. (Corning owns half of the besieged company, although each outfit is managed separately.) Du Pont has moved to improve its environmental record, but as of 1992 it was still one of the world's biggest polluters.

Financial Benefits of Work/Family Programs: Long-Term.
The future of American business cannot be isolated from the fate of America's children, our future labor force. The shortage of affordable, high-quality childcare severely threatens the quality of that labor

force. Early childhood experts tell us the first five years of a child's life, the preschool years, are when the foundation for lifelong learning is best built. By enabling employees to take advantage of quality child-care, which usually includes early childhood education programs, companies help protect their investment in the new generation's educational success and psychological health.

Family-Fair Program Alternatives

DEPENDENT-CARE POLICY OPTIONS

Childcare Options.
Having already noted the mounting demand for childcare, let's examine the supply side for a moment. We need only resolve one basic question: Is sufficient quality care available at affordable prices? And the answer is an unequivocal *no*.

Availability by itself isn't the problem in most parts of the country. Nationwide, childcare centers are 70 percent full, Jack Brozman, president of childcare chain La Petite Academy, told *Business Week* in early 1993. However, high land costs, which make building new centers prohibitively expensive in cities such as New York and San Francisco, have caused shortages in some areas. Plus, as CCAC and many other childcare experts have pointed out, the supposed surplus of care masks two other facts: the shortage of affordable care and the shortage of high-quality care. When parents can't find affordable, quality care, they must either accept lower quality care, which is often unlicensed and/or substandard, or withdraw from the labor force. Both of these alternatives should alarm the business community. Working parents who lack confidence in their childcare arrangements are likely to be distracted at work, and thus far from optimally productive. And parents who choose to stay home instead of work contribute to high recruiting and training costs for their companies.

Much of the quality shortage stems from the low wages and status and meager benefits typical of childcare work. Despite generally high educational levels, 60 percent of childcare workers earn five dollars or less an hour. Probably less than one half receive employer-provided health care coverage; only about half receive free or reduced rate care for their own children. No wonder, CCAC notes, that the profession suffers a 40 percent turnover rate (compared to 18 percent for all occupations). For many parents, the fear of leaving their children in a non–employer sponsored center provokes them to quit their jobs.

As for cost, annual fees can vary from fifteen hundred to ten thousand dollars per child, with an average of about three thousand dollars, reports CCAC. For many working women, the burden just gets to be too much. According to *Business Week,* "half of the women who return to welfare do so because of childcare problems."

In this as in other socioeconomic areas, the U.S. lags far behind many of its competitor nations. France, for instance, provides free, universal care for children over three years of age, and pays a big chunk of the burden for younger children. But the debt-ridden U.S. government won't likely be playing catch-up anytime soon. Nor are states, also hurting financially, likely to close the gap. That leaves parents holding a pretty big bag, unless they work for a company willing to help out.

The following options, several of which are combined in the best programs, show what companies, large and small, offer working parents these days.

Resource-and-Referral Service: Employers offering these services at minimum provide their employees with lists of childcare sources and sometimes provide activities lists for school-age kids as well. The more complete services also counsel employees on childcare options and care quality, keep tabs on which programs have vacancies, refer employees to quality providers in their area, and expand care availability by recruiting and training new providers. Some companies offer resource-and-referral services in-house; others contract with community-based or national services, such as Work/Family Directions in Boston or The Partnership Group in Lansdale, Pennsylvania (see Resources).

Business Week notes that resource-and-referral services cost little to provide—about nine to thirty dollars per employee for lists (late 1992 prices), upward from there for other assistance mentioned. But even the most complete services leave much of the logistical, and all of the financial, burden on employees' backs. Large companies with highly mobile work forces will find a national service a useful adjunct to their other relocation support.

Parent Education Seminars: Whether organized by staff or provided by outside consultants, these can vary from informational forums on community resources to support groups and topical discussions on work and family issues. A particularly family-friendly public agency, the Los Angeles Department of Water and Power, offers, in addition to its full slate of programs for moms, peer support groups for new dads plus a "Tips for Dads" hotline and loaned pagers during the last weeks of pregnancy so fathers won't miss the hallowed event. Seminars cost even less than an ongoing resource-and-referral service, but in the best programs, seminars simply augment a more substantial commitment to work/family assistance.

Employee Subsidies: Direct financial assistance helps ease a financial strain on most working parents, and for others, removes an obstacle to working. Some companies offer an equal subsidy to all employees; some subsidize progressively, helping most those employees with the least income. Companies such as NationsBank and Polaroid base their progressive scales on total family income, not just their employee's paycheck. A few employers include subsidies in a cafeteria or flexible benefits plan, in which the employee can customize an employer-subsidized benefit package best suited to his or her family's needs without necessarily increasing the employer's benefit costs. Large companies that offer, say, on-site childcare centers at some sites but not others sometimes use subsidies to balance the benefits.

Even smaller companies with low-skilled work forces have found subsidies cost-effective. Ding-A-Ling, a Fort Lauderdale answering and beeper service, has only 110 employees, but 95 percent are women, most of whom are single mothers. After owner Herman Shooster discovered that it was easier for employees to quit than pay for childcare, he began making childcare co-payments. The benefit has reduced turnover and absenteeism, improved employee loyalty and morale, and attracted new employees to the company. In a normally high-turnover business, Ding-A-Ling is now able to maintain quality because employees rarely leave.

Note that subsidies do not necessarily replace resource-and-referral services, because many working parents lack both the time and background to search out a proper caregiver. When setting up a subsidy program, employers should also disabuse themselves of the notion that a little financial help is better than none. If the company provides an insufficient amount for the employee to afford quality care, the employee still has a childcare problem, the employer still has a distracted and stressed employee, and a lot of money has been spent to little productive end.

Pretax Salary Set-Aside: Through its Dependent Care Assistance Program, the IRS allows employees to set aside up to five thousand dollars in income as nontaxable to cover dependent-care and medical expenses. However, any money remaining in the account at year's end must be forfeited.

Numerous companies offering family programs include the DCAP. However, since low-paid workers have little or no tax liability, a pretax set-aside is of little use to them. American Express found that only about 4 percent of an estimated ten thousand eligible employees utilized its set-aside accounts in the six and one half years before the company added direct childcare subsidies to the mix. Employers also should counsel employees to compare this benefit to the Child and Dependent Care Credit, which is available to all workers, since they must choose between this tax credit and the DCAP.

On- or Near-Site Day-Care Facilities: An increasing number of companies have determined that creating and subsidizing their own childcare centers is the best way to ensure quality, convenient care for their employees' children and a competitive benefit package to offer prospective recruits. Some companies operate their centers as an in-house department; some construct a center and then donate it to a nonprofit employee group to run it; some hire a for-profit provider such as Kinder-Care at Work, a division of the day-care chain Kinder-Care, to operate a company-built center. Under any of these alternatives, employers usually fund operating costs through a combination of parent fees and employer subsidies. (See Employee Subsidies above.) Ben & Jerry's sets a particularly high standard by offering the same pay and benefit package (including three pints of ice cream daily) to its on-site day-care workers that it does to other Ben & Jerry's employees.

On- or near-site care not only allows concerned parents to check on their kids, but also supports parent-child bonding, a major criterion for dedicated parents. For example, St. Paul Companies has set up an electronic mail system so that its childcare center staff can send messages about the children to their parents throughout the day.

Of course, this Cadillac benefit costs like one—from-scratch facilities for large companies can run from $500,000 to $1 million to construct. Although some companies fear the liability risks of providing direct childcare (particularly in the face of new, stricter childcare regulations in some states), contracting out management to a professional provider mitigates the legal worries.

The Bowles Corporation, a Petersburgh, Vermont, engineering firm with twelve employees, has proved that resourceful smaller employers can provide on-site care as well. The company purchased a mobile home for fifteen hundred dollars, located it next to its offices, spent another thousand dollars to renovate it consistent with licensing standards, and staffed it with two experienced caregivers. As of late 1991, seven children of employees used the facility, along with five other children.

Company-Financed Off-Site Care: Many companies, nervous about the financial, legal, and managerial challenges of entering a business about which they know little, prefer to finance new or existing childcare services off-site in return for guaranteed slots for their employees. AT&T typically pays an existing center to expand its capacity by, say, thirty children as a way of ensuring that half of those slots go to employees' kids. Some companies pay to develop childcare networks of caregivers working out of their homes. These arrangements have flexibility advantages over central facilities. For example, Phoenix-based America West Airlines, whose employees work irregular shifts, travel, and are spread out geographically, assigned a small staff to train and monitor home-based caregivers in employees' neighborhoods, often supplying caregivers with toys and cribs as well.

Supporting Community Initiatives: Companies can expand and improve the quality of existing community childcare services, and create new services where none exists, through partnerships with public and other community-based agencies. Support can be in the form of cash, expertise, or product. North Carolina National Bank, now part of NationsBank, made low-interest loans available to new and expanding childcare centers in South Carolina as part of its overall corporate dedication to work/family programs. Of course, without subsidies lower-paid company employees may not be able to take advantage. Plus, initiatives take time to produce results.

Care for School-Age Children: A comprehensive childcare program includes before- and after-school care for older children, and makes provisions for school vacations as well. Staff of the childcare facility at S. C. Johnson & Son, Inc., in Racine, Wisconsin, pick up children after school and drive them to the center, where the kids can take part in crafts, recreation, and tutoring. Some companies contract with professional summer camps to provide care during summer vacation and also provide bus or van service to the camp. Such companies as Fel-Pro, United States Hosiery Corporation, and S. C. Johnson operate their own summer camps in addition to regular childcare programs.

Childcare in Extraordinary Circumstances: Some conscientious companies arrange priority access for their children at local hospitals with sick-child facilities, easing their working parents' concerns considerably. Companies such as Fel-Pro, HBO, 3M, Merck & Co., and the Seattle Times Company arrange with outside providers to deliver sick-child care to employees' children in their own home or family day-care homes, and also subsidize all or part of the resulting fees.

When companies require working parents to travel or work after regular hours, they may present them with difficult and costly childcare choices. Wells Fargo Bank reimburses employees for extra expenses in both circumstances. S. C. Johnson's center is open, as of this writing, from 6:00 A.M. to 6:30 P.M., but provides staff to stay with a child whenever the parent works late.

Day-Care Consortiums: Pooling resources with other companies saves start-up and administrative costs and also enables smaller companies to offer a childcare benefit that is competitive with those offered by larger firms. Ten companies in Boulder, Colorado, combined efforts as the Boulder Business Dependent Care Association, which offers each company's employees sick and emergency childcare; school-vacation programs; and a childcare resource-and-referral service. Large companies often cooperate, too. Procter & Gamble, for instance, sponsored a consortium childcare center in Norwich, New York. In fact, a small company with limited planning resources is well advised to first see if a large local firm has a program and is willing to accept a partner. Obviously, the consortium approach can be applied to many of the options covered above and below.

Approaches for Multinational Companies: Overseas employees, whether U.S.-born or local, have the same family concerns as working parents in this country. But creating work/family programs for them means matching initiatives to sociopolitical circumstances that vary widely from country to country. European governments provide much more support for working parents than does the U.S. government and often mandate business co-payments. However, government social programs are beginning to erode in many EC countries in the face of persistent economic troubles. Outside of Europe, government supports and mandates are far less common. ITT, which operates in seventy countries and has nearly fifty thousand employees overseas, approves the basics of all of its subsidiaries' benefit plans in its New York headquarters, but relies on local managers to work out the details.

Eldercare Options.
Gloria A. Scherma, Eldercare program director for New York–based Harris Rothenberg International, calls today's working parents the "sandwich generation" because so many are caring for aging parents as well as children—20 to 25 percent of working parents care for elderly persons in some significant manner, and they're spending from six to thirty-five hours a week doing it. By the late 1990s, according to a *Wall Street Journal* report, 44 percent of employees may be caring for an elder. Yet a 1992 survey of 1,004 companies by the Society for Human Resource Management found that two thirds offered no eldercare benefits at all.

In general, work/family considerations regarding eldercare don't differ much from those related to childcare. Those companies with programs tend to select from about the same set of options available to them for childcare: resource-and-referral programs, subsidies, pre-tax salary set-asides, informational seminars, on-site day care, emergency in-home care, and so on. Thus, most of the discussion above on childcare policy options also applies to eldercare polices, with a few differences.

• Primarily because of medical complications, employees may find eldercare far more stress-inducing and otherwise difficult to manage than caring for their children. Recognizing this, popular eldercare providers such as Work/Family Elder Directions in Boston, Massachusetts, and The Partnership Group in Lansing, Pennsylvania, offer employee counseling in addition to referrals.

• To help employees cover the potentially devastating costs of long-term nursing home care, many companies now offer to their work force long-term care insurance at group rates. Employees can usually choose to cover themselves and their spouses, as well.

· The federal pretax salary set-aside program (Dependent Care Assistance Program) does apply to eldercare but is limited to situations where the dependent adult lives with the employee. Only expenses incurred during work hours may be offset.

Major American corporations that have made substantial commitments to eldercare include the following: IBM, which has contributed to community initiatives aimed at expanding the supply of quality eldercare and also offers its employees group-rate long-term care insurance; Procter & Gamble, which offers subsidies (as part of a cafeteria-style benefit package) and long-term care insurance; and Fel-Pro, which subsidizes emergency home care in addition to providing informational seminars. Stride Rite has widely publicized its intergenerational on-site center, but employees have been slow to utilize the benefit. As the program director admitted to reporters, this may be because the company has not promoted the center as energetically internally as it has externally.

Family Leave and Flexible Scheduling.
Vickie Dorsey, an attorney in NationsBank's legal department, had her first baby while in the employ of another company, one with few programs for working parents. When the child, Lydia, was nine months old, Dorsey returned to work full-time because her employer didn't offer reduced schedules. "It was awful," she remembers. "It was difficult to concentrate all day at work because I felt so terrible about having that tearful crying scene every morning. But the clincher came when she was about eighteen months old. I got home one day and my caretaker told me that Lydia had been standing at the front window for an hour and a half looking out at the driveway going, 'Mama, mama?' And I said, That's it! Either they allow me to cut my schedule back or I do not work."

After "a lot of hair-pulling and teeth-gnashing," Dorsey was able to convince her employer to let her work part-time, which she continued during the three years before joining NationsBank. At the latter, a model family-friendly company, she works about an 80 percent schedule through what NationsBank calls its SelectTime program. She says that if the option disappeared, so would she. "At this time in my life, rather than work full-time, I wouldn't work at all. If employers fail to recognize that in today's society a lot of families are dual working families, if they don't allow some flexibility to make sure that parents get good time with their children, then they're going to pay for it ultimately because there are going to be generations of ill-adjusted kids."

The working world is full of Vickie Dorseys—talented, valuable professionals who will sacrifice their careers and salaries or find a better deal at another company if their employers won't allow them adequate time with their children. This only underscores the fact that *all the child- and eldercare options listed above still don't add up to a caring work/family policy, not to mention a competitive employee benefit, without significant family leave and flexible scheduling.*

FAMILY LEAVE

Welcome as it is, the Family and Medical Leave Act signed by President Clinton as one of the first actions of his administration remains a modest gesture. The act requires employers to offer only twelve weeks of unpaid leave (to care for a new or sick child, a parent, or a spouse) and applies only to companies with fifty or more employees, which exempts 95 percent of all employers. By comparison, in their book *Companies That Care,* authors Hal Morgan and Kerry Tucker profile fifty businesses that offer leaves of six months or *more.* They note that IBM allows three years of parental leave, Hewitt Associates and U.S. West two years, and Merck and Joy Cone eighteen months. The list of companies with one-year leave polices includes AT&T, Arthur Andersen, Gannett, John Hancock Mutual Life Insurance, Pacific Gas & Electric, Procter & Gamble, and U.S. Sprint among several others. That lineup certainly makes one wonder whom President Bush was speaking for when he vetoed, in the name of business, the first version of this bill.

Clinton's signature ended America's notoriety as the only industrialized nation in the world without family-leave job guarantees. In fact, according to Sheila Kamerman, professor of social work at Columbia University, some 117 countries have parental-leave polices. Indeed, many industrialized countries not only mandate job-guaranteed leave, but also require that the employee be paid (either by the company, the government, or both) most of his/her normal compensation.

Clearly, leaders in other industrialized nations don't seem to feel that providing such support to working parents runs counter to their economic interests. A few farsighted American employers also have noted how their family-leave and flextime benefits help the company as well. Johnson & Johnson studied the effectiveness of its flexible schedules and family-leave programs and found that 58 percent of all employees surveyed, and 71 percent of those using the benefits, described the policies as "very important" in their decision to stay with the company. The company's research also showed that absenteeism among employees using family leave and flexible schedules was 50 percent less than for the overall work force.

Among other possible financial benefits for businesses that offer competitive, or better, leave and flexible scheduling options:

· Increasing leave and flexible scheduling for working parents decrease a company's need to provide child- and eldercare support. (For higher-paid staff, that is. Lower-paid employees are often unable to afford unpaid leave or part-time work.)

· If there is a relationship between responsible parenting and responsible work habits, the quality of the parent/worker lost to inflexible companies may be exceptionally high and difficult to replace. In fact, a University of Chicago study of the eighteen hundred employees at Fel-Pro did demonstrate a strong relationship between high benefit users and high performers. High benefit users led other workers in team problem-solving and were twice as likely to submit suggestions for improving the company's products and procedures.

Some companies have held off offering family leave for fear that employees would abuse the privilege. Not in AT&T's experience— the corporation allows up to one year off for parental leave, but has found that 60 percent of new parents return to their jobs within three months and all but 10 percent return within six months.

FLEXIBLE WORK SCHEDULING

Flexible scheduling flies in the face of a number of American workplace traditions. First, until recently, few American companies approved of their employees' caring as much about their families as they do about their jobs. Second, many corporate cultures today still value most the employees who work the longest hours. Third, many companies promote a culture of mistrust, in which constantly looking over the employee's shoulder and other micro-monitoring is considered effective management. Obviously, employees who ask to work at home or work odd hours when a supervisor may not be present go against that grain.

Progressive employers take the opposite stance: Supporting employees in being caring parents, valuing quality over quantity of work, and trusting employees helps, not hinders, a company in reaching its goals. They note that flexibility and trust nurture the creative process, vital in innovation-intense enterprises like computer companies, but also important in any company hoping to keep pace in a world of near light-speed change. They argue that evaluating work by task is a far more direct measure than evaluating it by time. And they acknowledge their role, and stake, in building a society of healthy children.

Among those testing some of these assumptions, a Continental Corporation unit studied the effects of its new flexible schedule option and found that productivity went up 15 percent in the program's first fifteen months.

Flexible scheduling options include the following:

Reduced-Time Options: NationsBank's SelectTime is a typical reduced-hours program for working parents. Employees with a track record of one year full-time service and satisfactory performance reviews may negotiate a reduced-hours schedule on a predictable, long-term basis in order to care for dependent family members. Often, SelectTime employees will contract to accomplish their assigned tasks in fewer hours than usual so they can devote more time to family responsibilities and still hold on to their current positions. Salary is adjusted to the percentage of full-time hours worked; full benefits and status for promotions are retained.

Many employers feel that part-time schedules for working parents are a terrific deal because the employee stays more focused than if working full-time, and the company often gets full-time accomplishments for part-time money. By contrast, Apple Computer employees have no strict time requirements, just an agreement to get the job done. The company does not save salary, but its approach simplifies the supervisor's role and creates a trusting work environment.

Part-Time Phase-In: Most American companies do not pay employees during parental leave except for a few weeks of maternity/paternity leave. A phase-in option allows parents to partially offset the financial hardship of forgoing their salaries by working part-time during the leave period. The employee retains full benefits when phasing in and receives a prorated salary.

Job-Sharing: Job-sharing means that two employees split the responsibilities of one full-time job. The two job-sharers may work alternating or overlapping schedules. Steelcase, Donnelly Corporation, and Patagonia are some well-known companies offering this accommodation.

Job-sharing enables a company to retain two valued, experienced employees that it might otherwise lose to family demands (although it will pay increased benefit costs for the privilege). Several companies have noted significant reductions in absenteeism in job-shared positions. Other conceivable company gains include reduced overtime pay and improved job coverage, although Robert Rosen, author of *The Healthy Company,* notes that job-sharing works best with "stressful work for which two heads are better than one." But the two heads must be compatible, so the challenge is finding effective pairs.

Compressed Work Week: In most circumstances, a compressed work week means working a 40-hour job in four 10-hour days. Levi Strauss offers another version, allowing employees to work longer hours during summer months so that they can leave earlier on Fridays. Employees love the extra time off and, in the case of four-day weeks, reduced commuting time, but the long days on often leave them exhausted. Management must evaluate whether the employees' productivity suffers in a compressed work week, although the extended "recharge" period on the weekends may well compensate. Some labor unions oppose compressed work arrangements.

Working at Home: Computers enable many working parents to strike an ideal balance between work and family by turning the home into a remote office. But working at home requires great discipline on the employee's part because of the distractions, and great restraint on the manager's part because of the challenges of supervising an employee off-site. Obviously, mature, self-starting employees perform better than others in this type of situation.

Many working parents actually work more productively at home, where they aren't beset by worries about their children or guilt over being separated from them. Also, the commuting time and day-care problems they avoid may make the critical difference between maintaining a full-time schedule and needing to reduce time or quit.

Companies with significant numbers of employees working off-site also save office costs, which is why some companies promote off-site work even when children aren't involved.

Flexible Time: This term encompasses all the other flexible work options considered above. As such, it connotes more an attitude—to negotiate whatever time arrangements work for both employee and company—than a specific program. Given the high state of computing and telecommunications technology, the difficult commuting conditions in overpopulated urban areas, and increased business sensitivity to working parents' needs, "flextime" arrangements are quickly becoming the norm in American companies, at least those that want to recruit competitively and retain good people.

Gretchen Fields, human resources manager at the flexible, ultra–family oriented Hanna Andersson (a Portland, Oregon, retailer of high-quality children's clothing), notes that turnover in the company's professional positions runs from zero to 2 percent annually in a company in which 76 percent of those positions are held by women. Fields, who has two young children at home, works about forty hours a week at Hanna, catching up on evenings and weekends at home when she needs to. "No one looks aghast if I walk out of here at five o'clock. At other companies, if you walk out at five o'clock, it's unacceptable even if your work is done."

School Volunteer Programs: As mentioned above, some companies, such as NationsBank, also support parents in volunteering at their children's schools, a program as much education-based as it is family-based. In *Companies That Care*, Morgan and Tucker bluntly summarize business's long-term stake in such initiatives: "Companies that do not permit parents to attend meetings with teachers are contributing to the failure of our schools."

SINGLE WORKERS IN A FAMILY-FRIENDLY COMPANY

A comprehensive work/family program solves a multitude of problems for an employee, but creates one as well—single-worker backlash! Single workers, particularly those without responsibility for elders, may resent what they perceive as special favors for workers with family responsibilities, particularly if they have to cover for workers on family leave or departing early to take care of family concerns.

While this may smack of little Susie griping that Billy got better stuff for *his* birthday, benefits can be apportioned so that no employee's circumstance is rewarded at the expense of another's. Here are some suggestions from experts:

- Offer work/family benefits as part of a cafeteria-style package, so that employees can customize their benefits to their circumstances.
- Make flexible scheduling available to all employees, as Spiegel, Inc., does.
- Offer special benefits for singles. Because they cost the company less in medical insurance, Quaker Oats gives childless workers an annual three-hundred-dollar credit that can be cashed in on extra vacation days or other benefits.

Finally, a company should consider its single workers when planning special activities. Just as free football tickets may not mean much to female employees, and a company softball game may leave out disabled workers, scheduling a company dinner dance is rude to single workers without partners. Yes, managing working parents requires some juggling, much like parenting itself. And part of master parenting is ensuring that Susie does score as big at birthday-time as Billy.

Sexual Harassment

When Anita Hill took on Clarence Thomas, the Bush administration, and the Senate Judiciary men's club before a national television audience, she single-handedly elevated sexual harassment to the top drawer of women's work issues, where it joined the glass ceiling and the gender pay gap. But whereas documenting the latter two charges is easy, sexual harassment remains as vague a concept to many managers, especially male managers, as it did prior to Hill's entry on the scene. This speaks volumes about the cultural barriers that women face in the workplace. Many men will debate endlessly about whether this or that behavior or comment constitutes sexual harassment. However, the victims are far less confused about why they're uncomfortable at work, why they're often too upset to produce much, and why they sometimes feel compelled to quit.

Of course, male employees sometimes get sexually harassed, too. In May of 1993, a jury awarded Sabino Gutierrez of Ontario, California, $1 million in his case against his employer, Cal Spas, a hot tub manufacturer. As reported by the Associated Press, Gutierrez claimed that on several occasions Maria Martinez, the company's chief financial officer, entered his office, closed the door, and fondled and embraced him. Although he complained to other managers, none took action. When he continued to reject Martinez's advances, he said, she threatened him and had his managerial duties assigned to another employee. He eventually left his $45,000-a-year job.

As more women assume leadership positions in American companies, there will undoubtedly be more Sabino Guiterrezes. But for now, the overwhelming number of cases involve claims by women against men. Even a potentially authentic romantic proposition can exert disorienting sexual pressures on a female subordinate. For example, suppose a company owner finds himself irresistibly attracted to one of his female employees and asks her out to dinner. Suppose further that she has no romantic or sexual interest in him, but does enjoy working in his company, and aspires to advance in her career there. Will she feel comfortable declining his invitation? If she declines, will that affect her future performance evaluations and advancement opportunities? If she accepts, how should she behave on the date?

As this hypothetical situation should make clear, sexual harassment is not usually about sex per se. *It is about power.* And given that most working women, even women executives, work for a male boss, women remain at a distinct disadvantage in the power equation.

Power plays in the form of sexual harassment also occur between employees at the same level on the flow chart. Consider that not only are women being promoted into management positions in unprecedented numbers, they are also being hired into jobs that previously only men performed—in construction, for example. When men feel threatened by women entering their domain, they may fight back with sexual banter and behavior, actions that emphasize their majority position, since they couldn't get away with those actions otherwise.

Male-bonding rituals being what they are, some men will also sexually harass a woman—with a lewd comment, an uninvited caress, or an obscene picture left on her desk—more to impress their male cohorts than to solicit a response from their unfortunate target. The male-dominated power structure and culture in many companies enables, and even encourages, such behavior.

While these incidents imperil working women, they increasingly threaten the bottom line as well. Sexual harassment can cost a company dearly in terms of absenteeism, employee turnover, low morale, reduced productivity, and, of course, lawsuits, because whether or not male managers take sexual harassment complaints seriously, the courts and federal government do.

In 1980, the U.S. Equal Employment Opportunity Commission issued guidelines defining sexual harassment as a form of sex discrimination, which was outlawed by Title VII of the 1964 Civil Rights Act. In 1986, the Supreme Court added muscle to the EEOC regulations when it held unanimously in the case *Meritor Savings Bank* v. *Vinson* that sexual harassment violates Title VII if it is unwelcome and "sufficiently severe or pervasive to alter the conditions of the victim's employment and create an abusive working environment." The passage of the Civil Rights Act of 1991 enables sexual harassment victims to receive punitive and compensatory damages. In cases decided since, some victims have won seven-figure awards.

As Susan M. Benton-Powers, a Chicago attorney who advises companies on employment issues, told *Business Week*: "[Employers] have to investigate complaints. Otherwise, they can be held liable." In fact, following a ruling by a federal judge in Nevada, employers also are wise to act even when the accused harasser is a nonemployee such as a customer, client, or vendor. When Carol Powell, a blackjack dealer at the Las Vegas Hilton, grew tired of a customer's crude behavior, she complained to her bosses, but ultimately felt compelled to admonish the customer on her own. As reported in *Business Ethics* magazine, she was fired for her impertinence, but the judge ruled that she can sue the hotel for failing to protect her.

Essentially, the EEOC guidelines distinguish between two types of sexual harassment. The most overt form is the "quid pro quo," your basic "sleep with me or else" or analogous proposition. The second form involves behaviors that create an "abusive working environment." These behaviors can be cumulative. That is, the pinches, raunchy humor, and girlie calendars may reach a critical mass. The basic test in either case: Was the behavior unwelcome?

According to legal experts, drawing upon the EEOC regulations, sexual harassment includes the following actions, *if unwelcome*:

- Verbal comments and questions about an employee's body or sex life, even remarks made as compliments, such as "I wish my wife dressed the way you do"
- Nonverbal gestures, such as eyeing someone up and down
- Physical acts such as fondling, hugging, touching, brushing up against and, of course, assault or restricting an employee's movement, including blocking a doorway
- Display of objects such as sexually suggestive posters, calendars, cartoons, and pictures. An office party with nude dancers also qualifies
- Terms of endearment, so-called, such as "honey," "baby doll," or "sweetheart"
- Requiring an employee to submit to a sexual or romantic advance as a condition for a work-related decision (the "quid pro quo")
- Actual or threatened retaliation against an employee who complains or intends to complain of harassment
- Conduct directed toward one employee which, although not reported or rebuffed by that employee, creates a hostile working environment for others

If men find the sexual harassment issue confusing in America, they should try France. As reported in *Business Ethics*, 45 percent of women polled by the French magazine *Le Point* did not consider it harassment for a male manager to ask a woman to spend the weekend with him to discuss her promotion request. Yet a supervisor convicted of harassing a subordinate can be punished with a 100,000 franc ($10,000) fine and up to one year in jail.

Increased public awareness of the nature of sexual harassment, especially since Hill/Thomas, makes claims—and convictions—even more likely.

- Harassment claims filed with the EEOC, which had already been steadily increasing for years, jumped 50 percent in the year after the hearings.

- Of 607 women surveyed by the National Association for Female Executives (NAFE) in 1992, 60 percent reported that they had experienced sexual harassment.

- Perhaps most tellingly, a ten-point majority of registered voters polled in 1992 said they believed Hill over Thomas. At the time of the hearings, sixteen- to twenty-four-point majorities sided with Thomas.

So how has business responded to protect its female employees, and its own liability? According to that same NAFE survey, hardly at all. More than half of those questioned said that their companies had not confronted the issue. Of those companies that had acted, many had simply thrown a new policy or do's-and-don't's handout at the problem with no follow-through.

That won't be sufficient in the eyes of the EEOC. Commission guidelines advise companies to establish an effective grievance procedure by which employees can register complaints. Additionally, the EEOC advises employers to protect victims' confidentiality, and to protect them from retaliation as well. If they don't do these things, they invite liability.

What the EEOC wants to see in a sexual harassment grievance procedure is key to any ethical company structure—that is, a complaint path that bypasses the employee's direct supervisor, in case the supervisor is the offender. Grievance procedures, of course, should be supported by thorough investigation and adequate penalties to discourage harassing behaviors. Northern States Power Company (Hazel O'Leary's stomping ground before she became President Clinton's Secretary of Energy) permits employees to file complaints either through their supervisors, the human resources department, or a panel of peers. The company makes investigation results, with names deleted, available by request to employees and publishes them annually. Palmer & Dodge, a Boston law firm with 360 employees, allows its staff to file complaints through an impartial mediator, and has designated an ombudsperson to privately counsel victims.

Because sexual harassment is a cultural blind spot about which many men in particular don't have a clue, some companies try the carrot-and-stick tack by sponsoring awareness seminars in addition to setting tough investigation and enforcement standards. FMC Wyoming Company, a mining company in Green River, Wyoming, with a twelve hundred–person work force, hired an outside consultant to train in-house workshop leaders, thereby accomplishing twin goals: first, making peer counseling out of what might otherwise have been an oppressive top-down program; and second, saving the cost of having the consultant do everything.

The final element that makes a comprehensive sexual harassment program click is no-nonsense support from the top. When Northern States Power expanded its programs post–Hill/Thomas, each employee received a letter from CEO James J. Howard communicating the company's "zero tolerance" for harassment.

Although no company can afford to neglect sexual harassment, some programs can lead to unpleasant consequences. Raising awareness in the work force may increase complaints, for one thing. Nor is it always easy to know where to draw the line. Some apprehensive companies have banned office romances entirely, for instance. While this step may seem extreme, there is no refuting the fact that romances involving a male manager and female subordinate can become complicated legally, particularly when the love sours. Of course, such bans also may be illegal in states prohibiting employers' interference in employees' private lives.

Sexual harassment, a high-stakes problem with deep cultural roots, defies employers' inclinations to treat it casually. No one-shot seminar is going make the problem go away. The good news about this problem is that as more and more businesses do protect themselves and their female workers through ongoing education of their employees, the workplace may become an important transmitter of much-needed social change.

Managing HIV/AIDS

Speaking of transmitting important social change, business today can no more deny its interest, legally and otherwise, in stemming the HIV/AIDS crisis than it can in combating sexual harassment. As of this writing, more than two thirds of large work forces (those with more than twenty-five hundred employees) and nearly one in ten small employers (less than five hundred employees) have already experienced an employee with HIV infection or AIDS. And the disease is spreading fastest precisely among those populations—women, adolescents, and young adults—from which business will recruit most of its employees in the future. In addition, polls reveal that most teenagers are practicing behaviors, mainly unprotected sex, that increase their risk of HIV infection.

Internationally, HIV/AIDS infections are increasing in some countries at rates that dwarf those in the U.S. For example, the World Health Organization projects that by the year 2000, more than one million adults will become infected in Asia each year, a pace that surpasses even that of Africa's. This fact, of course, should particularly alarm multinationals utilizing Asian labor.

News on the treatment front is equally bleak. As of this writing, not one of the current drugs used to treat HIV-infected persons significantly impacts the course of the disease. Education—teaching the public the importance of taking proper precautions during sex and when injecting drugs—remains the most effective preventive measure. Yet U.S. education efforts, inhibited by religious and other social conservatives, have been scattershot and far less than frank. The powerful conservative constituencies also object to appropriating resources for what they mischaracterize as a disease of homosexuals and addicts. So Americans remain shockingly naïve not only about the causes of HIV and AIDS, but also how to respond to the crisis.

Meanwhile, new infections are occurring at a current rate of fifty thousand per year. According to the National Leadership Coalition on AIDS, fewer than half of the one million people now carrying HIV know they are infected and can infect others. In a phone conversation from his Washington, D.C., office, Coalition president B. J. Stiles stressed that any company with more than a handful of employees can expect to confront HIV/AIDS in the form of an infected or ill worker sometime this decade. The consequences can be severe for businesses unprepared to deal with them.

· The AIDS crisis has precipitated more lawsuits than any other disease in American legal history. Under the federal Americans with Disabilities Act (ADA) and other current laws, an employer can be held liable for discrimination for refusing to hire people with HIV or AIDS or for firing them; for discriminating against them in job assignments, performance appraisals, or benefit eligibility; or even for failing to make "reasonable accommodations" (those that do not unduly financially burden the employer) that would allow them to continue working. The ADA also prohibits discrimination against people who associate with disabled persons, including people with HIV/AIDS. Thus, the ADA covers a job applicant or employee who is a friend, relative, lover, roommate, or caregiver to an HIV carrier, even if the association is through volunteer work.

· Panic can destroy workplace esprit de corps when an employee comes down with the disease or even is suspected of carrying it.

Workers may refuse to share offices and equipment with ill co-workers, productivity may suffer, and valued employees may leave.

· The productivity of AIDS victims can be severely compromised unless the employer understands how to make appropriate accommodations.

· Although national health reform (pending as of this writing) might change this, AIDS currently increases the health/life insurance costs for businesses that provide plans. However, treating an AIDS patient does not cost more, on average, than treating patients with other life-threatening illnesses like cancer, and may cost less.

Thanks to a number of public interest organizations that are anxious to help, AIDS education doesn't cost much to dispense in the workplace. "The cost of an HIV program is pennies, not dollars," says Lee Berry, HIV program coordinator for the American Red Cross chapter in my region. The Red Cross is one of several organizations that provides AIDS education assistance to businesses at minimal cost. Others include the National Leadership Coalition on AIDS and the National AIDS Clearinghouse. (For contact information, see Resources.)

Polaroid designed its own program, which includes all the elements recommended below, plus partnerships with nationwide and community AIDS organizations, promotion of employee volunteer efforts, and a specially created AIDS information and counseling office. Speaking before the New England Corporate Consortium for AIDS Education, CEO I. MacAllister Booth said the entire initiative "is one fifth the cost of treating a single case of AIDS."

Because experts have been fighting the disease since 1981, they now have a good handle on how to manage it in the workplace. The New York Business Group on Health, Inc., and the National Leadership Coalition on AIDS, with support from the American Red Cross and the Centers for Disease Control, recommend a three-pronged approach.

Write and Implement an HIV/AIDS Policy: The simplest approach is to adopt the "Ten Principles for AIDS in the Workplace," developed by the New York City–based Citizen's Commission on AIDS and endorsed, as of this writing, by over six hundred employers nationwide. Those principles are:

1) People with AIDS or HIV (human immunodeficiency virus) infection are entitled to the same rights and opportunities as people with other serious or life-threatening illnesses.
2) Employment policies must, at a minimum, comply with federal, state, and local laws and regulations.
3) Employment policies should be based on the scientific and epidemiological evidence that people with AIDS or HIV infection do not pose a risk of transmission of the virus to co-workers through ordinary workplace contact.
4) The highest levels of management and union leadership should unequivocally endorse nondiscriminatory employment policies and educational programs about AIDS.
5) Employers and unions should communicate their support of these policies to workers in simple, clear, and unambiguous terms.
6) Employers should provide employees with sensitive, accurate, and up-to-date education about risk reduction in their personal lives.
7) Employers have a duty to protect the confidentiality of employees' medical information.
8) To prevent work disruption and rejection by co-workers of an employee with AIDS or HIV infection, employers and unions should undertake education for all employees before such an incident occurs and as needed thereafter.
9) Employers should not require HIV screening as part of general pre-employment or workplace physical examinations.
10) In those special occupational settings where there may be a potential risk of exposure to HIV (for example, in health care, where workers may be exposed to blood or blood products), employers should provide specific, ongoing education and training, as well as the necessary equipment, to reinforce appropriate infection control procedures and ensure that they are implemented.

Require All Managers and Supervisors to Attend Special Training on Managing HIV/AIDS: Those with authority over other employees need to understand the facts about HIV/AIDS so they can encourage appropriate behavior toward victims, address co-workers' concerns, and help victims adjust. Obviously, managers and supervisors may have personal concerns about managing victims; the training is the proper forum in which to deal with those.

The training should also communicate in no uncertain terms the company policy, and upper management's support for it, so managers and supervisors understand the legal issues and possible consequences of discriminatory actions. In 1989, an air-traffic controller supervisor at Dulles International Airport apparently neglected to read a Federal Aviation Administration policy mandating that air-traffic controllers who take AZT be transferred to administration. As reported in *Business Week*, when controller Ron Wilkinson disclosed that he was taking the drug, the supervisor suspended him. Wilkinson sued, and although he died before the verdict was rendered, the Virginia judge awarded his estate fifteen thousand dollars, plus legal costs.

Conduct Comprehensive, Compulsory AIDS Prevention/Education Programs for Employees: The employee program ideally serves several functions: explaining the company policy; teaching employees how AIDS is transmitted (and how it is not); encouraging empathy for AIDS victims; and facilitating discussion. Making a program compulsory ensures that AIDS awareness permeates the entire work force, including those employees who might otherwise be shy about attending. Of course, the program should also respect every employee's feelings on the crisis. Employees' fears, however irrational, about working with infected co-workers deserve compassionate handling, even though a nondiscriminatory company policy will not isolate the ill employee.

One other hint: Tailor the programs to the audience. Levi Strauss found that a video featuring gay, urban men talking about AIDS didn't go over nearly as well in El Paso as it had in San Francisco. The company put together a new program featuring a video in which "average employees" asked all the important questions.

No matter how appropriate a company's standard, managers may face some tough decisions when enforcing it. Hanna Andersson's sensitively written policy emphasizes that HIV and AIDS cannot be transmitted through casual work contact, and promises that managers will counsel and educate employees concerned about working with an infected co-worker. However, the policy warns, if after counseling and education efforts, an employee still refuses to work with an infected cohort, the employee may be disciplined or even terminated. In fact, the policy grew out of a situation in which a janitor had to be let go after resisting all intermediate measures to resolve the problem. "He didn't even want to empty the garbage for [the ill worker]," recalled company co-founder Gun Denhart painfully in her Portland, Oregon, office. Management hasn't needed to go to such lengths since.

Confidentiality, to which an infected employee is legally and ethically entitled, may also cause problems. As an employee's behavior and performance become increasingly affected by the condition, employees and supervisor may become increasingly perplexed and irritated.

In fact, few if any issues have the power to disrupt that HIV/AIDS does. By the same token, through educating its work force about the disease, a company makes a profound impact not only on those individuals but also on the communities in which they circulate. HIV/AIDS cannot be spread through casual contact, but HIV/AIDS prevention can.

CHAPTER 4

Employee Rewards and Job Security: Honoring the Wealth-Creators

THROUGHOUT THE ECONOMIC SLUMP of the early 1990s, the demand for one product—management books—grew and grew. It wasn't hard to explain. Since few were applying the information in them, companies stumbled and bumbled, and their leaders went out and bought more advice that they could ignore.

It's management orthodoxy, at least as preached in books and seminars on the subject, that the company that treats its work force as a long-term investment invests in its own long-term success. How many millions of books have been sold in recent years praising the wonders of empowerment, teamwork, partnerships between management and workers, and the long-term view? Looking at recent economic developments, however, one has to wonder if those who bought the books ever took them from their bags.

Corporations have slashed and exported jobs, driven down wages, cut benefits, replaced permanent positions with temporary help, and busted organized labor, all in the name of reducing expenses and boosting profits. Job security has gone the way of the push lawnmower—nothing wrong with it, much healthier for the user in fact, but terribly unfashionable. Mainstream business leaders preach a gospel now about maintaining flexibility, avoiding long-term labor commitments, and cutting costs to the bone including pay, benefits, and the people that earn them. They haven't really rejected conventional management wisdom. They've just stopped paying attention to it.

Of course, without job security and the decent compensation associated with it, none of the things discussed in those management books and seminars works. Employees burdened with extra duties because of layoffs and fearful that their own jobs could soon disappear hardly feel like giving their all for the company. The resentment and insecurity also dissipate any sense of team spirit and common goals.

In remarks before a Social Venture Network conference audience in April 1993, Robert Rosen, president of Healthy Companies, a nonprofit organization that studies the relationship of company employee practices to high performance, noted American business's misguided attempts to become more competitive: "A lot of companies have been making major investments in TQM [Total Quality Management] in the last few years. But we're finding that the investments don't work if the companies don't have meaningful work and a sense of purpose, if there isn't valuable economic security, and people don't enjoy working inside the company. Why should they make commitments to TQM if they're going to lose their jobs?"

In yet another bid to lower labor costs, employers have pounded unions in earnest since 1970 or so, and in the Reagan/Bush era, with government's enthusiastic cooperation. But organized workers weren't the only ones to feel the pain. As social commentator William Greider has noted, organized labor's retreat accompanied a retreat in key causes for ordinary citizens: wages, health benefits, housing, progressive taxation, workplace health and safety, working hours, and other "civilized working conditions." The paired decline was no coincidence, Greider writes: labor had supplied much of the political power for those causes. But business has paid too, with more on-the-job injuries, sluggish productivity from disheartened workers, and consumers with little extra cash to spend or invest.

Unfortunately, if you don't examine them too closely, dominant economic measures seem to confirm the canniness of corporate America's disregard for the American working person. As I was writing this in early 1994, the economy had started to grow at a promising rate again after a several-year slump. Corporate profits and productivity were up. Even unemployment appeared to be abating.

But ordinary people weren't sharing in the celebration. Many of the new jobs were temporary, low-wage, or stripped of benefits—often all three at once. Productivity improved partly because corporations had taken advantage of low interest rates to invest in technology that replaces still more jobs, and partly because employees in downsized companies were forced to do the work of one and a half people. Besides, a prosperity uptick built on such conditions doesn't exactly spread the wealth around. The new corporate economics denies more and more Americans the means to buy the companies' products. In an economy largely built on consumer purchases, I can't understand where corporate America thinks this is all supposed to lead.

Excellent compensation packages and job guarantees certainly don't ensure business success. IBM's top-drawer pay and benefits and no-layoff policy didn't insulate the company from billions of dollars in annual losses early this decade. Over the same years, Delta Airlines led its industry in compensation, but was among the leaders in troubled finances as well.

However, many industry analysts assigned IBM's and Delta's problems to management miscalculations into which the rank-and-file presumably had little input. We'll examine the virtues of the participatory management approach in the next chapter. For our purposes here, let's just say that for every IBM or Delta, there's an employer that attributes its success to keeping its work force well-compensated, stable, and happy.

For example, Milton Moskowitz and Robert Levering, authors of *The 100 Best Companies to Work for in America*, rate Fel-Pro, a Skokie, Illinois, automotive parts manufacturer with two thousand employees, in their top-ten in pay and benefits, and also grade it tops in job security. As of early 1993, the company hadn't had an unprofitable quarter in thirty years—in an industry frequently troubled since 1980—and had a waiting list of five thousand people who wanted to work there. In 1990s America, Fel-Pro comes off as eccentric, building profits by keeping employees satisfied and secure. But it also has a financial track record that few if any of its downsizing, job-exporting, and labor-bashing competitors can match.

In the remainder of this chapter, we'll describe more such employers. We'll also note the inevitable ambiguities contained within compensation, labor, and job security issues. How does a socially responsible company compete with companies who pay bottom-dollar wages to Third World factory workers? What is the role of unions in a company that already takes good care of its people? The path of the generous employer is not always an unobstructed one, but it does lead to emotional satisfactions with which more Machiavellian companies are entirely unfamiliar and, frequently, admirable financial paybacks as well.

Pay and Benefits

In 1914, Henry Ford made national headlines when he raised his factory workers' pay to five dollars a day, twice the going rate. He had a ready explanation: "These are the people who will buy my cars."

Ford's simple reasoning has escaped most of today's business leaders, although even mainstream publications such as *Business Week* have begun to notice the correspondence between falling employee compensation and feeble consumer demand. In terms of real dollars, wages have dropped steadily—that is, failed to keep pace with inflation—since about 1973. In that year, political economist Walter Russell Mead writes, American workers averaged $315 (in inflation-adjusted 1982 dollars) in weekly pay, up from $196 in 1947. By the end of 1990, the average weekly wage had fallen to $258, or halfway back to the 1947 figure. Blue-collar workers have suffered the steepest slide—5.9 percent wage erosion for blue-collar males in the period from 1988 to 1992, according to an Economic Policy Institute study. But white-collar wages are tumbling, too—2.4 percent decline for males over the same period.

It's hard to fathom what conservative business leaders and their allied policy advocates want when they complain about the high cost of American labor. Census bureau statistics reveal that 14.4 million year-round, full-time workers (18 percent of the domestic work force) had annual earnings below the poverty level in 1990, compared to 10.3 million (14.6 percent) in 1984 and 6.6 million (12.3 percent) in 1974.

The real numbers of working poor dwarf even those figures, note Richard A. Cloward and Frances Piven, professors at Columbia University School of Social Work and CUNY, respectively. The average family spent one third of its income on food in the 1960s when federal officials first calculated the poverty line, so the line was drawn at three times food costs, adjusted for family size. By 1990, food made up only one sixth of the average family budget, mainly because such factors as health and housing costs had risen at much higher rates. A full-time worker receiving the minimum wage of $4.25 per hour makes $8,840 a year. The official 1991 poverty line for a family of four is $13,920; if recalculated to include the "real cost" of necessities, Cloward and Piven argue, the figure would be $21,600.

As real wages drop, benefits disappear. We can blame some of this on the costs of employer-provided health plans, which have risen so much faster than inflation that they have crowded out other benefits in many workplaces. But many employers have used the excuse of high health-plan costs to eliminate benefits altogether. They replace full-time workers with part-time or temporary employees or foreign workers or machines, and they strip new full-time positions not only of health coverage but of overtime pay, paid vacations, and sick days. Most of the new jobs in the domestic economy are in its fastest-growing sector, service industries. In many cases, these jobs offer only minimal benefits or no benefits at all.

Of course, some companies that pinch their workers' wages and benefits end up getting pinched themselves. In 1987, General Electric's electric motor division demanded that its hourly workers accept an 11 percent pay cut and forgo scheduled raises of $1.30 per hour. Threatened with their jobs, the workers capitulated, saving the company $25 million. The company saved another bundle by closing two motor plants, eliminating a thousand jobs. However, as a GE senior vice president admitted to *Business Week* writer Aaron Bernstein, worker morale collapsed and "productivity went to hell."

There are other ways of getting an edge on the competition—increasing productivity and improving quality, for example. In fact, after the dismal failure of its cost-saving programs, GE's motor division switched strategies in 1991 to an approach that stressed quality and productivity driven by work-team decision-making. Whether the company understands that such an approach depends upon satisfied, secure employees remains to be seen.

The temptation to economize on labor is understandable if one accepts the current business view of labor as just another business expense. However, many leading business thinkers don't. Irwin Kellner, chief economist of Chemical Banking Corporation in New York, noted in a *Los Angeles Times* business commentary how such misplaced priorities had undermined consumer purchases and now were destroying companies from the inside: "Employees should be treated as assets to be developed, not costs to be cut whenever possible. Capital and production can migrate across state and national borders, but people will always make the difference. For it is only from people that ideas, initiative, and commitment can arise that will help a company distinguish itself from its competition, and thus survive and prosper."

TOWARD A SOCIALLY RESPONSIBLE COMPENSATION POLICY

Kirk Hanson, first president of The Business Enterprise Trust, which promotes business responsibility, and senior lecturer at Stanford University's Graduate School of Business, suggests four criteria by which a company can assess the social responsibility of its compensation policies:

1) Adequate compensation to each employee to provide for a family
2) Preference for full-time employees over part-time
3) Executive compensation proportional to other employees
4) Gain-sharing system rewarding all employees for company success

Proving that his are neither empty nor unreachable ideals, Hanson abstracted his principles from exemplary policies of existing businesses. For instance, Ben & Jerry's "compressed compensation ratio" dictates that "the highest paid employee . . . (including corporate officers) may earn no more than seven times what the lowest-paid employee could earn for an equivalent work week, excluding overtime." The lowest-paid B & J employee, as of early 1993, made $16,339 (including $2,819 worth of benefits), setting the maximum total compensation paid by the company at $114,373. However, an additional policy plank states that no employee can make over $100,000 until all full-time employees with at least a year's seniority are earning at least $8.50 per hour (twice the minimum wage).

Admittedly, Ben & Jerry's is an almost uniquely equitable employer. Among companies of comparable or greater size, I know of only one other with a similar policy, office-furniture maker Herman Miller, which limits CEO cash compensation to twenty times the average company paycheck. That fact speaks volumes about the topsy-turvy compensation values of contemporary American business. In the typical American major corporation, *Business Week* notes, the CEO makes 157 times—an average of $3.8 million in 1992—what the average factory worker earns. His typical Japanese counterpart makes $872,646 (1991 figure), according to the same publication, less than 32 times the salary of an average Japanese factory worker, and that doesn't account for bonuses that can hike the factory worker's earnings by a third. True, a Japanese CEO usually stays for life, so there is no CEO market or raiding to bid up the price tag. Also, Japanese business culture stresses teamwork and consensus management, and de-emphasizes the role of the CEO. That's in stark contrast with the heroic American model, in which the new CEO rides into town to save the day. As for Ben & Jerry's approach, though they have had occasional difficulty filling senior management positions at their way-below-market executive pay levels, the process tends to attract people who care more about the company than the money.

But these considerations don't alter the underlying facts of American executive pay. While employee salaries continue to slide and more and more full-time workers are forced below the poverty line, executive pay skyrockets. Between the economically dismal years of 1991 and 1992, it rose over 56 percent! The latter fact points up another glaring disparity, the gulf between executive pay and performance. As *Business Week's* editors noted in an editorial savaging executive pay trends, when the economy was at peak power in 1960, CEOs of major corporations earned an average of $190,000, a "mere" 41 times the salaries of average factory workers. Today, most corporations acknowledge that employee input and teamwork is vital to company success yet structure their pay scale as if only the CEOs' contributions matter.

More than just unseemly, exorbitant CEO pay arguably bears part of the blame for America's deep economic and social troubles. Fortune 500 CEOs, for better or worse, exert a powerful influence on the country's national and state political leaders and thus help set the socioeconomic agenda. However, their wealth often insulates them from the needs and problems of ordinary citizens. For example, major corporate CEOs can afford the best private health care for their families no matter what the state of the national health care system. Yet many executives lobby against a national health plan and otherwise argue for shrinking the social safety net even as their actions, massive layoffs and cuts in wages and benefits, strain the net at its current level.

We can credit the corporate trend toward part-time workers for much of the strain. Part-time employment is a social positive when a company offers it as an option to working parents. But a company that pursues a part-time employment strategy simply to avoid paying benefits exploits workers who take those jobs because they have no other choice. Most part-time employees have to work at least two jobs to have any hope of paying for rent and food. Without benefits and with the increased costs of traveling to two workplaces, they may not even be able to reach that modest goal without public assistance.

Hanson's fourth criterion, a reward system for employees who help make the company successful, is discussed later in this chapter, in the section Sharing the Wealth. However, placing his other principles in contemporary social context reveals them as less an employee wish list than a prescription for basic workplace fairness and for social health.

Job Security

"IBM Will Reduce Workforce by 85,000." "GM to Cut 74,000 Jobs." "Sears Dropping Over 100,000 Employees." We hardly flinch anymore at headlines like these. With huge layoffs all the rage in corporate America, we almost expect to see four- and five-figure job cuts announced in the daily business pages (although carefully euphemized as "downsizing" or "restructuring"). Perhaps six-figure announcements like Sears's cause us to pause before the next sip of coffee, but only momentarily.

Farther down in the business section come the discussions of other job trends: shifting to part-time and temporary workers as noted above; "de-layering" corporate hierarchies, which wipes out numerous middle-management positions; jettisoning in-house professionals in favor of professionals hired on a per-project, contract basis; the ongoing export of manufacturing jobs to countries with cheaper labor and lax regulatory climates; replacing person-power with new, productivity-boosting technology. A few fast facts reveal the dimensions of the changes:

· A 1993 Economic Policy Institute study revealed that 60 percent of the jobs created in the year's first six months were part-time positions. Half of those were filled by people who had sought full-time work.

· Nearly 30 million Americans, over one quarter of the U.S. labor force, work in temporary, part-time, or contract jobs, according to a study published in *The American Prospect*. Most of these workers lack benefits, pensions, union representation, and job security, not to mention access to a career ladder.

· Since the mid-1980s, notes *Business Week*, American corporations have eliminated well over 2 million middle-management positions, in addition to the 8 million manufacturing jobs erased from 1979 to mid-1992. Few of the displaced white- or blue-collar workers are finding new positions at anything close to their previous pay.

Pessimists worry that job security has disappeared forever from the American job scene; apologists for the current trends "assure" them that they are correct, but claim it's a positive sign. Both groups misinterpret contemporary reality by making the same mistake that the job-slashers do, not looking far enough into the future.

First of all, the above-mentioned changes are not necessarily permanent, and not necessarily bad. A large share of American unemployment stems from government defense spending cuts in the post–Cold War era, an appropriate and necessary step (although public hysteria about government spending has thus far prevented the retraining and redeploying of these workers for socially useful projects, such as building light-rail systems in large cities). The flattening of corporate hierarchies, rough as it is on middle managers, means that top-down management structures are giving way to more democratic forms in which line employees can make meaningful input.

It is also hard to believe that the reliance on temporary, contract, and part-time help constitutes more than an extremely short-sighted fad. Undeniably, these "core-and-ring" companies save on benefits and wages, in addition to weakening unions. They also better equip themselves to deal with sudden economic shifts, or so they maintain. However, they lose in other areas that matter more—loyalty, commitment, productivity, suggestions, innovations, caring, customer service, and work quality—because terrorized and nonpermanent workers turn a company's vital human core into something fragile and quivering. As we've seen, these "cost-cutting" measures also destroy consumer demand and strain the public purse through lost income tax revenues and increased public welfare cost.

There's yet more backfire built into the current trends:

Doubts About Downsizing. Downsizing turns out to be more dud than magic cure-all for most companies. For example, Eastman Kodak

(Rochester, New York) spent $1.2 billion and sliced twelve thousand jobs in a major restructuring effort to improve profitability, but the "no pain, no gain" strategy produced only pain: profit margins reduced by half, mediocre stock prices, and near-imperceptible growth from levels reached a decade before. In 1992, the American Management Association surveyed 547 companies that had downsized within the previous six years and found that only 43.5 percent showed increased operating profits. Because companies that downsize are normally troubled to begin with, downsizing may stop the bleeding in the short term. But that often amounts to treating the symptom instead of the disease. The hundreds of thousands of employees cut loose by General Motors and IBM didn't cause their companies' problems. According to most analysts, bureaucratic inertia and poor executive decision-making did. Nor does job surgery produce growth, which comes from creative, not destructive, acts: new products, new markets, more market share.

In fact, downsizing can inhibit growth because it leaves a company ill-equipped to meet sudden new demand or even current needs. Several major corporations have reduced their work forces by offering generous early retirement packages, only to lose more—and often better—people than they anticipated. Centerior Energy Corporation, an Ohio-based utility, unexpectedly lost one fourth of its senior management corps to an early-1990s employee buyout initiative, stripping it of much of its experienced talent. Eastman Kodak miscalculated how many would bite on its 1991 buyout bid, and had to spend more money to refill two thousand positions. In fact, *Business Week* reports that, according to a consulting firm study, "two thirds of companies offering early retirement in recent years unintentionally lost particularly valued employees."

For Workers, the Last Straw. The Chicago-based National Safe Workplace Institute, in its 1993 report titled "Breaking Point," warns that downsizing, heavier workloads, and eroding compensation have caused many stressed workers to snap, contributing to 110,000 incidences of workplace violence and 750 deaths in 1992.

Cuts Cut Sales? Forced by financial circumstances to live more simply, many consumers seem to be discovering that they do just fine with less. This is good news for the environment, which is suffering from a heavy overdose of consumerism, but bad news for business in its current, albeit environmentally unsustainable, form.

Furthermore, many of the arguments put forth by those doing the restructuring don't wash. For instance:

What High-Priced Labor? To justify their new reliance on part-time and temporary workers, executives point to "unacceptably" escalating nonwage costs such as health benefits. Nonwage costs *have* risen faster than inflation, but declines in real wages plus higher productivity from new technology and streamlined processes have more than compensated. According to *Business Week* writer Aaron Bernstein, it cost less to hire new workers in 1993 than it had ten years earlier.

Workers Pay the Freight. At any rate, workers pick up the check for benefit cost increases with skimpier pay hikes. An MIT economist studied spiraling workers' compensation costs between 1979 and 1987 and found that they lowered real wages without costing jobs.

The Global-Competition Fallacy. When employers explain why they're sending so many jobs to Mexico and overseas, "global competition" is the usual excuse offered. Within this global contention lies only a partial truth. In light manufacturing, which requires minimal skills and machinery, it's true that a domestic company has a tough time competing with foreign products assembled at a fraction of the labor cost.

For example, the socially idealistic Deja Shoe, a new company making shoes out of recycled materials, found it could not compete with the Nikes and Reeboks of the world without having its product assembled overseas. Since they built the company on the principle of making new markets for recycled materials, founder Julie Lewis and her management team felt they had to go offshore as their competitors did. "If we make a shoe in the United States and it costs two hundred bucks, nobody is going to buy it and then what are you doing for market development?" she asserted as we talked in her office in Tigard, Oregon. As a socially responsible company, Deja monitors labor conditions in the foreign factories with which it contracts and has made improvements where it could.

The situation differs in heavier industries such as auto manufacturing, where American workers produce at much higher rates than do their lesser-trained and -equipped Third World counterparts. The productivity gap negates much or all of the wage difference. For example, while studies show that well-trained Mexican workers in modern plants such as the Ford plant at Hermosillo produce at levels equal to American labor, few such plants are on-line in the Third World, and thus few native workers are trained to operate them. An October 1992 study by the Congressional Office of Technology Assessment found that it was actually slightly cheaper, $8,770 to $9,180, to build a car in the U.S. than in Mexico. Why? Better-trained American workers and advanced plants totally offset the Mexican wage advantage, and transporting parts to Mexico and the cars from Mexico to the U.S. is expensive. Notice that when Mercedes-Benz decided to build a $300 million assembly plant away from home to escape highly paid German labor, it chose not a Third World country but Alabama.

Besides, many employers offer the same "global competition" rationale to explain away their campaign against "high" domestic wages. Japanese workers earn about the same as those in the U.S., German workers much more, and these are the global competitors we supposedly fear the most. The more truthful explanation, as many executives now admit, is that the job export threat makes a mighty hammer for driving down wages at home and winning other labor concessions.

Amid all the job turmoil, many of America's leading companies pursue a different tack, basing their performances on nurturing their most valuable resource, their people. Examine Moskowitz and Levering's list of the best companies for job security and you will find some of the nation's most admired firms, Federal Express, Southwest Airlines, automotive supplier Donnelly, and other household names such as Hallmark Cards and S. C. Johnson Wax. Consider the following examples:

· Instead of relocating plants overseas, Midas Muffler (Chicago) kept jobs home in the 1980s and increased its employees' value through participatory decision-making, incentives for injury-free performance, and training in automation and quality control. Despite wage and other overhead expense increases, the company produced a record number of exhaust pipes and tailpipes in 1990 at a unit cost unchanged from 1982.

· H. B. Fuller policy states that no worker will be laid off unless the company has a losing year. As of this writing, it hasn't had one yet. When the St. Paul–based company, which makes adhesives, sealants, and coatings, has closed plants, it has offered employees help in relocating to other Fuller plants or finding other jobs. Workers are guaranteed 32 hours of weekly work during work stoppages, and if that work can't be found around the plant, they are paid to do community service.

· While waiting in an airport on a research trip for this book, I asked a young man behind a Southwest Airlines check-in desk if everything I'd heard about Southwest as a good employer was true. I could hardly stop his gushing in time to make my flight. As of this writing, Southwest is the only profitable major company in its terribly troubled industry. Yet counter to much current business thinking, the company pays its employees well, offers them profit-sharing, runs a union shop (90 percent of the employees are unionized), and invests in its people through extensive training (most senior positions are filled from within the company). Not coincidentally, it appears, Southwest is an industry leader in customer satisfaction.

Sharing the Wealth

The notion of employers sharing the wealth with their employees rests on two principles, one ethical and the other pragmatic:

1) From an ethical standpoint, giving employees a stake in the business's success honors their role in helping to create that success.
2) Pragmatically speaking, the surest way to get employees to act like owners in terms of responsibility and motivation is to make them owners or otherwise enable them to share in company gains.

Of course, as anyone who's ever examined our welfare system knows, it takes more than good intentions to make an incentive program work. But any number of companies have discovered "the secret formula" of wealth-sharing with their work forces and boosted their fortunes as a result.

The most widely discussed—and to some extent, the most controversial—motivation/reward tool remains employee stock ownership plans (ESOPs). ESOPs have an ambiguous history when it comes to improving a company's lot. But that spotty record seems mainly due to the less-than-generous spirit with which many ESOPs are established. Particularly when the company gives employee-owners a say in decision-making (just as it would other owners), ESOPs clearly give a company the ability to pull ahead of its competition.

Research on ESOP companies virtually shouts this point. A 1986 study performed by the National Center for Employee Ownership (NCEO) and published in the *Harvard Business Review* examined forty-five companies five years before and five years after establishing their plans. NCEO also compared each company to at least five competitors. The employers that combined their ESOPs with participatory management showed performance gains of 8 to 11 percent over their preplan numbers, and also significantly outperformed their rivals. (Interestingly, the subject companies were beating their competition before going the ESOP route, but the plans widened the gap.) In companies that installed ESOPs without changing decision-making practices, the plans made little difference.

Subsequent studies, using a variety of methodologies, point to and expand upon the same conclusions: blending ESOPs with participatory management usually improves performance, but ESOPs—and for that matter, participatory management—alone don't necessarily make much impact. Corey Rosen, executive director of the National Center for Employee Ownership, offers the following explanation: "Ownership provides the incentive to share ideas and information but the structures to do so must also be present. Employees are not accustomed, and are rarely asked, for their ideas. Managers are not in the habit of asking. . . . Participation without ownership, by contrast, provides the structures, but not the motivation, and most participation programs, partially as a result of this, do not last very long."

As Rosen implies, the controversy surrounding ESOPs begins with the attitude with which plans are implemented. Because of employer concessions written into the regulations governing ESOPs, some companies have used the plans to enrich owners and senior managers without improving lesser-paid employees' compensation packages. Obviously, these more cynical applications of ESOPs can't be expected to advance the company's accomplishments. Other ESOP caveats include a web of federal rules, high administrative costs, and tax benefits that make sense only for companies with at least $100,000 in profits.

Still, dramatic ESOP success stories abound.

Springfield Remanufacturing Company. This engine rebuilder seemed graveyard-bound in 1983 when factory manager Jack Stack and twelve other employees negotiated an ESOP-based leveraged buyout to effectively "buy our jobs," as Stack now puts it. At the time, the company employed 119 people and had a debt-equity ratio of almost 90 to 1. Its stock was valued at ten cents a share. Three years later, the debt-to-equity had fallen to 5 to 1; by late 1992, it was 1.88 to 1, stock had risen to $18.20 a share, and the work force had grown to 720, a sixfold post-ESOP increase. Furthermore, Stack was able to craft a winning book, *The Great Game of Business*, by recounting the Springfield experience.

Stack divulged the secret of Springfield's resurrection in a talk at a Social Venture Network workshop at a spring 1993 conference in Atlanta: "What we stumbled into is the realization that all those management practices and all those things we did in order to try and live within this philosophy of wage, labor, and supervision might not even be needed at all. What we embarked upon was a philosophy that we would try and teach the employees to think and act like owners. We would show them the rules, keep score, and basically give them a stake in the outcome. And it's absolutely unbelievable what happened."

In essence, not only did the company give its employee-owners decision-making power, but it also gave them the information to use it wisely by opening the books and teaching employees what the figures mean. "I'll never forget," Stack told the workshop attendees, "the story of walking through the fuel injection department and a janitor who had been sweeping comes up to me and says, 'You know, you guys are always teaching us business and financials and you're always talking about the impact on job security. Well, I was looking at your balance sheet the other day and 76 percent of your receivables are in one marketplace, and that marketplace typically has a recession every seven years. What are you going to do about it if you really believe in job security?' " The statement stunned Stack, who had never before looked at the company's predicament in those terms. He called a management meeting, presented the problem; the company began to diversify from that moment forward.

In the mid-1980s, the company lost a GM contract and, with it, 40 percent of its business. Faced with making either drastic cutbacks or a miracle comeback, the employees voted to keep everyone on payroll and develop new products to fill the hole. They developed one hundred products, and annual sales jumped 30 percent. From the ESOP's inception through 1991, annual sales grew from $16.5 million to $70 million.

Avis. Avis may be number two in car rentals, but it is number one in employee ownership, America's only major corporation that is 100 percent employee-owned. Through highly structured employee participation groups (EPGs) and EPG-elected regional representatives, employees have decision-making input at every level of the vast company, based in Garden City, New York. Senior vice president Robert Salerno told *Business Ethics* magazine that the participatory scheme really started to produce results once managers saw that employees were more interested in respect and cooperation than hefty raises. In the year following the employee buyout in 1987, stock prices catapulted 300 percent; they rose another 15 percent the next year. Profits, $16 million in 1987, hit $79 million in 1988 and $93 million in 1989.

ESOPs are not the only way to reward employees for helping the company to grow. In fact, they're not even the only way to make employees stockholders. The following examples show various ways that companies profit from the subtle psychology and hard cash of incentives.

Donnelly. This automotive parts maker, perhaps the preeminent democratic company in the nation (see Chapter 5), pays employees back for their productive decisions through quarterly bonuses tied to the company's "return on investment" (the money made on investments by stockholders). Whenever the return exceeds 5.2 percent, management distributes the rewards. From 1985 to 1992, Donnelly sales tripled and employment doubled.

Cin-Made. Robert Frey, president of this packaging firm established near the turn of the century, wanted the company and its employees' union "to become worthy partners, not worthy adversaries," as he told me in early 1994; so he negotiated a creative incentive plan that has paid off for employees and owners alike. The union agreed to lock wages at the 1984 level. In return, the company established a merit increase system, jointly administered by union and management, for employees attaining additional skill levels, and set up a uniquely generous profit-sharing program. The program guarantees that at least 18 percent of pretax profits, without caps or qualifications, are distributed to union members. As at Springfield Remanufacturing, management also educates employees on the financial aspects of the operation, so they understand their stake in everything they do.

As of our conversation, the average profit-sharing over the previous four and a half years was 36 percent of base wages, or about $4,000, per employee. Nonunion employees and managers participate in a similar plan. Frey acknowledged, "Some businesspeople may think I'm nutty as a fruitcake giving this kind of money back to employees, but our profits have skyrocketed. I didn't do this just for social reasons."

Several companies have found ways to turn employees into owners without turning to ESOPs. For instance, Life USA, a Minneapolis-based life insurance company, pays employees 10 percent of their compensation in stock. PepsiCo offers stock options, totaling 10 percent of compensation, to all of its 120,000 employees. Under its SharePower program, the options, granted each July 1, give employees the right to buy stock at the July 1 price for the next ten years, no matter how high the stock flies. Since PepsiCo stock more than doubled in value between 1989 and 1993, employees can make serious money through SharePower. And employees need not invest cash. They can purchase shares with appreciated stock value as well.

Labor Relations

Writing on this section commenced on Labor Day 1993, not a happy time for American workers; in fact, many of them would have been glad to work that day if they only had a job with decent compensation and security. Determining social responsibility in labor relations is a complicated task, but there is no denying, as implied earlier, that the twenty-year-plus slide in the American wage-earners' lot coincides with the decline in organized labor's strength.

As of 1992, union membership had fallen to 15.5 percent of the work force, down from a 1954 peak of 35 percent and 23 percent in 1980, according to a Labor Day 1993 Associated Press story. In the private sector, membership totals a scant 11.5 percent. According to several social analysts, the tumble began when antagonistic corporations realized they could profitably violate the 1935 Wagner Act protecting workers' right to organize. Because of inevitable legal delays, lax enforcement by the National Labor Relations Board, and insignificant penalties, they suffered minimally if at all when they fired workers attempting to organize. With the election of Ronald

Reagan as President, government's aggression against organized labor came to match that of union-busting executives.

To some extent, these executives, and later, government, simply took advantage of public anti-union sentiment for which the unions themselves are partially culpable. For example, the public holds unions partly responsible for past inflation. (Unquestionably, in better economic times, employers did simply pass on to consumers whatever wage and benefit increases they negotiated with workers. On the other hand, nonunion workers also benefited from the upward pull on wages, and more money was pumped into the economy, also benefiting wage-earners.) Mainstream unions alienated minorities and liberals because they were slow to accept minorities into their ranks. Nor has it helped that, brought up in an individualistic society that treats "socialism" as a swear word, Americans evidence none of the class consciousness of European workers and their unions.

Even many of the exemplary employers mentioned in these pages, including some of the country's otherwise most progressive companies, attempt to end-run around organized labor when they can. Typically, they defend their stance by pointing to generous wages, benefits, and work conditions. We take such good care of our people, goes the usual line, that they have no need to organize. In some cases, this may well be true. Fel-Pro, one of Moskowitz and Levering's top ten, has no unions, and its highly paid and benefited workers apparently couldn't care less. The same seems to be true at fellow top-ten company Beth Israel Hospital in Boston.

But Federal Express, another top-ten employer with a nonunion history, had a different experience, with one segment of its work force anyway. In January 1993, 51 percent of the company's twenty-two hundred pilots voted to join the pilots' union, the Air Line Pilots Association (ALPA), despite a vigorous campaign against unionization by management. The vote shocked the company, which justly takes pride in its excellent pay and benefits, its domestic no-layoff policy (still in force as of this writing despite tough times for airlines), its openness and fairness with its employees, and especially, its esprit de corps.

Granted, pilots are not typical employees at Fed Ex or elsewhere. Elite in both skills and salary, they make up but 3 percent of the company's work force. Still, the situation raises serious questions about the role of unions in exceptional companies like Federal Express and also mainstream companies striving to increase productivity and quality through teamwork and other cooperative employee/ management relationships. One has to wonder, as a Federal Express employee suggested to me, if the real intent behind the generosity of companies like Fel-Pro, Beth Israel, and Fed Ex is to keep the shop union-free.

Paternalistic employers such as Fed Ex try to mimic, or surpass, the advantages employees would gain through unionization. For example, in addition to its excellent compensation and job security polices, Fed Ex offers a grievance procedure, called the Guaranteed Fair Treatment process, that supposedly goes beyond even typical union-pushed systems in allowing an employee to appeal a manager's decision before a panel of peers. According to Moskowitz and Levering, fairness permeates nearly every company action. For instance, in the early 1990s, to help keep its no-layoff record intact, the company cut executive salaries. CEO Fred Smith claimed the cuts dropped his compensation by 50 percent.

Let's hypothesize how organized labor advocates and paternalistic employers might contest this issue. Even fervent laborites might commend such gestures as Fed Ex's salary cuts for high-earners. However, they'll counter, the problem is that employees in paternalistic companies have no power, and thus no recourse against a change of heart by management. The entire relationship is built on trust and, in the case of established employers like Fed Ex and Fel-Pro, track record.

So what's wrong with trusting the trustworthy? the "enlightened management" school would counter. Besides, they say, the adversarial character of organized labor would compromise the team spirit that companies like Fel-Pro and Fed Ex try so hard to achieve. That's exactly why Fred Smith resisted unionization at Federal Express, according to his biographer, Vance Trimble. Union supporters will then argue back that companies get the relationship with labor that they deserve, and that unions work with, not against, good employers. In other words, Trust *us*.

Obviously, this is a controversy without clear rights or wrongs. If you run a workplace democratically and generously, unionization may well be beside the point. But as Stanford Business School MBA Eric Weaver wrote in a thoughtful essay to the Social Venture Network membership, which includes many of America's most benevolent employers, "If we are good-guy managers, we may be under the illusion that [employees] will tell us everything on their minds. The fact is, it just ain't that simple. When workers live from paycheck to paycheck and interact with someone who has the power to take their jobs away, how can they be expected to be totally open about their problems and disappointments on the job, especially in today's job market?"

Another troubling aspect of employer paternalism concerns how the company behaves in troubled times. IBM, one of the enlightened models studied by Fred Smith when he built Fed Ex, grew fat and happy while cutting its employees a big slice of the pie. But when business soured, the employees had neither a union nor the democratic structures of a Springfield Remanufacturing through which to funnel their input on how to reform the company. Management's unilateral input: eliminate 85,000 jobs.

Indeed, as reported in *Business Ethics* magazine, Fed Ex's row with its pilots originated in the pilots' fears about their job security without a union. Many Fed Ex pilots lost seniority, endangering their chances for promotion, when the company merged with Flying Tiger air freight and absorbed its pilot corps (who, by the way, were represented by ALPA). Despite the company's domestic no-layoff record, the bumped-down pilots got more nervous when three thousand European workers, although none of them pilots, were let go. Though ALPA had lost badly in previous efforts to organize Fed Ex flyers, the new circumstances turned the tide.

The argument that unionization has no part to play in "good" companies does not hold up. Solidly unionized Southwest Airlines, notably successful in a staggering industry, joins Fed Ex, Fel-Pro, and Beth Israel Hospital in the Moskowitz/Levering top-ten list of best workplaces. The list of five runners-up includes Merck, another immensely profitable and strong union company. In all, twenty-three companies among their one hundred best employers make Moskowitz and Levering's "strongly unionized" list.

The Federal Express example yields yet one more useful point about the role of unions in employee-friendly companies. As these companies grow, they usually become less friendly, however unintentionally. (Remember that Fed Ex's problems began following a merger.) Once-charming informalities become bureaucratized, and once-close management/employee relationships grow more remote as the company expands its perimeters. In such circumstances, employees may well feel they need a formal intermediary to keep their interests on the company's front burner. Besides, when they look across today's landscape, they see management slicing and dicing work forces in company after company to satisfy anxious stockholders. With management obligated to look out first for shareholders' interests, employees can hardly be blamed for wanting a union to look out for theirs.

CHAPTER 5

Personal Fulfillment in the Workplace: Life During Work

ARETHA FRANKLIN HAD IT RIGHT. According to a comprehensive study released in 1993, what American workers want—more than money, more than "getting ahead"—is a little R-E-S-P-E-C-T.

The National Study of the Changing Workforce, conducted by the Families and Work Institute and sponsored by corporations and foundations including AT&T, American Express, Johnson & Johnson, Du Pont, and the Rockefeller Foundation, examined the attitudes, aspirations, and concerns of working people in a time of economic and workplace upheaval. As compensation continues to slide and job security vanishes altogether, the typical employee of the thirty-seven hundred surveyed measures work success in terms of respect from supervisors and peers, open communication, autonomy, and support from management. Sixty-five percent ranked open communication as "very important" in choosing a job, compared to only 35 percent rating wages and salary that highly.

The study's results won't surprise any manager who has asked similar questions of a company's staff. While the American workstyle has progressed since "efficiency" guru Frederick W. Taylor was

espousing his authoritarian, worker-as-mindless-machine management gospel in the early 1900s, the transition is far from complete.
Companies that treat their workers as intelligent, creative individuals
with valuable insights are still the exception, which is one reason you
read and hear so much about them in the business press. The other
reason is that many are among the highest-performing companies in
the nation.

In the previous chapter, I told the story of Springfield Remanufacturing, in which management empowered worker/owners with both
economic literacy and decision-making authority, to spectacular effect. We also explored the example of Donnelly Corporation, the
leading participatory workplace in America. We'll learn more about
Donnelly's methods in the next few pages, and those of other companies that found that the keys to employees' satisfaction are also the
keys to success.

But there's a far more basic reason for affording employees respect
as thinking beings. Management/employee relationships are human
relationships within a democratic society. It's hard to understand,
then, why the rules governing those relationships should be other
than humane, democratic rules.

In a 1992 speech before the Commonwealth Club of San Francisco, progressive business founder and author Paul Hawken proposed a "commercial bill of rights" that would articulate "not the
rights of corporations—which already have many rights, perhaps too
many—but the rights of the people who work within them." Most of
the rights he listed pertain to issues we will examine in this chapter,
including:

The right to create products and participate in processes that do not
    harm others.
The right to a job that is meaningful, worthy, and constructive.
The right to be told the truth about the company and its products.
The right . . . to participate in critical and substantive decisions that
    affect the work force.

Although many business traditionalists may view Hawken's perspective as "antibusiness," many newer, profitable American companies have been built with similar values at their cores. Thus,
marrying profits and humane, respectful management practices is no
mere ideal. But in this case, profits are the by-product, not the point.

Empowerment

The strategy of empowering employees (also called "participatory management" or "democratizing the workplace") goes back much farther than the Japanese management mania that has overtaken this country over the last decade or so. The Chinese sage Lao-tzu wrote some twenty-five hundred years ago of the transformation that occurs when one who governs gives up some of his power to those under his command:

> A realm is governed by ordinary acts,
> A battle is governed by extraordinary acts,
> The world is governed by no acts at all.
> And how do I know?
> This is how I know.
> Act after act prohibits
> Everything but poverty.
> Weapon after weapon conquers
> Everything but chaos.
> Business after business provides
> A craze of waste.
> Law after law breeds
> A multitude of thieves.
> Therefore a sensible man says,
> If I keep from meddling with people, they take care of themselves,
> If I keep from commanding people, they behave themselves,
> If I keep from preaching at people, they improve themselves,
> If I keep from imposing on people, they become themselves.

Lest anyone doubt that empowerment is nonetheless *management*, he noted:

> A leader is best
> When people barely know that he exists,
> Not so good when people obey and acclaim him,
> Worst when they despise him.
> "Fail to honor people,
> They fail to honor you";
> But of a good leader, who talks little,
> When his work is done, his aim fulfilled,
> They will all say, "We did this ourselves."
>
> (Translation by Witter Bynner)

Progressive educators have long noted that when teachers treat students as if they are intelligent and creative, they begin to perform that way. In this regard, workplaces are no different. Employees who are respected feel more respect for themselves and tend to put their energy into proving their worthiness instead of punishing management for slighting them.

Those companies that empower employees by allowing them to participate in decisions and help solve problems do so for any number of less subtle reasons as well.

• Employees who do the work daily know far better than those who manage it how to squeeze more efficiency, quality, and productivity out of company processes.

• Employees' input can be crucial in preventing costly ethical and safety lapses.

• Employees who have input into company processes feel more pride in having helped create the company's products and services. Frequently, that pride spurs them to also take more responsibility for the overall success of the company, giving it a crucial edge over its competition.

• Empowerment keeps employees alert to ways they can make a difference. At its most effective, empowerment creates an entrepreneurial, inventive, excited workplace atmosphere, a vital attribute in the rapidly shifting conditions of today's economy.

The connection between empowerment and performance isn't automatic. Empowerment by itself no more predicts high performance than does employee stock ownership by itself. University of California-Berkeley business professors David I. Levine and George Strauss surveyed the research and found that empowerment almost never hurts performance and more often than not improves one or more of the following: satisfaction, commitment, quality, productivity, turnover, and absenteeism. However, the positive effects often fade over time, probably because, Levine suggested to writer Matthew Hermann for an *East Bay Express* (Berkeley, California) story, "Most attempts at worker participation in this country have not been serious. They have been attempts to trick workers into thinking they have some control when, in fact, they are given almost none."

Thus, statistically anyway, giving empowered employees a stake in the outcome remains a far more surefire way to boost accomplishments. Indeed, financial incentives play a role in both examples below. However, what's particularly notable in each case is the degree of decision-power shifted to employees.

Texaco. Poor attendance, brittle union relationships, inferior quality, and an abysmal safety record dogged the Texaco Refining and Marketing plant in El Dorado, Kansas, when, in 1985, management decided that only radical surgery could save the patient. With the aid of a consultant, they defined goals, including inspiring a sense of ownership in the work force. They then designed a number of initiatives to achieve those goals. The strategy boiled down to one overarching change: eliminating the old management-by-decree system and involving the employees in running the shop.

Reform began with extensive training programs to teach employees how to solve problems. Management gave even lower-level employees decision-making power and encouraged them to question methods and make suggestions. Top managers began discussing previously secret performance data with line workers. Performance incentives—some monetary, some not—sweetened the deal.

The transition wasn't frictionless. Jealous managers resented underlings venturing onto their turf. Some union leaders feared employee participation would usurp their influence with members. But over time, managers grew less petulant and more trusting; executives soothed the union by involving its leaders in the planning.

Meanwhile, creating powerful employees produced powerful results. Morale shot up and plant performance with it. The plant became an industry leader in refining efficiency and decreasing fuel loss to evaporation and leaks. Pump performance tripled. Finally, as of this writing, the Chemical Manufacturers Association has acknowledged the plant's safety record for two straight years.

Donnelly Corporation. Fad followers won't find Donnelly among the herds of employers drawn toward Japanese management techniques because the company was already so far out front. Donnelly instituted participatory management techniques back in the mid-1940s when the autocratic schemes of Frederick Taylor were a corporate religion and Japan a war-making, industrial primitive.

Donnelly-style democracy, which the company calls its "equity structure," works like this: All employees, blue- and white-collar alike, belong to work teams, which elect representatives to "equity committees." The committees meet monthly to conduct their regular business, handling disputes and interpreting personnel policies, and also elect representatives to the Donnelly Committee, a council of fifteen that makes all company policy and recommends the wage-and-benefit package to the board. Although the company president or another senior officer automatically sits on the committee, the elected representatives dominate the rest of the membership. Thus, the committee's makeup reflects the company's ratio of managers and rank-and-file.

Donnelly's for-the-people approach to problem-solving sets an outstanding example not only for other corporations but also for the American democracy at large. When the company went through a demand slump in 1989, it consulted the equity structure for cost-cutting ideas. The committee recommendations, adopted by management, spread the pain fairly among the staff. Workers submitted to mostly voluntary, short-term layoffs of two to three weeks, and sixty office jobs were eliminated. All employees making more than $40,000 a year took pay cuts, which ranged from 3 percent at the bottom of the scale to 17 percent for top managers. Under the terms of the plan, original salaries would be reinstated when conditions improved, which they did six to eight months later.

Although in a different manner than Springfield Remanufacturing, Donnelly empowers its employees with information as well as decision-making input. The company brings in a continual stream of management, production, and future experts to stimulate new thinking throughout the work force and protect management from its isolated perspective. For example, when prominent manufacturing expert Dr. James P. Womack spoke on efficient car production, he addressed an audience of five hundred employees from all levels of the company.

The Donnelly management theory resembles what we saw earlier with Springfield Remanufacturing: When employees are entrusted to make important decisions, they bring a uniquely informed and broad point of view to bear, and when they understand the game being played and their stake in it, they'll play to win. It seems to work for Donnelly. With most of its competitors dead and buried, in trouble, or downsizing, the company has been expanding: its U.S. work force more than doubled from 1983 to 1993, from 1,000 to 2,300. Its earnings growth has averaged 20 percent compounded even though its industry has suffered three downturns since 1980. And during the industry doldrums still current when this was written in early 1993, the company's profitability and earnings continued to improve.

Another way to understand the attributes of empowerment is to look at the problems created by its antithesis—autocracy. One of the biggest dangers in an autocratic company is vulnerability to disastrous safety and ethical lapses. The words "Bhopal" and "breast implant" still cause shudders in boardrooms across the country. When employees don't have a mechanism for making suggestions to improve ethical or safety performance, they may assume that the company just doesn't care to hear about them. If line workers in a top-down management structure have no alternative to going through their supervisor to register a complaint or note a problem, they have no way to respond if the supervisor is the problem. If employees do not feel that the company shows them proper respect for their contributions and abilities, they may decide to punish the company by holding back vital information that could prevent a problem, or otherwise sabotage operations. And certainly, if they feel they will suffer retribution, with no possibility for appeal, if they report a problem, they aren't too likely to open their mouths.

In a 1993 article, Jim Kouzes, president of the Tom Peters Group/ Learning Systems, drove home the conflict between authoritarianism and safety with his example of "cockpit management strategy." "Authoritarian leaders only intensify danger. Air safety depends on whether those in the cockpit can talk back to the boss. So does business survival. If you want people to act with a shared sense of urgency, make certain they feel safe in challenging authority."

The court doctrine of "collective knowledge" reinforces Kouzes's point with chilling authority. According to this principle, as related by Joel Makower in *The E Factor*, a company is considered to have acquired the aggregate knowledge of all of its employees even if no single employee is aware of a legal violation. Thus, if one employee knows of a leak of a toxic substance but doesn't know the applicable legally allowable limit, while another employee knows the limit but isn't aware of the leak, the company is considered to know of, and be liable for, the problem. Obviously, a company's best protection against a collective-knowledge violation is a management structure in which information is openly shared with the entire work force and employees are supported in suggesting needed change.

Of course, while empowerment is crucial to ethical business, it doesn't define it. Conceivably, encouraging employees to feel responsible for the company's products and services could even backfire if employees don't feel good about the company's impact on their world. For instance, an empowered employee for a tobacco company may feel terrible about his or her part in pushing that product at innocent youth.

Authority also conflicts with flexibility, yet no attribute is more crucial than flexibility in today's competitive circumstances. Imposing change on a work force without first garnering its input and ultimate consent is a recipe for rejection, covert or otherwise. Frank Navran, an Atlanta-based consultant utilized by many major corporations, guarantees his work, but only when the client company involves its employees in the process. "The only way that you're going to get systems that work is to get the people to design the systems," Navran told me as we spoke in his office in an Atlanta suburb. "You've got to go to the people who are going to be impacted by the system and say, 'Here's what we're trying to accomplish. Do you accept the legitimacy of that as a goal? If the answer is yes, then how do we do that? Help us get there.'"

Of course, increased competition and a tough economy have caused many companies to shed layers of middle managers, forcing some decision-making on the rank-and-file simply because the managers who used to make those decisions aren't there anymore. But, Navran points out, when a company dictates such structural changes from on high, workers don't feel so much empowered as they do stressed, angry, and frustrated. Suddenly, they're being asked to take on more responsibilities and work more hours to compensate for those who've left, for the same pay and in a meager job market that leaves them no means of improving their condition. In these circumstances, Navran says, an aggressively participatory management style helps alleviate the tension and negative feelings.

Ideally, of course, participatory management serves as more than mere palliative. Involving employees at earlier and more central stages of planning may eliminate the need to make later changes born of desperation. As we've already seen, Donnelly's employee committees kept layoffs to an absolute minimum during a rocky period for the company. Springfield's employee/owners did an end-run around the layoff option in times when mainstream managers would have cut jobs left and right. With employee input playing a crucial role, both companies, in the same embattled industry, accomplished rapid turnarounds, while the downsizers surrounding them continued to struggle.

Autocracy also inhibits, and often outright *prohibits,* a company's ability to improve quality. Increasing quality requires an increase in effort, but employees don't work harder just because they're commanded to, particularly in today's frequent conditions of overwork, job insecurity, and eroding compensation. Quality is nearly inseparable from empowerment. To cite just one example, as many empowering executives will attest, employees tend to treat customers with the same consideration and respect with which management treats employees.

Before leaving the topic of autocracy versus empowerment, let's acknowledge that "empowerment" usually falls short of true democracy in most cases. Thus, the term "democratic workplace" is a misnomer in most cases to which it is applied, because employees in most such companies still don't participate in all significant decisions. Even Donnelly is not a democracy in the final sense. The company sets its overall direction according to 10-year-forward plans; these are developed by a committee of the top five officers. Of course, the plans are then reviewed by the top fifty senior managers, revealing the company's basic aversion to top-down decision-making, and shared openly with all staff.

For all its clear benefits, empowerment can't solve all of a company's problems. For one thing, it won't change the behavior of the incorrigibly immature, irresponsible employee. Then again, such behavior isn't always what it seems. Says Navran, "I operate from the assumption that human behavior is not random. If we see a pattern of undesirable behavior in an organization, that is a symptom of an organizational problem. If we see an individual going against the mainstream, that's an individual issue." To look at it another way, empowerment quickly reveals who's playing team ball and who isn't because it organizes the work force into a team. Effectively, it actualizes the work force, and no company can perform near its potential until its people are performing close to theirs.

Work Teams—Sometimes Empowering, Sometimes Not

True empowerment encompasses much more than forming work teams. Nevertheless, many companies first experiment with empowering employees through the teamwork approach. The logic behind teams goes beyond merely giving workers more say in what they do. For instance, a team that includes designers, engineers, production staff, marketers, and salespeople can eliminate problems in the idea and development phases that might not otherwise emerge until much time, material, and money had already been wasted. Such broadly representative teams also tend to move a product from conception to market much more quickly than the usual department-by-department gauntlet. And because teams take over many of the functions previously left to middle managers, they reduce the need for high-salaried layers of management between themselves and the top, saving the company lots of expensive jobs.

When companies create teams, they also hope to create team spirit. Hypothetically anyway, organizing groups of employees to work toward a common goal develops in them that sense of pride, ownership, and commitment of which every employer dreams. For the sports-minded in the executive suite, "team" evokes memories of great athletic squads of recent vintage like basketball's Los Angeles Lakers and Boston Celtics who won championship after championship, generating buckets of dollars for their owners and themselves.

In its eagerness to harvest the other above-mentioned benefits of teamwork, however, management sometimes forgets the role that empowerment plays in making teams effective. At Donnelly, where teamwork is fundamental to the company's success, workers are primarily accountable to their teams, not the usual managerial pyramid. They don't punch a time clock. If they're late or absent for some reason, teammates cover for them. Teams set their own production goals and the company openly shares information with them so they know what to shoot for.

Management may also overlook the role that rewards can play in inspiring effective teamwork. Beth Israel Hospital of Boston, a great employer by most measures, exemplifies the power of the reward-plus-empowerment approach. In 1989, Beth Israel combined participatory management with financial incentives in its version of something called the Scanlon plan (developed by Massachusetts Institute of Technology professor Joseph Scanlon in the 1950s and also utilized at Donnelly and Herman Miller). The scheme organizes the staff into teams to identify ways the hospital can trim costs, and improve productivity and efficiency. When team-generated ideas lead to dollar gains, as determined by calculations shared with staff, the hospital and work force share in them equally. In its first two years, management figured the gains at $3.74 million, half of which was distributed to employees.

Authority-sharing and role-sharing, another attribute of successful work teams, create the sense of unity vital to effective team-play. The Lakers and Celtics won because, beyond being collections of outstanding talents, they were consummate *team players*: unselfish, sacrificing self-starters whose combined efforts dominated those of less cohesive groups of stars. No Laker or Celtic was too great a scorer to pass the ball to a more open teammate or do the dirty work of playing tough defense. Similarly, successful work teams learn each other's jobs and share duties, leadership, and decision-making authority depending upon who is closest to the task at hand.

When teams disappoint, it's often because management isn't willing to let go—of power, of mistrust, of profits—to support the team process. The business press has lathered much attention on companies that flatten hierarchies and organize employee teams; it's also quick to pan the innovations when they fail to yield swift results. The blame is often misplaced. Many companies establish work teams not out of a commitment to empowerment but because the failure of the authoritarian, pyramidal American business tradition in which they are steeped has left them few other alternatives. Unfortunately, old habits die hard.

In fact, this syndrome may well explain the problems that sprang up in early 1993 in General Motors' otherwise well-regarded teamwork experiment at its Saturn plant. Saturn cars, leaders in quality and customer satisfaction, were so good that the plant couldn't keep up with the spiraling demand. To get more cars rolling down the line, management put workers on 50-hour-and-up workweeks. To get new workers, most of them transfers who were laid off at other GM plants, on the line more quickly, they also cut back on the training in cooperative work methods that they previously had given all Saturn initiates. The stress of overwork and training cutbacks have eroded new workers' support for the cooperative arrangements, *Business Week*'s David Woodruff notes. According to Woodruff, workers also distrust the cozy management/union relationship. (Union leaders fully cooperate with the teamwork arrangements and participate in decisions at every level.)

It could well be that, despite its overall success, the Saturn experiment hasn't gone far enough. Teams do their own hiring and prepare their own budgets, but the 50-hour weeks and scaled-back training were management's doing. Letting workers help solve the problems or otherwise first enlisting their support might have prevented the dissent. In the opinion of the sage editors at *Business Week* and many industry experts, GM would be well advised to remake the rest of the stumbling dinosaur in nimble Saturn's image, rather than abandon the experiment because the bugs haven't been worked out quickly enough.

Meaningful Work

As economists Robert Heilbroner and Lester Thurow remind us, Adam Smith, guru of capitalism, warned more than two hundred years ago that the outcomes of his favorite economic structure are not all sweetness and light. While a capitalist society grows richer overall, Smith wrote in his masterpiece, *The Wealth of Nations,* it does so at the expense of the working population, made duller and less intelligent by the monotonous labor it performs.

Henry Ford knew exactly what Smith meant. In Chapter 4, we noted how Ford raised his work force's pay so his employees could afford to buy the cars they made. Ford had another reason for boosting wages: it was the only way to keep his employees from storming away from his dehumanizing assembly lines.

Modern developments such as teamwork, with rotating job responsibilities and participatory decision-making and employee ownership programs, have transformed the work experience for those lucky enough to work under such arrangements. Applauding these developments, consultant/author Peter Senge advocates job definitions that enable all employees "to bring their whole selves to work." Ironically, the contemporary Ford Motor Company is one of the corporations that saved its bacon by involving line employees in everyday management. Teamwork helped the once-floundering automaker raise its assembly-line productivity 36 percent between 1980 and 1993, matching Japanese levels in some of its plants.

However, many Americans still toil in conditions not unlike those that existed at Ford's. When Moskowitz and Levering visited a Levi Strauss 501 jeans plant in El Paso, Texas, in late 1991, they found the sewing staff of mostly Hispanic females performing crushingly dull, repetitive work. "Six different sewing machine operators, each doing one single task, were needed to sew a pocket on to the pants," the authors recorded. "And most operators did the same task, hour after hour, day after day, year after year." What's worse, the company paid them by the piece at a rate established by Frederick Tayloresque time-and-motion studies. The sweatshop workstyle stood in stark contrast to the numerous commendable actions of Levi Strauss, in most ways one of the most generous, community-minded large corporations in the nation.

Answering the question "Why are there so few meaningful jobs in America?" is like solving the chicken-or-egg puzzle. The applicant force for lower-paid jobs is neither well educated nor trained. But the jobs for which they're applying aren't asking much from them, either. Economist Robert Kuttner points out that, according to the Bureau of Labor statistics, the largest number of new jobs continue to be in such undemanding categories as janitor, data-entry clerk, fast-food worker, nurse's aide, and similar positions with no career ladder and minimal pay. Today's economy increasingly produces high-skilled jobs and the low-skilled jobs just mentioned, but few others. One has to wonder: if the schools turn out the better-educated workers that business craves, will it structure enough jobs worthy of them?

At the same time, some trends in the modern workplace help make work a more engaging, challenging experience, even for employees whose usual tasks are mundane and repetitive. And some sensitive employers have found ways of simultaneously making work more meaningful for their employees, and their employees more valuable to the company.

Cross-Training.
Ever-changing global developments and high technology keep the workplace and the economy at large in a constant state of transformation. Those employees who know only one task have limited long-term value to their company, or themselves for that matter, because that task could soon become obsolete. At the same time, companies are flattening hierarchies, reducing the chance for employees to improve their economic lot by rising through the ranks. Thus, some companies now base pay raises on *horizontal* rather than *vertical* advancement—that is, for mastering new skills instead of climbing a ladder that may no longer exist.

Other companies offer liberal transfer and job-sampling arrangements to retain employees who may be bored with their current assignments. At Lands' End, a Dodgeville, Wisconsin–based mail-order marketer of high quality clothing, bedding, and other soft goods, there need not be an opening in another department before an employee requests a "job enrollment" there. If the employee likes the new work, and the department can accommodate another person, the company arranges a transfer. Whether or not they ultimately transfer, horizontally mobile employees broaden their knowledge and skills, and introduce more variety into their daily work. And by making themselves more versatile, they not only increase their worth to their companies but, in the best cases, also transform work into a form of self-development.

Again, teamwork approaches also generally involve some degree of cross-training. For example, all Donnelly employees work in teams of typically ten to twelve members, each of whom is expected to learn the jobs of everyone else on the squad.

Job-Related Training, General Education, and Other Opportunities to Grow.

In addition to the approach mentioned above, many companies support their workers in improving themselves in both job-related and more general ways. For instance, The Body Shop reimburses half the costs of job-related courses and exams at the course's start and the other half at completion. Rhino Records also pays for job-related courses, promoting employee education by making course catalogs and brochures available through its human resources department. Ben & Jerry's offers career-planning seminars and counseling; paid (upon approval) two-to-four-day internships at other jobs in the company; tuition aid for up to three courses per year, of which the third may be non–job related; and, through "Ben & Jerry's University," other courses, seminars, and tutoring in computers, business writing, basic education, management development, job development, and financial planning.

Of course, for some employees, the meaningfulness of work ultimately depends upon the effect of that work on the world at large. Most of us want to feel that our daily toil somehow makes this a better place to live. Thus, employees who are proud of the products or services their company offers may well find even tedious jobs satisfying. This seemed to be the case at Shaman Pharmaceuticals when I visited the company's offices in late 1993. Shaman makes pharmaceuticals from traditional tribal remedies, harvested primarily in tropical forests. However, unlike many of its competitors, Shaman's policies protect the biodiversity of the rainforest and ensure that the native communities that are the drug's source share in the profits. When you walk into Shaman's headquarters in South San Francisco, you feel the sense of mission, whether you're speaking with a receptionist or a department head.

You feel a similar sense of calling at Nolo Press, a Berkeley, California, publisher of legal self-help books and software (including the popular do-it-yourself package, WillMaker). The progressive purpose, to empower people and protect their wallets, is evident in everything from the equitable compensation structure (all staff salaries are posted for employees to see, and the money paid to company owners Ralph Warner and Linda Hanger is a mere five times the lowest Nolo salary) to the dedication and familial congeniality that everyone seems to bring to work with them.

Conversely, at workplaces with more exploitive or destructive end-products, employees with challenging jobs may still leave work each day ill at ease, even bitter, because of the cynical manner in which their company regards its social responsibilities.

To look at it another way, the company that serves a positive purpose in the world, beyond the lowest common denominator of providing jobs, can draw on a wealth of goodwill with its employees, who may well forgive the occasional transgressions against their interests and self-respect. The company that serves no productive purpose other than adding dollars to the economy may find that even when it tries to sweeten the pot for its employees, it's pouring down a bottomless hole.

PART III

Social Responsibility in the Wider World

CHAPTER 6

A New Ecology for Business: Emergencies and Opportunities

IN AN ESSAY published in his Ventura, California–based company's 1992 catalog, Patagonia founder and president Yvon Chouinard wrote:

> Last fall, we underwent an environmental audit to investigate the impact of the clothing we make. . . . To no one's surprise, the news is bad. Everything we make pollutes. Polyester, because it's made from petroleum, is an obvious villain, but cotton and wool are not any better. To kill the boll weevil, cotton is sprayed with pesticides so poisonous they generally render cotton fields barren; cotton fabric is often treated with formaldehyde. Wool relies on large flocks of sheep that denude fragile, arid areas of earth.
>
> We are pursuing other alternatives, like buying wool only from temperate regions . . . and using "organic" cotton. Another conclusion we have reached is simple: We need to use fewer materials. Period.

These conclusions, Chouinard continued, had led the company to drop 30 percent of its clothing line, with more cuts in the future. What's more, "we are limiting our growth in the United States, with the eventual goal of halting growth altogether. . . . What does this mean to you? Well, last fall you had a choice of five ski pants; now you may choose from two. This is, of course, un-American, but two styles of ski pants are all anyone needs. . . . We think that the future of clothing will be less is more, a few good clothes that will last a long time. We have never wanted to be the largest outdoor clothing company in the world, we only wanted to be the best."

Far from admitting defeat, Chouinard announced that when the company decided to scale down, "we also committed ourselves to a life span of a hundred years. A company that intends to be around that long will live within its resources, care for its people, and do everything it can to satisfy its community of customers."

The fact that even Patagonia, one of American business's most environmentally conscientious citizens, could not find another way to make its endeavors ecologically sound should give every businessperson pause. So severely is the environment threatened by ordinary human activities, far from the least of which are business activities, that living conditions as we know them can no longer be assured beyond the next decade or two. The Worldwatch Institute suggests that only a turnaround in values and results more "profound and pervasive" than the collapse of Soviet-style communism can prevent catastrophe on a massive, and perhaps irreversible, scale. And that turnaround must begin in large part with business.

Of course, the flip side of urgency is opportunity—in this case, incredible opportunity. And not just in the obvious areas of environmental cleanup and "green" products but in whole new ways of thinking about production processes, energy usage, packaging, product design, raw materials, and even ownership. In most cases, the environmentally sound way of doing things turns out to make economic sense as well—long term in most cases, short term in many. For instance, most forms of environmental protection—whether pollution control, waste reduction, energy conservation, recycling, or packaging reduction—also increase business efficiency, and efficiency means saving labor, time, energy, materials, and money, often all at once.

Still, the economic side of the environmental crisis is like one of those good news/bad news jokes where the bad news is the punchline. If every company in the world were as environmentally responsible as the best corporate examples, the planet would still be hellbent for ecological disaster. Certainly, environmental business reforms such as recycling, waste reduction, pollution control, and other environmental initiatives covered in chapter 7 help to reduce a company's environmental impact. These reforms are significant, pragmatic, and environmentally necessary.

However, they don't come close to eliminating the problems, or even reducing them to a level that could be termed sustainable. I call this the Patagonia Principle, but Chouinard's views are more zeitgeistian than idiosyncratic. In their book *Your Money or Your Life*, Joe Dominguez and Vicki Robin recommend that we drastically scale back our frivolous consumption for reasons of both personal fulfillment and conservation; their book was a national best-seller for two months. Reviewers are calling Paul Hawken's 1993 tome *The Ecology of Commerce: A Declaration of Sustainability* visionary, as it is in many ways, but World Bank economist Herman Daly, Worldwatch, and systems analysts Donella and Dennis Meadows (see below) are among the many who blazed the path on which Hawken now walks.

As for Chouinard's message to his customers to buy less, Esprit suggested the same to their customers years ago and Seventh Generation's similar message predates Patagonia's as well. Hanna Andersson also urges customers to purchase fewer items. While the company emphasizes the durability and quality of its clothing over the ecological benefits, Swedish-born founder Gun Denhart is fully aligned with the embedded environmental message: "In Sweden, you have maybe six outfits and you don't change clothes every day. We don't need all this stuff we have." Not even Fortune 500 CEOs surprise us anymore with their calls for "full-cost pricing" and other ideas central to a sustainable business future.

Despite these hopeful indications, however, we are galaxies away from having the infrastructures in place to transform the economy into a sustainable one. Our government's reluctance to support international gestures toward sustainability shows how far we remain from even a broad-based understanding of the crisis, for those global gestures are themselves tentative and inadequate.

In a review of Hawken's book in *The Nation*, Working Assets Funding Service founder Peter Barnes captured the essence of the dilemma perfectly: "The root cause of this march toward ecological oblivion is our much-hailed market system, which does a fantastic job of churning out goods but fails to pay the social and environmental costs of this production. Now that statist economies have been exposed as inefficient, ugly, and demoralizing, no one dares challenge the primacy of the market."

A detailed consideration of the sustainable-development idea is beyond the scope of the present work, although we'll put to "the sustainability test" much of what we examine throughout the book regarding environmental practices and products and services. The sections below focus on the way the environmental crisis affects business conditions today, including the economic opportunities implicit in ecological emergencies.

The State of the Planet

For years, the Worldwatch Institute had been warning in its annual *State of the World* reports that Earth was fast approaching its biological ability to support the human population. After analyzing 1993's data concerning global food and water supplies, the group announced in January 1994 that the critical limit had been reached. From 1950 to 1984, world grain production increased 260 percent and the seafood catch per person doubled. "But in recent years, these trends in food output per person have been reversed with unanticipated abruptness," the 1994 report says. Already, the institute noted, fresh water shortages are occurring in the U.S., Mexico, China, India, and the Mideast. The following details only part of the damage.

• Every year, Worldwatch notes, 42.5 million acres of tropical forest are cut down. China has nearly exhausted its harvestable timber. Brazil's Atlantic coastal rainforests, once a vast resource, are 95 percent gone, destroyed by logging, agriculture, and urban expansion. In the United States, under 10 percent of old-growth forest remains. Much of that is either scheduled to be cut or has otherwise been left unprotected, even though the timber industry decries current controls as far too restrictive.

• Atmospheric ozone, which protects the earth from the harmful effects of ultraviolet radiation from the sun, has thinned much faster than thought only a few years ago. As such, even recent international treaties designed to mitigate the problem are proving to be inadequate and in need of drastic revision. Ultraviolet radiation can cause skin cancer and cataracts, damage marine life, and reduce agricultural crop yields. In the U.S. alone, depletion of the ozone layer over the northern hemisphere is expected to cause an additional two hundred thousand skin cancer deaths over the next fifty years, an Environmental Protection Agency statement reveals.

· The earth loses 25 billion tons of topsoil annually, primarily from erosion caused by deforestation and high-tech agricultural practices, a *Business Week* environmental feature observed. Every year, nearly 6 million hectares (one hectare equals 2.4 acres) of previously fertile land become desert—that is, unable to produce food.

· At least 140 plant and animal species are doomed to extinction daily.

· The global population increases by 92 million people per year, 88 million of these in developing countries where population pressures force intensive land clearing, cattle grazing, and destructive agricultural practices. The current population of 5.3 billion will double by the year 2030 at current rates, according to United Nations projections.

Threatening environmental conditions also include the effects of air pollution, water pollution, toxic waste, acid rain, and radioactive waste. And none of the above considers the global warming theory, left off the list because of a still-raging controversy over its validity. Many scientific experts remain skeptical of the concept—that heat trapped by industrial gases accumulating in the atmosphere will raise temperatures on earth to dangerous levels. Conservative business and political lobbies rely on such testimony in their campaigns against global warming treaties and regulations. However, they also conveniently ignore the near consensus of international scientific opinion advocating substantial preventive measures.

In essence, the scientific community feels that the signs pointing toward the theory are sufficiently tangible, and the potential consequences sufficiently horrifying, to warrant immediate action. Among those potential consequences: the partial or complete submerging of low-lying island nations as ocean levels rise, the flooding of agriculturally productive coastal lowlands, and the destruction of other crops already growing near their limits of temperature tolerance.

The anti–global warming contingent overlooks one other important fact. The major culprit in the global warming scenario is the burning of fossil fuels. Fossil fuel burning pollutes the air of our urban areas, compromising health sometimes even to the point of death. It also causes acid rain, which destroys plant and animal life in streams and rivers and damages forests. About these harmful effects of fossil-fuel burning, there is no debate.

Understanding Environmental Markets

In a global polling undertaken by the George H. Gallup International Institute prior to 1992's Earth Summit, 51 percent of Americans polled rated environmental problems as severe, and 67 percent believed that environmental problems affected their health "a great deal or fair amount." Notably, these attitudes survived twelve years of White House snickering at scientists' environmental concerns.

Americans hardly stand alone in their apprehensions. In fact, the poll's results varied little whether the countries were rich or poor, developed or not. Brazilians expressed the greatest personal concern. Two out of three residents in both Mexico and Poland rated environmental problems in their countries as "very serious." And in all but one country (Russia, where nine out of ten residents seemed more concerned about how environmental problems affected their health now than their offsprings' later), residents said that environmental degradation would impact their children's lives more than their own.

How does this concern translate into buying preferences and other economic attitudes? In sixteen of twenty-two countries, those surveyed said they were willing to pay higher prices for environmental protection, including 65 percent of Americans. In twenty of twenty-two countries, majorities favored environmental protection over economic growth, including 59 percent of Americans.

However, somewhat smaller numbers of Americans have put their money, or their votes, where their mouths are. During the recessionary early 1990s, the majority of consumers bought value, not green, a fact as painfully clear to brand-name manufacturers as to environmentalists. Environmental issues also fared poorly at the ballot box, particularly when overwhelmingly well-financed campaigns by business coalitions were able to portray the measures as costing jobs or increasing taxes.

Still, the numbers of committed environmental shoppers, those who *will* make a sacrifice for their values, constitute a market that few companies can afford to ignore. A late 1992 Roper poll sponsored by the S. C. Johnson company found that 25 percent of consumers were dedicated enough to change their lifestyles or pay more for "green" products, with another 31 percent of consumers potentially ready to follow their lead. These are huge numbers, noted Roper's Brad Pay, considering that half a percent makes a difference to some product manufacturers. And consider with these totals a 1993 *Advertising Age* study in which 73 percent of those surveyed said that environmental marketing claims affected their buying decisions either sometimes or often.

One message jumps from the above data: Any product that is both green and price-competitive enjoys a substantial advantage over its rivals. Meanwhile, all that keeps many products, such as recycled paper and sustainably harvested lumber, from being price-competitive is an economy of scale.

Clearly, we sit on the cusp of an industrial transformation. If the federal government, with its $200 billion in annual buying power, as well as state governments would back up their environmental declarations with purchasing preferences for such products as recycled materials and energy efficient technology, some green products might well be made competitive in short order. On occasion, the federal government has purchased conscientiously, with promising results. For instance, after first paying a premium of seven thousand dollars per car to jump-start the alternative-fuel vehicle industry, the White House reduced the premium by 90 percent by placing a larger order and applying a year's worth of buying experience.

As of mid-1993, the Clinton administration had pledged a big boost in Uncle Sam's green purchases. An order that went into effect in October 1993 required federal agencies, which make up 3 to 5 percent of the U.S. computer market, to buy "Energy Star" computers whenever they replaced equipment. The Energy Star is the Clinton EPA's green seal of approval, applied to computers that use 60 percent less energy when idling than standard models. As of this writing, the administration was also endeavoring to up the government's purchase of paper with recycled content. The government program by itself won't eliminate the premium paid for nonvirgin paper, but may set an important example for corporate purchasers and convince previously reluctant manufacturers in this and other areas to begin designing products for the green market.

Unfortunately, few large companies are willing to let go of the "other" consumers, those who buy for value or convenience first, environment be damned. According to an Associated Press story citing data from Marketing Intelligence Service Ltd. (Naples, New York), the number of new single-serve products—individual portions of food and drinks enclosed in multiple layers of packaging—jumped 30 percent in 1992, perhaps because Americans were taking their lunch to work 25 percent more than in the more prosperous mid-1980s. General Foods' Oscar Mayer Lunchables—small portions of ham, cheese, and crackers packaged in a segmented plastic tray, plastic wrap, and an outer cardboard—typify this trend. Lunchables sales rose 8 percent in 1992, to $151 million.

By the same token, while General Foods was counting its Lunchables money, it was paying in other ways for its lack of social ethics and long-range business vision. Lunchables, along with eight other products, "won" a Wastemaker award handed out by a coalition of consumer and environmental groups pressing for tougher enforcement of waste management laws. And in addition to outraged citizens, General Foods can anticipate more and more state laws clouding Lunchables' future, some pushed by its more forward-looking corporate colleagues.

For example, California passed a law in 1991 that requires strict new packaging standards. By 1995, plastic packages sold there must contain at least 25-percent recycled material, be smaller in size, be recycled most of the time or be reusable or refillable. Procter & Gamble and Clorox supported the California measure and fought hard for its passage.

Not coincidentally, of course, both companies were simultaneously readying important new package concepts in line with the new California requirements. Procter & Gamble now pours its Ultra Downy and Spic & Span into bottles made from 100-percent recycled plastic; debuted its Liquid Ultra detergent line in refillable containers that save 40 percent in materials usage and are made from 50-percent recycled plastic; and uses recycled cardboard in 90 percent of its packaging of laundry and cleaning goods.

Clorox packages bleach products in containers with the California 1995 minimum of 25-percent recycled plastic, and makes its Pine-Sol bottle from 100-percent recycled plastic. (Apparently working both sides of the street, Clorox contemplated a plan by its public relations firm to undermine the environmental movement. According to 1991 story in *Greenpeace News,* Clorox's "Crisis Management Plan," an antienvironmentalist document leaked to Greenpeace, called for labeling Greenpeace members as violent "eco-terrorists," suing newspaper columnists who recommend non-toxic household cleaners and bleaching agents, and sponsoring so-called independent scientists to discredit research findings unbecoming to Clorox products. Clorox rejected the plan, but didn't deny commissioning it.)

As of this writing, at least fourteen states require minimum recycled contents in newspapers and packages. Meanwhile, more and tougher legislation moves down the pipeline, pressed for by municipalities and some businesses laboring to find new recycling markets for their plastic trash. (With scant infrastructure in place to recycle plastic, costs of curbside programs are high and prices for the material low.)

As one other measure of green purchasing power, about a million individuals or households now own a Council on Economic Priorities socially responsible shopping guide. As of August 1993, some 800,000 copies of *Shopping for a Better World* and 100,000 to 200,000 copies of *Students Shopping for a Better World* were in circulation, with a big new marketing push for the students' guide about to begin. Each book grades product manufacturers in a number of social categories, environmental responsibility prominent among them, and promotes boycotts and "buy-cotts" as the appropriate consumer response. Consider CEP's minions and Roper's 25 percent as the vanguard of a new consumer responsibility movement and you'll understand predictions of an increasingly bright future for greener businesses and an increasingly troubled one for those that are "brown."

An Itemized Invoice for Business as Usual

The most visible costs of "brown" behavior come from violating government environmental standards. With every passing year, the national, state, and local environmental regulation books grow thicker and enforcement gets tougher. Paradoxically, conditions got especially uncomfortable for business violators during the antiregulatory, and largely antienvironmental, Bush administration. Between 1989 and

1992, the Justice Department not only dramatically increased its number of indictments (to about eight hundred, more than in the previous eighteen years), but also zeroed in more than ever on the culpability of senior executives. According to Joel Makower in *The E Factor,* those indictments resulted in convictions of 578 corporate presidents, officers, and other managers, with over a hundred and fifty years of jail time actually served.

Dollar amounts of fines climbed during that time, too—topped, in early 1992, by Rockwell International's $18.5 million settlement with the government after it pleaded guilty to illegally dumping radioactive and other hazardous waste at the Rocky Flats nuclear weapons plant in Golden, Colorado. That amount actually stirred considerable controversy in Congress, which questioned whether the fines were stiff enough considering the $200 billion estimate for cleaning up the mess. In another example, Wheeling-Pittsburgh paid $6.1 million for violating the Clean Water and Safe Drinking Water acts, and had to put out over an additional $20 million to install court-mandated pollution control equipment.

As business extends its reach around the world, so does the long arm of environmental enforcement. The most notorious and chilling instance involved Union Carbide (Danbury, Connecticut) in the 1984 industrial disaster in Bhopal, India, in which more than four thousand Bhopal residents died and some two hundred thousand suffered injury after toxic gas escaped from a pesticide factory. A long and ugly international legal battle ensued, in which Union Carbide's cost-containment mindset seemed far more obvious, in media coverage anyway, than its compassion for the victims and their families. In 1989, the company agreed to pay $470 million, a still paltry sum when apportioned among the families and individuals harmed. But the Indian courts weren't finished with Union Carbide. In 1992, they charged Warren Anderson, company chairman at the time of the accident, with homicide, charged plant officials as well, and began extradition attempts.

Even if, as expected, Anderson and his Bhopal managers never spend a day in Indian court, this case and others in which corporate officials have been indicted have shaken officers and executives in boardrooms across the country. We can measure the repercussions in more than just antacid tablets. Premiums for director- and officer-liability insurance have soared. And, of course, legal fees for defending a company accused of ethical violations can exceed even the cost of substantial penalties.

The potential costs of brown business far exceed the direct risks of fines and convictions, exemplified below.

· A slew of sophisticated environmental groups—assisted by legal, scientific, and technical experts—exert pressure on corporate behavior through litigation, legislation, unsavory media coverage, alliances with environmentally sensitive political candidates, and so on. And as author Makower points out, the efforts of a few outraged local citizens can cause even more disruption than those of the high-profile national groups.

· A variety of laws give citizens the right to know how a corporation's environmental behavior might affect them. The 1986 Superfund Amendments and Reauthorization Act requires companies to publicly disclose any toxic substances they use or transport in local communities. While the information is reported to state and local authorities, most of it is available to any citizen through databases or upon written request. Concerned citizens can also comb through annual reports. The Securities and Exchange Commission (SEC) requires publicly owned companies to disclose their environmental records, including violations and lawsuits, to investors because legal defense and, especially, judgments against a company can affect financial performance. Both the Superfund and SEC data, Makower warns, often become fodder for investigative journalists, local activists, and national environmental groups.

· Poor environmental performance now affects a company's ability to borrow money through public investment in its stocks and bonds. Moody's Investors Service, whose bond ratings powerfully affect the interest rates companies must pay to borrow money through corporate bonds, now figures environmental liabilities into its determination of a company's creditworthiness. (A creditworthiness rating is the rater's informed opinion of a company's ability to pay back borrowed funds; investors want higher returns if they are going to invest in a low-rated company's bonds.) And stock analysts often figure environmental performance into their stock recommendations.

Planning Now for a Transformed Tomorrow

This is easy to say when it's not your money, but if I were running a company I wouldn't wait long before remaking it for an environmentally transformed world and global economy. To hand our children a world worth living in rather than a world in steep decline, we'll need a global revolution in habits, incentives, and priorities unprecedented in human history. As an optimist, I think consumers and producers alike will, sometime in this decade, stop denying the state of environmental emergency that we've been in for years and begin the real work of converting to sustainable habits and practices. When that happens, the economy as we've known it will begin fading from view.

I base my optimism in part on the fact that everything we need to bring about the changeover is in our hands. As Worldwatch Institute president Lester R. Brown puts it, "We know what we have to do and we have the technologies needed for the Environmental Revolution to succeed." We also have the economic incentives because somewhere in that mix, there's a lot of money to be made doing exactly what is wanted and needed.

Something else I'd be doing in my company is developing products and services that are not material-intensive and not polluting, because current rates of material consumption, production, and pollution have exhausted nature's ability to maintain them. Dartmouth environmental studies professor Donella Meadows is principal author of the seminal environmental book, *The Limits to Growth,* and its sequel, *Beyond the Limits,* both of which have been compared to Rachel Carson's *The Silent Spring* for their ability to shock us into environmental enlightenment. But even she proposes some forms of growth as compatible with a sustainable future. Although she applauds Patagonia's decision, sheep farmer Meadows noted in a newspaper editorial commending the company that sheep can be raised "even in arid lands in ways that don't destroy land" and "cotton can be grown without pesticides."

In Meadows's vision, a sustainable world would furnish "all basic material needs" and would also "supply our important nonmaterial needs—for love, for self-confidence, for belonging, for purpose, for challenge, for transcendence—in a nonmaterial way, instead of offering cheap material substitutes that satisfy only temporarily and therefore set up the need for more and more of themselves." In other words, growth isn't the real problem. Material consumption is.

Assets on the Line—A Clear-Cut Sign for Material-Intensive Industries

After the Clinton administration announced in the summer of 1993 its plan for "sustainably" logging Northwest public forests, a frustrated timber executive complained to a reporter that if the government didn't soon allow bigger harvests, alternative building products companies would establish themselves in timber's place. It was a delicious moment, the executive unwittingly acknowledging what many experts outside the business have seen for some time, the increasing irrelevance of an industry that has eaten itself out of house and home.

Of course, the forestry industry would like to blame all of its troubles on the federal Endangered Species Act. Its unspoken anxiety, of course, is over its own endangered status. Although I focus here on timber as an example, you don't have to be a seer to understand that businesses dependent on the extraction or manufacturing use of vanishing natural resources like old-growth trees have no place in a sustainable future. For one thing, society is unwilling, despite allowing industries to push resources to the brink of extinction, to let them take that suicidal final step. For another, once such industries devour their supplies down to dangerously low levels, prices go up, and markets for alternative products develop. In a market economy, it can't be helped.

Thus, the forestry industry must now contend not only with powerful environmental constituencies but also plausible substitutes for their products. For example, Boise-based TJ International, Inc., synthesizes construction "lumber" by laminating wood strips from small, fast-growing trees; its engineered wood products are as strong and true as old-growth boards and beams, have no knots or other inconsistencies, and don't warp. Increasingly, contractors are also framing buildings with steel studs made from recycled cars. Plastic lumber, made from mixed plastics collected in curbside recycling programs, has entered the scene as well; the city of Los Angeles is building park benches and fences with it. In Sante Fe, New Mexico, people are building homes from pushed-together bales of straw. In Napa, California, builder David Easton has constructed his and a hundred other homes from rammed-earth, essentially the same technology used to build the Great Wall of China. Not incidently, straw-bale and rammed-earth homes have natural insulating properties that the average wood-framed home can't touch.

Granted, most of the above technologies compete for a small piece of pie; even the hard-charging TJ International held only 10 percent of its potential market as of early 1993. But the future clearly favors viable alternatives to wood wherever feasible, and this particular future is just around a very near corner.

The timber wars are being fought on another front, the paper market, and there too, companies that fail to adapt to environmental demands face long-term defeat. Woodless paper is already commercially available in the U.S., produced from hemp, the same furiously growing weed from which rope, and marijuana, is made. (Although growing hemp in the U.S. is illegal, Tree-Free Ecopaper of Portland, Oregon, imports "drug-free" hemp pulp from China, which is legal, and combines it with waste cereal straw to make its product.) In fact, about 8 percent of the world's paper pulp comes from materials other than wood, including hemp, jute, bamboo, rice straw, wheat straw, and other annual crop fibers in countries where wood is scarce. At least one timber giant, Weyerhaeuser, has taken note and is studying the economic feasibility of using rye-grass waste straw from Oregon's Willamette Valley in its paper products.

Besides, as long as paper production takes a heavy toll on the planet, pressures to cut its use will continue. The microcomputer revolution was supposed to lead to the "paperless office." Instead, shipments of free-sheet, uncoated paper almost doubled from the time the Apple II was introduced in 1976 to the end of 1990, largely because so many of those microcomputers were wired into laser printers. Software documentation also eats trees; the first 10 million units of Microsoft Windows sold contained at least 21 million pounds of virgin paper.

But several computer giants, feeling guilty about their role in exploding paper demand, have done what they can to reverse the trend. Microsoft, IBM, Apple, Sun, and others now ship documentation in CD-ROM form whenever possible, which also saves them postage and eases use for customers with the hardware to take advantage. Meanwhile, the computer revolution has enabled new processes to replace paper use in several business and personal applications. Companies are increasingly storing data electronically without automatically printing it out as well. Makower notes the dramatic upsurge in electronic data interface (EDI) use, by which companies can electronically communicate billing, sales, and inventory information.

Through electronic bulletin boards, many other companies and individuals also communicate electronically what they would otherwise have committed to paper. AT&T, for instance, has conscientiously increased applications for its worldwide on-line information exchange system to reduce waste paper. For example, by electronically listing job openings within the company, it saves 2 million pieces of paper monthly. Through computer networks like CompuServe, many now receive their news and stock reports electronically. It is not hard to imagine a near future with such networks supplanting much of the paper use now going into personal mail and newspapers.

Among other steps that businesses are taking to ease the strain on the world's vanishing forest resources, AT&T has set a photocopying goal of 50 percent "duplexing" (copying on both sides of a sheet), which could reduce paper use by 6.44 million pages per month at a cost savings of $385,000 annually. Home Depot uses recycled content products for forms, register tape, shopping bags, store signage, newsprint catalogs, and computer paper. Kmart headquarters stores its current sales records on-line and files older information on microfiche. With staff now printing only what they need, the initiative saves paper by the hundreds of millions of sheets annually, and reduces the company's need for filing cabinets and space to accommodate them.

I offer the above stories not really as a jab to timber and other material-intensive industries but as further evidence that the transition to sustainability is already underway. The timber industry knows where it stands; that's why giants like Weyerhaeuser have themselves begun investing in more sustainable product development. The game is no longer about being green. It's about staying alive.

Meat Products—A Poor Fit with a Sustainable Economy

If the current practices of the timber industry are ill-adapted to a sustainable future, timber companies retain eco-friendly options, as we've seen—sustainable harvesting, engineered lumber, alternative fibers for paper, and fast-growing trees such as poplars and cottonwoods that can replace more precious varieties for various uses. Thus, the big timber companies will change dramatically in coming years, but they won't disappear.

Other industries face a more problematic fate. For instance, what are agricultural chemical companies to do with a product that is increasingly discredited for its main application—growing food—and spawns grievous environmental and health consequences besides? Environmentalists have long emphasized the environmental obsolescence and social bankruptcy of the industry and worked to hasten its demise. They've also taken aim at other environmentally passé industries such as fossil fuel–burning utilities and transportation. But prior to Jeremy Rifkin's wave-making efforts in the early 1990s, another critical case of unsustainable and otherwise socially destructive enterprise, the raising of livestock for meat products, received far less attention.

On February 24, 1992, author and activist Rifkin publicly launched his international Beyond Beef campaign, with goals "to reduce the consumption of beef by at least 50 percent, radically restructure world agriculture and food policies, and lessen the influence of the worldwide cattle complex." Rifkin smartly timed the announcement to spotlight the release the following month of his book, *Beyond Beef: The Rise and Fall of the Cattle Culture*. However, the industries he targets won't lightly dismiss his efforts, for they've seen his act before and it scares them silly.

Rifkin's 1980s campaigns against BST, a gene-spliced hormone that makes cows give more milk, rallied small farmers en masse to the cause, led several large grocers to boycott milk from BST-injected cattle, and provoked three states to temporarily ban the hormone. In 1992, Rifkin and his organization declared all-out war on genetically altered foods, filing lawsuits, lobbying Congress for stricter regulations, and framing the companies in the media as greedy villains contaminating both the food supply and the environment. Whatever the pertinent legal and regulatory outcomes, consumers, already skeptical about the quality of industrially farmed produce, will determine the ultimate winner.

But Rifkin's credibility derives from more than his track record as industrial pest, for he is far from the first to note the socially destructive consequences of beef consumption. For instance, the much-respected Worldwatch Institute, in more sober language, has asserted many of his same points for years.

Rifkin also speaks to a highly receptive national audience. Heeding warnings from their personal physicians (and the U.S. Surgeon General, American Heart Association, and World Health Organization) to dramatically reduce fat in their diets, Americans have cut consumption of one of its primary sources—beef—from 83 pounds per person per year in 1975 to 63 pounds per year as of 1992, according to U.S. Agriculture Department data.

Meanwhile, medical research has blessed vegetarian diets as not only healthful, but perhaps the most effective dietary path to warding off numerous major lifestyle diseases. (The beef industry fought back with its "real food for real people" campaign but suffered an embarrassing setback when campaign spokesman James Garner called in sick to have a real quintuple by-pass operation.) In addition, many environmentally concerned citizens now make the connection between burgers sizzling at the corner fast-food joint and forests burning in Brazil, in part because the environmentalist ranks are full of vegetarians happy to point it out to them.

Ominously for the cattle industry, the considerable decline in beef eating has occurred despite a still limited public awareness of the socially deleterious effects of cattle production. For example, beef's adverse effects on health only begins with its high fat content. And the environmental damage wrought by modern livestock raising goes far beyond the clearing of precious rainforest. The following list of social problems caused by livestock raising, and the meat eating that drives it, by no means exhausts the subject.

MEDICAL ISSUES

· The lifestyle diseases partially caused by overconsumption of meat include heart conditions, strokes, colon cancer, and breast cancer. The American Dietetic Association's 1988 position paper on vegetarianism states that vegetarians are at lower risk for not only the above-mentioned diseases but also obesity, high blood pressure, osteoporosis, Type II (noninsulin dependent) diabetes, kidney stones, gallstones, and diverticulosis. Colon cancer alone kills about fifty thousand Americans a year; the incidence of this disease is roughly ten times as high in the beef-eating cultures of the West as it is in Asia and the developing world, where little beef is consumed.

The China Project, a massive study of diet, lifestyle, and health in China involving the joint efforts of American, British, and Chinese institutions, concluded that lowering fat consumption to 15 percent of calories (Americans average about 37 percent) would prevent most of the diseases of affluence just mentioned. The Project's co-principal researcher, Cornell University's T. Colin Campbell, stated publicly that "we're basically a vegetarian species" and should be "minimizing our intake of animal foods." About 70 percent of protein in the Western diet comes from animal sources, with 30 percent from plants; the ratio among the much healthier Chinese is more than reversed— 11 percent from animal sources and 89 percent from plants.

· An unfortunate myth about the benefits of protein has exacerbated the health consequences of beef eating in industrial societies. Citizens in affluent countries eat perhaps twice as much protein as they should for optimal health, according to numerous health experts.

· Obtaining maximum profits from beef cattle means obtaining the maximum weight gain in the minimum time, and that requires drugs, lots of them. The drugs, of course, end up in the meat sold to consumers. In the U.S., growth-stimulating hormones are administered to over 95 percent of feedlot-raised cattle. Feedlot managers also spray toxic insecticides around the lots to kill flies, since cattle can lose weight fending them off. Herbicides are another unrequested but inevitable ingredient in beef-rich diets. Feedlot cattle eat lots of corn and soybeans, by far the most heavily sprayed crops in the U.S. and the reason that beef is the most herbicide-contaminated food in the country.

HEALTH CARE COSTS

· Beef eating is rarely mentioned as a cause of out-of-control health spending but it should be. A 1989 U.S. Surgeon General's report stated that 1.35 million of the 2.1 million American deaths in 1987 were caused by diseases associated with dietary factors, a primary one of which is overconsumption of fat.

ENVIRONMENTAL ISSUES

· Nearly half the energy consumed by U.S. agriculture goes into livestock production. If Americans and other citizens of industrial nations would switch to a healthier, plant-based diet, gasoline use by agriculture would drop dramatically since vegetarian foods are a significant step lower on the food chain. (It takes 6.9 kilos of grain to produce one kilo of pork, 4.8 to produce one kilo of beef, the Worldwatch Institute notes.)

· As potable water becomes more and more precious, the environmental bill for livestock production soars. Production of one kilo of American beef requires more than 3,000 liters of water, since half the hay and grain fed to U.S. beef cattle grows on irrigated fields, observes Worldwatch.

· Then there's the poop problem. As Worldwatch's Alan Durning and Holly Brough write, "Manure is a valuable organic fertilizer and soil-builder in modest quantities but a dangerous pollutant in excess." Overwhelming excess, of course, is the rule of thumb at current levels of livestock production. Manure pollutes rivers and groundwater when more is layered on the land than the land can absorb; the gaseous ammonia that escapes from manure piles adds to the contamination in the form of acid rain and deposits. According to Worldwatch, manure accumulation has already wrought serious ecological damage in the Netherlands, the pork-producing center of Western Europe. Water is contaminated in many areas and the livestock industry has deposited more acid on Dutch soils than either the country's cars or factories.

· While we're more or less on the subject, another excretory by-product of cattle raising—methane, the second most significant greenhouse gas—may be heating up the atmosphere. With nearly 1.3 billion cattle stomping around the planet, the release of methane from cow belches and flatulence plus the methane emanating from manure piles totals about 15 to 20 percent of global methane emissions, says Worldwatch.

· Cattle raising plays a major role in the advancing global desertification crisis. The incredible proliferation of beef cattle in recent decades has caused overgrazing on the planet's remaining grasslands, leaving the topsoil poorly anchored and thus vulnerable to erosion by wind and rain. Compounding the problem, the cattle's pounding hooves compact the ground, making it impermeable to rainwater, which then washes away the topsoil. Downstream, the syndrome increases flooding and clogging of waterways, dams, and estuaries with sediment. According to the United Nations, about three quarters of the world's dry rangeland is now at least moderately desertified. In the U.S., as much as half of our rangeland has been severely degraded.

· The clearing of the planet's rainforest for cattle raising perpetuates yet more clearing because of the way it destroys the ecosystem and the soil it protects. Weeds soon take over, destroying the pasture's utility; thus, within a decade's time most pastures are abandoned and more forest destroyed to create new graze lands.

· As rainforest disappears, so do the plant and animal species that live there.

HARM TO THIRD WORLD POPULATIONS

· Escalating demand for beef in the industrialized northern hemisphere has encouraged many farmers in developing nations to switch from food crops to feed crops. This not only reduces the amount of food staples available for poor citizens in those countries, but also causes some of the most fertile land to be converted to pasture, far from its best agricultural use.

· Newly industrializing nations have bought into the historical association of beef eating with power and success, to their own economic detriment. During a period of rapid industrialization from 1950 to 1990, note Durning and Brough, Taiwan increased its consumption of meat and eggs six times over. By the end of that period, this former grain exporter was forced by livestock feed requirements to import 74 percent of its grain.

None of the above is to suggest that livestock production is inherently evil. Throughout human history, meat animals have supplied human culture with not only protein food but also fertilizer, clothing, fuel, transportation, and even agricultural "labor" in the form of beasts of burden. Besides, livestock can be, and for thousands of years was, raised in harmony with the carrying capacity of the land. In traditional cooking in many nonindustrial cultures, meat in small portions is added as a delicacy to meals primarily prepared with grains and vegetables. At such modest levels, meat consumption strains neither health, economies, nor ecologies.

But as Worldwatch and Rifkin stress, the modern affluent diet, heavy as it is in meat and protein generally, destroys people and planet with equal abandon. I might also add that it speeds the onset of a starvation catastrophe for the Third World's poor. Plot on a graph the shrinking planetary supplies of arable land and usable water. On the same chart, draw lines to indicate the rate of population expansion and economic development in the Third World. Note how soon the various lines converge. To head off a hunger crisis of cataclysmic proportions, millions of us who can afford all the meat we want will have to wean ourselves off the habit, because the international cattle industry is unlikely to reform its methods and drop back to sustainable scale until a contracting market forces it to.

Of course, the market will continue to contract, because meat supplies nothing to the diet that is not easily replaced. Nor will future consumers likely be sympathetic to the industry's economic contribution, for given such offsetting factors as health care costs and environmental damage, that contribution is highly overrated. In fact, the only social utility I can find for modern rates of meat consumption is as a metaphor—the sacrifice of Third World lands and economies to raise food for rich northern hemisphere plates makes a powerful symbol for the current state of North-South relations.

True, it hardly seems fair to brand meat-related industries—and the human dietary habits that drive them—as socially irresponsible, given that the connection between meat eating and human and planetary destruction has only recently been recognized. But with the facts now on the table, so to speak, the beef industry may in coming years be viewed much as tobacco companies are today, as intentional purveyors of destruction for a profit.

By the same token, it is no accident that the health food industry includes many of America's more promising small companies, because the future clearly favors their products. In 1993, the stock of Wholesome & Hearty Foods, makers of the meatless Gardenburger that appears on many mainstream restaurant menus, grew faster than any other stock on the NASDAQ.

Conversely, the "cattle complex," as Rifkin calls it, illustrates one of the main theses of this work—that socially irresponsible business increasingly becomes bad business as we head farther into the future. The trendlines for the industry all point downward because one cannot project a sustainable future in which the industry survives at current levels. So place your bets where you may, but mine are on tofu.

❖   ❖   ❖

Those who are cynical about business's capacity to reform its ways have plenty of basis for their skepticism, but they should also note the words of Frank Popoff, chairman and CEO of Dow Chemical. Speaking before Bill Clinton and Al Gore's "economic summit" prior to the 1993 inauguration, he said, "We must begin to develop and employ full-cost accounting and pricing of our products based on complete life-cycle analyses, ensuring that the full product cost, including the environmental cost, is incorporated in our products. And then [pointing his finger for emphasis] pass on that full cost to an ultimate consumer so that they can decide to consume or not consume your product based on full information and freedom from hidden costs and subsidies."

Popoff also called for "making pollution prevention versus end-of-pipe treatment our ultimate goal" and full-cost penalties for all violators in business, government, and households alike. If his company walks his talk and brings some similarly influential friends along for the exercise, environmental incentives will change the world.

Of course, there's a matter of phenomenal economic opportunity at stake here as well. For a preview, domestic companies and industries need only gaze across the oceans, where more forward-thinking nations than ours are already manipulating economic forces to create a more sustainable economy. As *Business Week* writer Emily T. Smith has reported, Japan and some European nations are employing environmental policies to force their industries to develop technologies that will be more competitive in an environmentally threatened future. In another move to get a jump on international competition, Tokyo established in 1990 a Research Institute of Innovative Technology for the Earth, backed by an initial $37.5 million budget, just part of its new 100-year game plan for sustainable development.

CHAPTER 7

The New Economics of Environmental Practices: Preparing for a Sustainable Future

''IF YOU'RE NOT PART OF THE SOLUTION, you're part of the problem." That political slogan, a carry-over from the activist 1960s, has never rung truer than when applied to the environment in the 1990s. All of the strategies covered in the sections below are "part of the solution." In addition, many contain embedded financial advantages, some of which are substantial.

In the previous chapter, I mentioned that if a company were to adopt all of the conventional practices for reducing its environmental impact, those practices would still not add up to sustainability. While that is true, I want to reassert here that most sustainable-development scenarios include the practices discussed below. For example, while sustainable development ultimately implies a transition to renewable energy inputs, the energy efficiency strategies discussed in this chapter are a vital first step before renewable energy technology is installed. Renewable energy equipment costs money. Companies that have first reduced their energy needs will pay less for "RE" hardware.

The other approaches covered in this chapter play similarly important roles in retooling the market economy for a sustainable future.

Recycling

At the edge of the parking lot of a Home Depot home center in Atlanta, staff in a bright yellow drive-through facility called Recycling Depot trade dollars for discards. Tradespeople, Home Depot customers, and other local residents drive up to the building—which opened in February 1993—with their home improvement scrap, copper pipe, water heater carcasses, electrical wire, and ordinary household recyclables. Some of them, mainly tradespeople with large quantities of recyclable metals, drive away with checks in the low-four-figure range.

But Recycling Depot is no simple green promotion. "Our target is a 30 percent profit margin, just like the home center stores," shouts Home Depot's Mark Eisen to me over the roar of trucks hauling the sorted materials to their next incarnation. Eisen, the company's innovative environmental marketing director who conceived and then developed Recycling Depot as a joint venture with Atlanta-based Mindis Recycling, adds that Recycling Depots will be cookie-cuttered at other Home Depot locations, of which there are 220-plus, once the profit goal is reached.

On the other side of the country (and other end of the recyclables "food" chain), a new footwear company in Tigard, Oregon, pushes shoes made from some of the same stuff that Recycling Depot collects—plastic milk jugs, cardboard boxes, and magazines—plus other refuse such as old tires, used file folders, exhausted seat cushions, and trim waste from disposable diaper, coffee filter, and wetsuit manufacturing. Company founder Julie Lewis, who still describes herself as more recycling activist than savvy entrepreneur, not only conceived the product but also the company's perfect-fit moniker—Deja Shoe. A sign of the eco-chic times, Deja Shoe overcame its more-than-humble beginnings to make its mid-1993 debut in such tony retailers as Nordstrom and Bloomingdale's.

Critics hailed the first *Star Wars* movie in 1975 for its "used future" look. Creator George Lucas proved even more prescient than critics thought. The used future has arrived. Not only do recycled materials show up in nearly every product type imaginable but recycling has become the feel-good environmental exercise of the 1990s for consumers and businesses alike.

Recycling also satisfies our essential sense of thrift. We don't like to throw things away if they still have useful life. And for that reason, recycling seems to imply an internal economic as well as environmental logic. Surely it must be cheaper to use recovered rather than virgin materials, particularly when those materials are "donated" by consumers in curbside and other nonreimbursed collection programs.

If only the economics were that simple. True, discarded metals command strong prices in all markets. Plenty of buyers prize used white office and computer paper as well. But for most other recycled commodities, supply far exceeds demand. Of all the recyclables, newspaper costs the least to process, but as anyone who recycles their local daily can well imagine, the quantity available overwhelms its salability in many regions of the country. New glass costs relatively little to produce, so used materials rarely command much of a price. Plastics present a multitude of problems. Scant infrastructure exists to process used plastics; what infrastructure there is accepts only a very few of the varied resin types. Because of their bulk and light weight, plastics are costly to transport. They're also labor-intensive to sort.

In some cases, politicians who have wrapped themselves in green have caused more immediate damage than good to the recycling cause. Capitalizing on recycling's popularity, legislators in many areas of the country pass heroic recycling mandates to the cheers of their constituents without considering how the resulting influx will affect markets. States and cities could expand markets by mandating that their own offices purchase recycled products whenever possible, but few have acted on that long-range perspective.

Nor have many businesses, beyond the usual cast of green idealists, rushed to help the situation. Most manufacturers, including the majors, built their businesses using virgin material and are hardly inclined to change habits or machinery now for as "ethereal" a reason as environmentalism. In some industries, government policy still favors those using virgin material. For example, paper manufacturers receive subsidies for cutting the trees in their private forests and tree farms.

Clearly, the public and private sectors must work together if recycling is to make more economic sense. Fortunately, some movement has begun in that direction. As of late 1992, at least twenty-four states and many cities were offering some form of financial incentive to businesses to stimulate markets for recyclables. Among the opportunities, New York makes available grants and loans to help businesses study and test new technologies. The program mainly targets small- and medium-sized businesses. As part of its now codified goal to reduce its waste stream by 50 percent, California has created a dozen "Recycling Market Development Zones" in which businesses can access tax credits, low-interest loans, marketing help, technical assistance, and other benefits if they will, say, purchase equipment that makes products with at least half recycled content.

Meanwhile, despite the market problems, there is money to be made in recycling the old-fashioned way: collecting and selling. Mark Eisen says that Recycling Depot gets enough money for its metals to subsidize the rest of the operation. Waste disposal giant Browning-Ferris has made its recycling operations profitable by paying close attention to price and buyer trends.

Here are some other outposts of the used future, most with built-in economic advantages.

Office Recycling.
Most big companies have programs that justify themselves in a dual-green manner—that is, environmentalism and hard cash. Large waste haulers generally charge less to pick up bins of recyclables than they do for trash because they can sell the former, particularly metals and white office papers. The recyclables gathered in four Seattle offices of U.S. West saved the company fifty thousand dollars in disposal costs in 1991 alone. Nonmanagement employees who call themselves the "Green Team" run the U.S. West program, which donates to charity the profits from glass and aluminum can collection. Whirlpool Corporation in Benton Harbor, Michigan, decided to contract out its recycling in a way that increased employment opportunities for people who had problems finding work. For a modest charge, employees from a local organization, Gateway Sheltered Workshop, collect and process Whirlpool's recyclables. As of this writing, the Gateway work force had increased from eighteen to about seventy since the Whirlpool contract was signed in 1990.

International Recycling Mandates.
Noting that environmental laws in countries such as Germany and Japan are much tougher than those at home, forward-looking American computer companies often adopt the standards of the strictest

country both because they can then sell a single model in any international market and because they recognize that tough laws in one nation often become the model for others to follow. German lawmakers, for instance, have proposed legislation that would require electronics manufacturers to accept back from customers products that have reached the end of their useful lives. The manufacturers would then be required to either recycle or reuse the parts and materials.

Such developments have provoked the computer industry to become a recycling leader. Since March 1991, when you buy a laser printer toner cartridge from Apple, you also get a prepaid shipping label to return the cartridge when it is spent. Apple claims to recover 95 percent of the returned cartridge. It also donates one dollar to environmental organizations for every cartridge returned in the U.S. In Japan, Canon was reprocessing cartridges at the rate of 150,000 per month by late 1992.

Hand-Me-Downs.
The computer industry also beats most in another form of recycling: donating or selling old or outmoded equipment to less discriminating users. For example, the East-West Development Foundation in Cambridge, Massachusetts, exports donated, intact equipment to Russia and Eastern Europe (see Resources). A company can also sell its old systems to brokers who recondition them for Third World buyers. Other networks and hotlines exist for donating used equipment to charities or contacting manufacturers who will reclaim the systems for parts.

One soft goods manufacturer has matched the recycling mindset of the hardware makers. Customers of the charitable-minded Hanna Andersson, marketer of durable, high-quality children's clothing, can return used "Hannas" and receive 20 percent credit toward their next purchase. The Portland, Oregon, company then donates the clothing to organizations serving needy children.

Hanna Andersson's Gun Denhart explained to me, "It makes people feel good to have a channel where they can return the clothes and have them used for another baby, and it's of course good for the people who receive the clothes. Finally, something I didn't think about in the beginning is that people love being in a company that has a social conscience."

Manufacturing.
Although not yet a Deja Shoe in its overall social/environmental profile, Nike claims to be developing a totally recyclable production system. A current process grinds and pulverizes discarded whole shoes, turning them into outsole material for new shoes. The resulting outsoles, with 20-percent recycled material, perform as well or better than regular outsoles, the company says.

General Electric has designed an experimental refrigerator, the Totem, that can be easily disassembled so that its parts can be reused or recycled. All mechanical elements are encased in a single unit rather than scattered throughout the appliance. Thus, owners can easily remove worn-out parts and replace them rather than trash the entire Totem. Even the insulation, made from an alternative material, recycles. Plus, notes design magazine *Metropolis*'s Janet L. Rumble, companies like GE are discovering that designing for easy disassembly also creates a cost-effective side benefit, easier *assembly*.

Customer Buy-Back Programs.
Xerox offers a twenty-four-dollar next-purchase discount to customers returning spent copier cartridges. To facilitate the return, Xerox also provides a prepaid mailing envelope. The company, which salvages the cartridge's recoverable parts and works them into new units, began the program at the urging of recycling-conscious customers.

Packaging.
Moulded Fibre Technology creates custom-designed interior packaging from 100-percent recycled newsprint and water. (See Resources for contact information.) Real Goods, a mail-order marketer of renewable energy equipment and green consumer products, packs its shipments in shredded documents collected from government offices and banks in its Northern California county.

Rejuvenation Lamp & Fixture cushions its mail-order products in Styrofoam popcorn recovered from vendors' packaging. But as president Jim Kelly told me, the company has revised the procedure slightly since starting it. "The first two or three times we did it, we got nasty notes saying, 'You guys say you use recycled packaging. What am I doing with popcorn?' So we printed up a little thing saying, 'When this happens to us we send it on. Sorry. You do the same.' We haven't received any nasty letters since," he said, laughing.

Buying Used.
When I visited Deja Shoe in the summer of 1993, Julie Lewis pointed out to me that Deja's office space was furnished entirely with used office furniture. While the economics are obvious, buying used whenever possible is also a Deja policy, one not likely to change even as this green-leader's fortunes rise.

Home Depot also buys used in at least one sense. As of this writing, approximately one third of Home Depot's 226 stores are refurbished "takeovers"—that is, reused buildings.

Waste Reduction and Pollution Control

When it comes to reducing waste, all businesspeople have a little Jack Benny in them. But waste reduction conserves more than money. These days, it also conserves public goodwill because it saves natural resources and slows the stream of toxics pouring out of industrial plants. However, before looking more closely at the subject, we need to define our terms. In normal usage, the term "waste reduction" encompasses all forms of minimizing solid waste, including recycling. Having already examined recycling above, we won't revisit it here.

Besides, recycling needs to be separated from coverage of other forms of waste reduction for another reason, economics. The economics of recycling, as we've seen, is complicated. The economics of waste reduction is not. Studies confirm what logic already tells us— that reducing waste improves product yields, saves material costs, and decreases disposal costs. Because waste reduction often involves reducing the use of hazardous materials that, as waste, would require special treatment or disposal methods, it also saves waste management costs, minimizes regulatory hassles, and reduces the potential for accidental spills. Having fewer toxics around also makes for safer workplaces, and safer workplaces lessen employer liability. What's more, many waste reduction programs cost nothing to initiate. Of those that do require some capital expenditure, the cost is usually minimal and quickly recovered because of the savings fostered.

By the same token, I consider waste reduction and pollution control together in this section because they're often functionally inseparable. First, as mentioned above, reducing the use of hazardous materials automatically reduces pollution. Second, even when considered alone, pollution is still a form of waste to be reduced. The subjects don't always overlap—for example, a company replacing an ozone-layer-harming chlorofluorocarbon (CFC) with a less harmful chemical merely makes a substitution. It doesn't necessarily reduce waste, and as a result doesn't necessarily save money. Still, such cases are the exception.

Executives in the large corporation universe well understand the financial benefits of reducing waste, as the examples offered below demonstrate. Unfortunately, many small and medium-sized companies often lack the expertise to analyze their processes for potential savings or the financial resources to capitalize a waste reduction initiative. However, the federal government has pitched in to help in various ways. For example, the EPA makes grants to companies demonstrating innovative pollution control methods, including waste reduction that reduces pollution. In one case, a Maryland firm received $25,000 for its reduction of heavy metals in its offset printing inks. The EPA also grants money to assist states in establishing pollution prevention programs. Most states now have such programs, which actually do more direct work with industries than does the EPA, according to *In Business,* a magazine about environmental issues in business.

The following examples show how several companies, large and small, have profited by cutting waste and polluting less.

· The 3M company pioneered pollution control as a financial strategy when it began its Pollution Prevention Pays (3P) program in 1975. These 3P projects begin with employee suggestions, and employees receive monetary awards if their suggested solution meets certain qualifications. Those qualifications include preventing pollution rather than controlling it, saving money, and yielding an adequate return on investment. The company estimates that the program has saved it $573 million, and slashed pollution almost in half, giving 3M the confidence to declare that by 1995 it will reduce air and water pollution by 90 percent and solid waste 50 percent from 1990 levels. Undoubtedly, the fact that the company, one of Moskowitz and Levering's 100 best employers, tries hard to keep its work force happy and motivated plays no small part in the 3P success story. Contented employees are far more likely to make productive suggestions than are disgruntled ones. And 3M's financial incentives don't hurt, either.

· Following 3M's lead, Dow Chemical's Waste Reduction Always Pays (WRAP) program also recognizes employees who suggest ways to cut the company's wastes and toxic emissions. In 1990, the top five WRAP initiatives saved more than $10.5 million by eliminating 13.4 million pounds of waste from production processes. Dow has declared a goal of reducing toxic waste emissions by 50 percent by 1995, based on 1988 levels.

· The Robbins Company, an electroplating firm in Attleboro, Massachusetts, forked over $220,000 to create an on-site, closed-loop system to treat wastewater. That's much more than the average cost of a waste reduction project, but the company's problems were much worse than average, too—the company was close to bust because of pollution fines, toxic waste disposal fees, and insurance against hazardous leaks. The new system uses 82 percent fewer chemicals, produces 89 percent less toxic sludge, and has cut lab costs by 87 percent. Not only did the investment pay for itself in four years, but the turnaround helped repair the company's public image, with local orders multiplying as one result.

Ultimately, of course, waste reduction and pollution control constitute only a temporary solution to the permanent problem of environmental degradation. For example, the introduction of catalytic converters reduced the pollutants emitted by automobiles, but air pollution has increased anyway in most areas because more cars now travel the roads and they cover more miles per trip. Most of the changes illustrated above represent *improvements* in processes, not fundamental *transformation*. As such, the financial and ecological gains, however significant, may be a short-term benefit with no certain role in a sustainable economy. Wholesale rethinking of products and processes, not incremental alterations, are required. Some of the industrial developments mentioned below entail more substantial levels of investment and risk, but promise far bigger long-term returns.

· In an industry powered by rapid obsolescence and sexy new technology, Compaq, AST, Acer, and other computer makers have answered with an innovation that is both wallet- and eco-friendly: expandable personal computers that allow their owners to update and expand the systems without discarding still-functional equipment.

· Environmentalists have never felt much affection for so-called biodegradable plastics used in trash bags, disposable diapers, and so on, because once the organic starches in the discarded products break down, an inorganic plastic dust remains that may be more trouble-some than massed plastic. But friends of nature are considerably more excited about polylactides, polymers made from organic mate-rials only. Ecochem, for instance, has tested one made from cheese whey and corn. Once a cost-effective manufacturing process is per-fected, the compostable material will show up as truly biodegradable trash bags, grocery bags, medical packaging, frozen food packaging, and plastic utensils, plates, and cups.

· When it comes to air pollution control, the rubber literally hits the road this decade in California, where state laws require the sale of zero-emissions vehicles by 1998 to comply with Clean Air Act man-dates. Detroit automakers have never been known for environmental responsibility of any stripe, but they know a huge market when they see one and are developing viable electric cars for it. While the vehicles probably will have limitations, such as a less than 150-mile cruising range, they still figure to be ideal for urban commuters. Manufacturers figure most people could drive an electric car to work and back each day and still have enough juice left in the batteries to run a few errands before the necessary overnight recharge.

This too, however, will be only an interim environmental solution unless a minor modification is made. As writer J. Baldwin, a green-car expert, points out, the automobiles might more accurately be called Elsewhere Emissions Vehicles, because at the other end of the charging device in most cases is an environmentally nasty elec-tric utility, whether hydroelectric, nuclear, or fossil-fuel burning. The automakers haven't tried to solve *that* problem. The forward-looking Sacramento Municipal Utility District (SMUD) is working on it, however. SMUD employees now travel their rounds in electric vehi-cles charged photovoltaically. In addition, the utility has added re-newable energy technology to the grid backing its solar recharging station.

Waste Exchanges, Closed-Loop Recycling, and Industrial Ecosystems

Reportedly, the late whole-systems guru Buckminster Fuller contem-plated the problem of smog and concluded, "What a resource!" Bucky would be pleased to know that some industrial citizens today are thinking along similar lines. Through a variety of arrangements, companies with an industrial by-product or overstock, or off-specification, obsolete, or damaged goods, are finding other companies that can use the stuff as their raw material. These relationships extend all the way from simple, one-directional applications—by far the most common form, in which one company utilizes something another doesn't want—to complex "industrial ecosystems," in which several companies interlock products and by-products in a series of industrial food chains.

Even in one-direction relationships, each participating company gains, as does the planet. The company with the unneeded commodity saves disposal (and possible liability) costs of landfilling or incinerating the material. The receiving company gets something it wants at a below-market price, often just the cost of transportation. And the environment ends up with a lighter trash load.

Of course, supplier and user first have to find each other. That's where matchmaking organizations called "waste exchanges" enter the picture. These organizations, most of which operate as nonprofits, list and categorize wastes, generally according to a standardized scheme (acids, alkalis, oils, organic chemicals, and so forth). Materials listed usually include everything from hazardous wastes to cardboard to manure. In my part of the country, a Washington state–based nonprofit, the Pacific Materials Exchange, supported by an EPA grant, has electronically linked every industrial waste exchange in the U.S. to help promote industrial recycling and prevent pollution. Several Canadian exchanges have joined as well. Subscribers can access the databank 24 hours a day through a computer and modem by calling a toll-free number. Members of affiliated waste exchanges can use the service for free. (To contact them, see Resources.)

Conceptually anyway, "industrial ecosystems" constitute the most elegant way of closing waste loops. Consultant Hardin Tibbs coined the term to describe networks of businesses that align their processes to minimize each other's wastes, optimize the network's use of materials, and reevaluate by-products as feedstock for other processes. Industrial ecosystems also strive to incorporate recycled material in new production wherever possible, and even recycled power released as heat, steam, and so on.

At a seminal conference called Ecotech, held in Monterey, California, in November 1991 and featuring many of the nation's leading futurists and economic visionaries, Tibbs described a living example of such a network in Kalundborg, a Danish town eighty miles west of Copenhagen. The story began in the early 1980s, when a coal-fired electrical utility in Kalundborg arranged to supply process steam to an oil refinery and a pharmaceutical plant. The web spun from there.

At roughly the same time, the utility started furnishing surplus heat to help warm Kalundborg homes. The scheme has eliminated thirty-five hundred home oil-burning systems from the town's environmental burden. The utility sends some of its remaining surplus heat to warm its own saltwater fish farms, from which local farmers take sludge to use as fertilizer. The utility will pipe yet more surplus heat to greenhouses in a planned 37-acre horticulture project.

In 1991, the oil refinery began selling to the utility what surplus gas it was not already selling to a local wallboard producer. The exchange saved the utility thirty thousand tons of coal a year, but to make the gas clean-burning enough for the utility's needs, the refinery had to remove its excess sulfur. The process generated yet more revenue for the refinery, which sold the sulfur to a sulfuric acid plant in Jutland.

The utility is now preparing to desulfurize its smoke. That refinement will leave calcium sulfate as a by-product, eighty thousand pounds of which the utility will sell to the wallboard manufacturer, which will use it instead of the mined gypsum it normally imports.

Among other exchanges, the utility also sells fly ash to local cement makers and road builders; the pharmaceutical plant supplies local farms with fertilizer—330,000 tons annually, made from treated sludge yielded by the company's fermentation methods; and the refinery sends cooling water and purified wastewater to the utility.

Although the Kalundborg history reads like something out of an eco-science fiction tale, Tibbs notes that most of the early transactions were negotiated for mundane economic reasons. More recently, environmental considerations have driven the arrangements. Nevertheless, the numbers still pan out. And while proximity made many of the materials transfers easier, it was not always vital. For instance, the fly ash and sulfur went to distant buyers.

Tibbs uses the Kalundborg tale to illustrate his theory of industrial ecology, a vision of how a sustainable economy can also be a growing economy. You can evaluate Tibbs's ideas for yourself in his writings (begin with his piece in the Winter 1992 issue of *Whole Earth Review*), but it should be clear that if there is to be such a thing as a sustainable, growing economy in our near future, waste exchanges, particularly those that "close loops," will play an indispensable role.

Reducing Packaging

You need only visit your local supermarket or music store to witness the local impact of an international green packaging revolution. You need only visit your favorite fast-food outlet to see where the next battles will be fought.

Lined up on the supermarket shelves, you'll find such signs of greener times as the earlier-mentioned Procter & Gamble and Clorox products in their recycled and/or refillable containers. You'll notice that P&G's Secret and Sure deodorants are no longer encased in paper cartons, saving 6 million pounds of paper pulp and keeping some 80 million cartons out of landfills, the *Wall Street Journal* notes. Near them, you'll see Gillette's Dry Idea and Soft and Dry, their dispensers similarly naked to the world. Over in the film section, the Kodak rolls you purchase will be in canisters made with 20 percent less plastic, inside of boxes with 100 percent recycled paperboard. The Kodak Ektar line of films will not be boxed at all. If on the way home you stop at the music store to buy a compact disc, you'll find it packed in reusable packaging instead of the old longbox, saving some 25 million pounds of paperboard waste annually, according to Gary Strauss of *USA Today*.

If by chance, however, you should stop for a quick meal at a fast-food restaurant, you'll quickly understand why landfills are still overflowing across the nation. While in Atlanta researching material for this book, I ventured from my motel room for a late dinner. I found that my only choice for a semihealthy meal within walking distance was a Subway store four blocks away. The sandwich and salad I ordered included so much waste in the form of plastic foam boxes, utensils, individually wrapped condiment servings, napkins, and a plastic bag that it far exceeded the not inconsiderable bulk of the meal itself.

Fortunately, the fast-food industry trails behind the packaging curve. (A notable exception, McDonald's has collaborated with the Environmental Defense Fund to reduce the corporation's solid waste impact.) Packaging as a whole is clearly moving in the direction of the environmentalists' "three R's"—reduce, reuse, and recycle.

The push comes from varied directions. Environmentally concerned consumers have implored product manufacturers to cut back on excessive wrapping. Many companies, noting the fierce competition for supermarket shelf space, and increasing costs for raw materials, production, and shipping, see the wisdom of at least two of the "R's," reduce and reuse. Marketers have also latched on to environmental qualities as a way to differentiate products from their otherwise similar competitors. In the recording industry, high-profile, activist performers such as Bonnie Raitt and Peter Gabriel made waves.

As mentioned earlier, state and local laws designed to preserve scant landfill space have also played their part. And laws in the U.S. trail the environmental consciousness of European and Japanese mandates by years, a fact of which multinational companies are well aware. For example, in Germany, companies bear ultimate responsibility for the collection and recycling of packaging enclosing their products. Retailers there must also take back any packaging not accepted by their suppliers, which pressures suppliers to "three-R" their packaging to satisfy *their* customers, the retailers. Clearly, the direction of international packaging and recycling laws are changing the very concept of ownership, with governments making companies responsible for not only a product's packaging but also the product itself once it has exhausted its useful life.

With such laws in place "across the pond," U.S. companies can see the domestic packaging future manifest and many are making the inevitable changes now. It's true that short-term costs of converting existing processes can offset immediate cost savings. And for now, recycled materials don't necessarily cost less than virgin ones. Nor have mainstream American consumers been as quick to abandon convenience packaging as environmentalists wish. Still, the long-term prospects in all of these areas make the green packaging movement one revolution that business can support unequivocally.

Making Markets

In 1983, Mel Bankoff, a former natural foods store operator and restaurateur, started his natural foods product company Emerald Valley Kitchen with his last two hundred dollars and admirable intentions. He wanted to use the healthiest, tastiest ingredients possible and he wanted to support agricultural methods that didn't ravage soil, water, and farmworkers. One problem: even as a start-up, he couldn't find organic beans and tomatoes—the main components of his primary products, premium bean dips and salsas—in sufficient volumes.

He can now, thanks to his own persistence. Without a viable market in which to shop for his ingredients, he helped make one. By finding and sticking with small organic growers who could at least partly meet his needs, he helped keep their operations viable. They in turn were able to expand their operations to the point that they could supply his growing business and others at decent prices. I visited Bankoff and his operation in the summer of 1993. "We're able to get a large enough contract where the price is competitive now," Bankoff told me while relaxing in the small lunchroom of his Eugene, Oregon, plant.

The ripples from Bankoff's concerted efforts have radiated in all directions. For instance, Bankoff's tomato supplier, buoyed by Emerald Valley's substantial orders, is spreading the gospel of organic agriculture throughout the farm belt in California's Central Valley. Said Bankoff, "He's showing farmers who have grown commercially for years with tons of chemicals that they can do it organically and show a profit and actually have a better yield than they had with chemicals."

Emerald Valley has made headway in another important area—getting a healthy, alternative product into mainstream supermarkets like Safeway and Albertson's. There, it's snatching market share from its blander, less quality-conscious competitors. That paves a road on which other alternative products may eventually travel. To more discriminating customers, natural foods products often stand out in both quality and taste, regardless even of the health advantages. "That's how I first became aware of Emerald Valley," recalled Pat Fagan, the company's sales and marketing director who joined us in the lunchroom. "It was my favorite salsa." He added that Emerald Valley's pledge, printed on its packaging, to give 1 percent of profits to "ecology and hunger projects" also swayed his product choice.

Breaking down the chain supermarket barrier also promotes Bankoff's campaign on behalf of sustainable agriculture. Explains Fagan, "Unless you have a market pulling on the other side, you're not going to have any growth in the organic food industry. By getting into mainstream markets, Emerald Valley is helping the organic farmers survive and it's a self-perpetuating process."

Gary Hirshberg and Samuel Kaymen started Stonyfield Farm Yogurt with ideals similar to Mel's, supporting organic agriculture and environmental causes in general. But the realities of the marketplace soon deferred two of their goals, producing an all-organic yogurt and packaging it in recyclable containers. Organic milk costs about 50 percent more, according to Hirshberg, whereas research and experience had shown that consumers would not pay more than about a 15 percent premium for a pure product. Counterintuitively, as Gary puts it, they also discovered that plastic containers were the most ecologically sound packaging solution if the plastics industry would recycle them. However, as we know from an above section, it won't.

"That was humbling," Hirshberg recalls, "having sat on the sidelines and criticized business for its decision-making priorities and then suddenly being in the position to have to make some of those decisions. How we came out of it in both cases was to dedicate resources to solving the bigger problems."

Stonyfield now pays a premium to family dairy farmers who use sustainable practices that the company hopes will eventually become wholly organic. For their containers, they've worked with other manufacturers using similar containers to help fund a recycling infrastructure. As of this writing, two pilot collection/recycling efforts that will turn the discarded plastic into another product were set to debut in mid-1994. (Mel Bankoff, by the way, was working on a similar effort for his company's plastic packaging when I toured his plant.)

Given the potential power of its impact, the most intriguing example of market-making I've seen is that of Home Depot. Home Depot, the nation's largest home center, is a $7 billion-plus per year operation with well over two hundred stores. It's also the environmental leader of its industry, although the nature of its operation forces on it several constraints. Explains Mark Eisen, "Retailers are real good at responding to customer demand. They are not good at, nor do I think they should be, telling shoppers, 'That's wrong to buy that.' Maybe if we had a little eco-store, we could do that, but when you're the mass market, you get customers who don't care. So what you have to do is point out the alternatives."

The latter is what Home Depot does better than any other mass retailer in the country. With Eisen supplying the environmental guidance, company buyers have identified truly environmentally sound garden, household, and building products, which the company stocks beside their mainstream competitors. As I walked through one of the Atlanta stores with Eisen, he pointed out to me such environmentally appropriate alternative products as cellulose insulation (made from recycled newspaper or telephone books), organic seeds, xeriscape plants (to reduce water consumption), compact fluorescent light bulbs, and engineered-wood products.

In order to assist its customers in making informed choices, the company has produced an informational handout called "Environmental Greenprint," which educates customers about environmentally appropriate garden and home projects and points them toward related products carried in the store. Home Depot is developing more elaborate environmental educational booklets, displays, and signage as well. And where the company can make an outright substitution of a green product for a brown one, it has done so. For example, Home Depot now carries only lead-free solder in voluntary cooperation with the EPA's waterborne lead abatement program, and sells only non-halon (that is, non-CFC) fire extinguishers.

Not everyone forgives Home Depot for all the brown goods that pass by its registers, but Eisen maintains that an organization of Home Depot's magnitude is trapped by its market: "I've had people come to me at these eco-trade shows and say, 'Why don't you get rid of those pesticides and just sell the good stuff?' You can't. You'd be out of business, and your customers would just go across the street. What good would that do?

"You can't be the total solution. If science, the media, schools, and public agencies beat the environmental message into people, they'll start to think differently and things will start to shift. The retailer can be part of that in terms of guiding people, but the number one way we tell them is by selling the alternatives."

Renewable Energy and Energy Efficiency

When physicist Amory Lovins makes his pitch for energy efficiency, you wonder if his favorite fuel isn't snake oil. That's not because of his presentation, appropriately documented and professional. But Lovins, the nation's leading energy efficiency expert, claims he can save most of the electricity now used in almost any building or facility while *increasing* effectiveness, all with an investment that will pay back in one to three years. He's got a ready retort for the skeptics, however: "Check my utility bills."

In the early 1980s, Lovins equipped the 4,000-square-foot headquarters of his Rocky Mountain Institute (RMI) with efficient light bulbs, lighting hardware, and appliances. That dropped the building's electrical consumption tenfold. RMI also cut its water use by half and the energy needed to heat space and water by 99 percent. (The superinsulated building needs no furnace even though it sits in the subarctic Colorado mountains.) Total electrical bill after the changes: five dollars per month. Payback time on the technical installations: under a year.

Today, because of the heated pace of technical developments in energy efficiency, it's much easier and cheaper to accomplish what RMI did then. In the years from 1985 to 1990 alone, RMI estimates that the potential to save electricity about doubled and the average per-kilowatt hour cost of doing it dropped by about two thirds. As we'll see below, some businesses have saved endangered jobs by cutting electrical needs instead. Some have saved their own skins.

Of course, Lovins and his nonprofit RMI serve a broader mission than monetary thrift. Ultimately, our wasteful electrical appliances and light bulbs are plugged into electrical utilities. None of the currently prominent energy-generation technologies do any favors for the environment. Yet, the simplest interventions substantially mitigate the damage. A consumer replacing a single 75-watt light bulb with an 18-watt compact fluorescent lamp that lasts 10,000 hours saves energy equivalent to what a typical U.S. power plant would produce from 770 pounds of coal, Lovins notes. Not burning that coal in turn saves 1,600 pounds of carbon dioxide and 18 pounds of sulfur dioxide from release into the atmosphere, reducing both global warming and acid rain.

As Lovins and other experts such as physicist Donald Aitken of the Union of Concerned Scientists make clear, sustainable development depends upon full implementation of these technologies. That means that ultimately we can't afford development without them. We are running out of oil and can't afford the environmental cost of burning fossil fuels much longer anyway. Nuclear power is a failed dream, having shown an even more pronounced capacity for financial catastrophe than it has for human and environmental disasters like Chernobyl.

Although massive political resistance from the conventional energy lobbies has kept the facts largely hidden from the American public, renewable technologies such as solar-thermal and wind have advanced sufficiently to entirely meet the nation's power needs, now and in the future. But the economics of investing in new infrastructure makes most sense when commercial and individual ratepayers first implement efficiency strategies like Lovins's.

Ignoring the long-term global perspective for a moment, we can see that energy efficiency also makes profound sense today for virtually any business. What's more, American business as a whole continues to suffer for its failure to take advantage of this technology. With no domestic oil industry to supply cheap fuel, Japan invested in efficient technology decades ago, a not inconsiderable factor in its industries' ability to compete in world markets. European nations such as Germany and Sweden also far outstrip ours in setting, and achieving, efficiency goals. In Germany, for instance, compact fluorescent light bulbs are the lighting appliance of choice.

The opportunities to save through energy efficiency stem both from improved technology and incentives, from public utilities and states, that reward energy-efficient purchasers. Let's first examine the state of the former.

The greatest technical advances from a cost-savings standpoint have been made in lighting, motors, and refrigeration. Writing in *Scientific American,* Lovins and other efficiency experts note that lighting accounts for about two fifths of the power used in the typical commercial building, and more than half when considering the air conditioning required to offset the heat emitted by regular lights. The Electric Power Research Institute in Palo Alto, California, estimates that 55 percent of that power can be saved cost-effectively by installing compact fluorescent bulbs and many other types of efficient hardware, with no loss of light, less glare and noise, and no flicker. The bulbs cost more initially but pay back not only through energy savings but also because the bulbs last many times longer than traditional lamps. Companies can squeeze additional energy savings from improved maintenance; lighter-colored wall finishes and furnishings to better distribute light; top-silvered blinds; and glass-topped partitions, which let sunlight penetrate farther into the building.

Significant design advances have increased electric motor efficiencies as well. Motors account for 65 to 70 percent of the energy consumed by industry, and over half of all electricity produced in the U.S., Lovins observes. Installing electronic adjustable-speed drives alone can save 10 to 40 percent of that power, he argues, with average paybacks of a year. Replacing the motors altogether with more high-efficiency systems and making other improvements that RMI suggests can increase the savings to 50 percent, with paybacks for the new systems typically completed in about sixteen months.

Superefficient refrigerators that use only 15 percent of the power of conventional models have been around for years, cooling foods in backwoods "off-the-grid" homes (homes generating all their own power from renewable energy sources). Sunfrost, the outfit that makes them, achieves the savings through extra insulation and such simple improvements as mounting the compressor on top of the unit, where the heat the motor produces rises into space instead of up through the appliance that it's trying to cool. Unfortunately, the improvements make the Sunfrost wider and squatter than conventional models, so it doesn't fit in a normal home or office refrigerator slot. That hasn't stopped companies such as Sony's Columbia and Tri-Star studios from installing Sunfrosts in its buildings, along with other state-of-the-art efficiency technology, but it does explain why you don't see more of them around.

Until 1993, major appliance companies always pointed to the same configuration problems faced by Sunfrost to explain why they couldn't manufacture a more efficient refrigerator of their own. However, once a consortium of twenty-four utilities and several environmental groups offered $30 million in prize money for a breakthrough in efficient design, Whirlpool managed to build an energy-miser unit with normal dimensions. The winning refrigerator exceeds federal energy standards by 25 to 50 percent and contains no CFCs. As of this writing, the company planned to offer its first public model in early 1994. Frigidaire, which finished second in the contest, will sell a competing model. Of course, food companies have long had an efficient option. Commercial refrigerators that yield 50 percent energy savings have been available for years, Lovins notes.

That utilities would put up the money for the great refrigerator race might sound strange to those not yet familiar with the industry's "demand-side" management approach. Why should utilities promote the development of a product that will use less of what they sell? The answer, in a Lovins-coined word, is *negawatt*, meaning "unit of saved energy." The negawatt concept has led to a paradigm shift in utility planning and substantial rebates for commercial ratepayers in many regions of the country.

To put the negawatt approach in most basic terms, a number of forward-thinking utilities have, with the help of Lovins, Aitken, and other experts, figured out how to make more money by selling less. That is, it's cheaper for utilities to save energy than make it. For instance, a program to save commercial and industrial electricity costs about half a cent per kilowatt-hour. The utility would have to pay several times that to generate the power saved, and ten to twenty times the negawatt cost to build a new coal or nuclear plant, Lovins calculates. The latter figure is key. As utilities look down the road at future demand (more people, more air conditioners, more gadgets, and so on), negawatts present a far more attractive alternative than building costly new plants that no one wants near their neighborhoods anyway.

Thus, as of early 1993, some two thousand utilities were offering energy-efficiency programs of some kind, including programs for businesses and commercial construction. These initiatives have reduced peak demand by over 21,000 megawatts since 1977, or about 42 times the power drawn by Richmond, Virginia, observes Frank O'Connell, writing for *Nature Conservancy*. The best programs often include design assistance and financial incentives for companies to build more energy-efficient buildings, technical support in upgrading lighting systems, and even gifts. For example, in 1991, San Diego Gas & Electric sent teenagers door to door to ratepayers' homes throughout the county to distribute free compact fluorescent bulbs, water heater blankets, and low-flow showerheads.

Whether or not your local utility has jumped on board the demand-side bandwagon, your business can still profit by taking advantage of the considerable technical advances in energy efficiency. Energy efficiency may, in fact, be just the medicine your company needs to cure what ails its cash flow. Compare, for instance, the total economics of layoffs with those of becoming more energy efficient. Downsizing wreaks havoc on balance sheets because of severance packages, early retirements, administrative costs, and the like. A company that downsizes also terrifies its remaining employees, and sometimes overstresses them physically by piling more duties on their shoulders. Should demand for its products and services increase in the future, the company will need to start hiring again, incurring recruitment and training costs.

By contrast, the investment a company makes in energy efficient technology and building design may save enough money from reduced utility bills to keep a work force intact. Saving jobs preserves morale and productivity, and also saves the short- and long-term cash costs of cutting jobs. Lower utility bills improve cash flow and reduce production costs, too.

The following examples show how several companies retooled their finances as well as their physical plants through energy efficiency.

· J. C. Penney pays $120 million a year in utility bills for its fourteen hundred stores, a pretty penny by any measure but not nearly what it was spending before it began an energy conservation program in 1982. When constructing new stores or renovating old ones, the company incorporates efficient lighting technology and computers that control heating and air conditioning use. Average annual energy use in many stores has been cut nearly in half.

· Caught between high manufacturing costs and a slow market, Southwire, the nation's largest rod, wire, and cable company, suffered with the rest of its industry in the 1980s until it mined its negawatt mother lode. Over eight years, the energy-intensive company saved about 60 percent of its gas and 40 percent of its electricity per ton of product. In the rugged years between 1980 and 1986, negawatts accounted for virtually all of the company's profits, and may have saved as many as four thousand jobs in six states, according to Lovins.

· In Lawrence, Kansas, Wal-Mart has opened an environmentally considerate store with energy attributes that lowered the 121,264-square-foot facility's utility requirements by 54 percent. The design-for-efficiency approach includes: an extensive skylight system, complete with electronic daylight sensors that dim or brighten fluorescent lights; superinsulated windows; a non-CFC cooling system that makes ice at night, frozen with cheaper off-peak electricity, to cool air by day; and a solar-powered exterior sign. Among its other eco-friendly features: a parking lot made from recycled asphalt; landscaping with native plants, which reduces watering needs; a wastewater and runoff recovery system that irrigates the landscaping; and an on-site recycling center for customers. Plus, architect William McDonough, one of the world's leading environmental designers, made the entire building "recyclable"—that is, convertible to apartments should Wal-Mart ever abandon it. (To contact McDonough's firm, see Resources.)

Certification Processes

When "green" products did disappointing business during the recessionary early 1990s, some marketing experts suggested that consumers mistrusted manufacturers' claims of eco-friendliness. The Hartman Group, a Newport Beach, California, environmental consulting firm, surveyed consumers and found that only 13 percent believed what manufacturers say about the environmental attributes of their products.

To what extent consumer skepticism affected their buying habits is open to speculation, but the theory does provoke the question, What *is* an environmentally concerned customer to believe? First, consumers were told that "biodegradable" meant "good." Not necessarily, environmental experts retorted. If a product or packaging ends up in a landfill, there isn't enough oxygen present for it to degrade. Consumers were also told that disposable diapers were "bad." My wife and I went to considerable effort to diaper our baby in cotton exclusively, only to find out once she was through the diaper stage that, considering the pesticides sprayed on cotton fields, the caustic chemicals with which cloth diaper services clean the diaper, and so on, we'd gone to a great deal of effort for a debatable environmental improvement.

This is not to say that all green claims are bogus. As Joel Makower has pointed out, many manufacturers have made substantial changes in product formula, design, manufacturing process, and packaging to make their goods more ecologically sound. Other products, such as the energy-efficient appliances discussed above, represent important advances critical to a sustainable environmental future.

Still, few consumers have the time, background, or inclination to sort the real from the hype regarding meaningful manufacturing and product standards. Given the varied efforts already underway to develop such criteria, it seems clear that recognizable standards will eventually emerge. As of this writing, the following consumer rating initiatives compete for credibility and effectiveness.

· Although no federal regulations exist, the Federal Trade Commission has issued voluntary guidelines.

· In the absence of federal standards, several states have passed laws regulating green marketing claims, others have passed laws requiring state agencies to develop such regulations, and still other states have similar legislation pending. For example, California's Truth in Environmental Advertising law limits use of such words as "recycled" and "recyclable" depending upon recycling opportunities in the state; defines "biodegradable" and "ozone-friendly"; and nails violators with a misdemeanor, punishable by up to six months in jail, $2,500 in fines, or both. Of course, the problem for manufacturers marketing nationally is making products that both conform to varying regulations in different states and anticipate regulations to come. Companies committed to minimizing their environmental impact rather than trying to cynically green-market their goods certainly face less of a dilemma, since their internal standards may well exceed the most stringent state requirements.

· As of this writing, two nonprofit groups have attempted to provide independent, third-party verification of green product claims. Scientific Certification Systems, Inc. (Oakland, California), offers two services, one that assesses specific product claims (those products that pass can display an SCS "green cross" label) and one that performs a "cradle-to-grave" life-cycle assessment. The latter evaluates not only product claims but also the energy and resources used, the pollution generated, and solid waste produced in the product's manufacture, distribution, sale, use, and disposal.

The second organization, Green Seal (Washington, D.C.), creates industry-wide environmental standards and then evaluates individual products against those standards, awarding the Green Seal to products that measure up. Through Green Seal's public hearings, the public, environmental groups, government agencies, and the industries themselves all have the opportunity for input into the standard creation process.

· On the international front, the European Commission implemented a voluntary eco-label in late 1992, applicable to a wide range of similarly used products that the commission has had evaluated. Each manufacturer pays to have its product tested, and to use the label if the product passes. The International Standards Organization (ISO), which earlier developed a body of worldwide standards called ISO 9000 that encourages product and design quality, has been working up a new compendium of principles to promote environmental excellence in both manufacturing and end-product. Companies that make the ISO grade will be permitted to label their products as "environmentally sound." Numerous American companies have already signed on with ISO 9000, a promising sign for the new effort.

Unwilling to have its customers confused or deceived by superficial environmental product claims, Home Depot has taken matters into its own hands under Mark Eisen's leadership. Home Depot requires all vendors to prove any environmental claims they make about products sold to Home Depot customers by submitting those products to the SCS life-cycle analysis. "We've got to protect the integrity of what we sell," notes Eisen, "because people will think we endorse it when it's on our shelf, which we in fact do because we say, 'Buy it from us.' But every time we clean a product up and help them do it better, we clean it up on every other retailer's shelf."

Other Practices to Lessen Negative Environmental Impact

A business can take plenty of other steps to reduce its negative impact on the environment without a massive shift in infrastructure. Most of the actions discussed below cost little to implement and some have built-in cost advantages.

Buy a Plain-Paper Fax Machine.
The faxes come out on plain paper and don't fade, eliminating the need to photocopy them for storage. The faxes are also recyclable, as opposed to standard thermal fax paper, which usually is not. The machines cost more to buy, but less to use—about three cents per fax compared to six cents for thermal faxes.

Use Less Toxic Cleaners.
Many institutional cleaning products, as well as regular household cleaners, contain hazardous chemicals that cause indoor air pollution, harm the health of those who use them, and contaminate the water supply when washed down the drain (since breakdown and waste treatment of the chemicals may be incomplete). "Greener" cleaners may cost more initially, but save money in the long run because they are concentrated and versatile (eliminating the need for separate floor cleaners, glass cleaners, and so on). They must usually be purchased from alternative sources or direct from the manufacturer rather than through janitorial supply houses. The Nature Company, a Berkeley, California–based retailer of educational, art, and gift items with nature themes, makes its green cleaners and other alternative supplies used by its janitors available to employees at significant discounts.

Support Transportation Alternatives.
In St. Paul, Minnesota, 3M operates more than a hundred vans to carry groups of employees to work. Employees drive the vans, and use

them on off-work time for a small fee. Riders pay a monthly fee that covers all expenses. As suggested in the Earthworks Group's *50 Simple Things Your Business Can Do to Save the Earth*, vans can also do public relations duty if painted with the company's logo and an environmental message. Parking price breaks for carpoolers make another useful incentive.

Eliminate Wood Pallets.
American businesses buy 500 million wood pallets a year. Home Depot uses recycled plastic slipsheets in place of pallets. A German company that Mark Eisen has been developing as a potential Home Depot vendor makes pallets from recycled plastic that last years longer than those made from wood.

CHAPTER 8

Corporate Giving and Other Forms of Community and Planetary Neighborliness

THE FOLKS BEHIND PROCTER & GAMBLE'S Crest toothpaste know how to make every advertising dollar count, even when they're not advertising. In Crest's name, P&G committed $4.7 million in 1993 to its Caring Team of Athletes program. The program works like this: First, the company selects a star hitter from each of the twenty-eight major league baseball teams. Then, based on each player's statistical performance that season, P&G donates money to provide free health care for children of the working poor (specifically, parents who earn too little to afford health insurance but too much to qualify for public assistance).

We see so many similarly high-visibility corporate sponsorships splashed on the television screen and on signs at community events that we tend to take business's community involvement for granted. In fact, less than 30 percent of all corporations give anything at all, although the major corporations are far more likely to give something (between 1 and 2 percent of pretax profits on average).

The nongivers have their own distinguished defender, economist Milton Friedman. Friedman insists that publicly owned companies that *don't* contribute or involve themselves in their communities are the ones behaving most responsibly, for when executives divert money or energy—no matter how worthy the cause—from the company's primary business activity, they short-change their primary public, the stockholders.

In a 1993 issue, *The Utne Reader* asked a group of prominent business leaders and social commentators to offer their thoughts on business's role in solving social and environmental problems. Several made comments that not only bear directly on the subject of this chapter but answer Friedman's famous objections.

For example, author Andrew Bard Schmookler confronted head-on Friedman's argument on behalf of stockholders. He proposed a law requiring "large corporations to submit to their shareholders those decisions in which corporate profits and societal impact significantly conflict." Intriguingly, Minneapolis-based Dayton-Hudson Corporation did in fact poll its stockholders in 1983 on their support of its philanthropic philosophy (the company gives an extraordinary 5 percent of pretax profits to charitable causes, a total of $11.2 million in the year prior to the poll). Nearly three quarters of those polled favored either maintaining or increasing the 5 percent policy. Only 5 percent favored reducing the percentage so dividends could be increased.

In fact, Dayton-Hudson CEO Kenneth A. Macke was one of those queried by *The Utne Reader.* He defended the business viability of the company's largesse, noting that when a community becomes more "liveable and productive," everyone benefits, including retailers like D-H. He also argued that the company's philosophy has given it a competitive advantage by positively affecting everything from sales to purchasing to recruiting to takeover defense.

Author Milton Moskowitz stated that "it's ridiculous to expect business to solve social and environmental problems. That's a job for all of us, especially the governments we elect." Nevertheless, he too contended that acting on behalf of local communities is smart business, because it helps a company "stand out from the crowd."

Anita Roddick, founder of The Body Shop International, expressed her notion of business's responsibility to community and society with a simple equation: "We believe that business has to put in what it takes out." Finally, Ralph Nader restated what some call the "proximity and capacity" argument: "Businesses have great economic and political power in their community. Their exercise of that power for good citizenship can prevent problems from arising and festering and can help bring together other forces in the community for the common good."

We'll encounter other notions about business charity and community involvement in the following pages.

Just Neighbors—Involvement in the Local Community

> *ELLIOT HOFFMAN, president of Just Desserts, a San Francisco Bay Area baker and retailer of premium desserts and other bakery items: "I never got involved in the community or social issues with the conscious thought that if I do this, it will help my business. You do this because you believe in it, and if you're lucky maybe it will come back to you."*

I had long since circled Just Desserts on my Bay Area map before I met Elliot Hoffman. On an early 1970s trip to Berkeley with a musician buddy, the two of us decided to sample every good cheesecake in the region—in one night. We started in San Francisco on a frigid evening and worked—that is, ate—our way to the East Bay. We tried at least a dozen cheesecakes that evening, many of them memorable: by common agreement, Just Desserts tied for Best of the Bay.

I've learned in the nearly twenty years since that Just Desserts, founded by Hoffman and his wife, Gail, in 1974, stands out in a different way—its company citizenship. The uncompromising quality that distinguishes its products extends to every other facet of the company's activities. As you approach the company's central bakery and offices in industrial South San Francisco, its environmental commitment calls to you from the rooftop, where eighteen solar collectors provide the facility's hot water needs. When you step inside, the first thing you notice is the multicultural work force. Although Just Desserts has no formal diversity program, the work force reflects the city's potpourri of cultures and lifestyles.

The Hoffmans' public citizenry only begins with creating a model and environmentally conscious workplace. Indeed, the company's reputation these days owes almost as much to its civic leadership as it does to its irresistible bakery goods. One of Just Desserts' most intriguing social projects takes place daily on a strip of company-owned land behind the South San Francisco facility. When I meet Elliot in October 1993, we begin our conversation at a redwood picnic table at the edge of the strip. Just beyond us, organic fruits and vegetables grow in parallel rows traversing the full length of the tract's narrow rectangle: toward the back of the garden, a tall, slender African-American man breaks up the soil with a long-handled cultivator. The man, looking cool in jeans and blue workshirt despite unseasonably warm weather, has recently been released from jail. If all goes as hoped, his participation in the "Garden Project" will help release him from the life that put him behind bars.

Hoffman didn't invent this particular community endeavor, although he's initiated many others. While home recovering from a serious illness several years ago, Catherine Sneed, a counselor at San Francisco County Jail, conceived the idea of using organic gardening as a counseling aid. As she envisioned it, the garden experience would be rich in metaphors. The inmates would nurture life instead of harming or destroying it; use organic—that is, drug-free—methods; and donate the yield to homeless shelters and soup kitchens, giving back to the community instead of stealing from it.

Intrigued by the idea, County Sheriff Mike Hennessey made available some land on jail property; Sneed and some inmates cleared it, and the Project was born. After meeting Hoffman when both were speakers at a community program, she invited him to the jail for a look-see.

"I'd frankly never been in a jail before," Hoffman says, recalling the day. "There's three people living in a cell made for two people—really more like half a person. Their kitchen table is a piece of cardboard that's put over the toilet. And they're locked up there twenty-four hours a day except for maybe four hours a week when they exercise. And that's with probably the most progressive sheriff in the United States doing the best that he can.

"So then they took me out to the garden. Cathy asked one of the students to give me a tour, a big African-American guy who a year ago might have slit my throat just as soon as give me the time of day. And you could tell from talking to that guy that he was serious about wanting to change his life. He didn't want to go back to the 'hood, didn't want to get back into the drug scene. But how many people want to hire an ex-criminal?"

That's when the business and public-citizen gears in Hoffman's brain engaged each other. "I said to Cathy, 'I've got this piece of dirt that's just a garbage dump. Why don't you grow fruits and vegetables there that I can use at the bakery? I'll buy them at market prices and maybe we'll create a job or two. Maybe we'll create a model of what can be done wherever there's a piece of dirt.' And that's exactly what happened."

Clearing of the Just Desserts plot began in November of 1990. On April 30, 1991, the students, as the recently released inmates and occasional homeless and other troubled participants are called, harvested the first strawberry crop, which ended up on Just Desserts cheesecakes sold throughout the Bay Area. Other Garden customers now include the noted Berkeley restaurant Chez Panisse and, of course, Ben & Jerry's.

Once they've graduated to the Just Desserts site, the students not only receive counseling in personal issues but also attend what the Project calls Real Life University, where they learn such basics as how to open a bank account and the importance of coming to their job (they are paid better than minimum wage for sixteen hours per week in the garden) on time each day. "And when we're going to hire somebody," adds Hoffman, who has six ex-Garden students working for Just Desserts when we talk, "they go through an interview and they have to get recommendations and so on. It's very important that that happen."

The Garden Project has forged a link with the city's Department of Public Works, which now hires Project graduates to plant and tend trees around the city. Unfortunately, Hoffman frets, there still aren't enough jobs for the worthy applicants that emerge. And without jobs, many will disappear back into the only other economy available to them, the economy of the streets.

Using the Garden Project as a springboard, Hoffman has organized other community endeavors to assist his company's indigent neighbors. On Earth Day 1993, following four months of planning, he and a group of eight hundred business volunteers including the chair of Pacific Telesis and the vice chair of Chevron descended upon an elementary school located in a disadvantaged neighborhood near the bakery, armed with $280,000 worth of donated supplies. They built gardens, retaining walls, and automatic watering systems; painted classrooms and hallways; cleaned and scrubbed around the school; upgraded the laboratory and gym facilities; and so on.

Hoffman has also served on the board of the local chamber of commerce for the sole purpose of educating other members about the social side of business. "There are a lot of people out there," he says, "who don't know how [to involve themselves in the community], but would like to, and they need what you might call on-ramps. That's what the school project was about in a sense, showing eight hundred people an on-ramp."

While Just Desserts' civic activities have certainly not gone unnoticed, public relations has never been the point. The company made that clear in 1990 when, with eighteen other companies (including Ben & Jerry's, The Body Shop, Stonyfield Farm Yogurt, Rhino Records, Patagonia, and Working Assets Funding Service), it declared its opposition to the Persian Gulf conflict in a full-page ad (titled "An Unnecessary War") that ran in *The New York Times*. A popular radio talk show host tore into the company and all but called for a boycott of its products, but Hoffman wasn't fazed.

"Our staff was so proud that we took that stand," he says smiling, "and yet we got blasted from some customers. We also got some wonderful calls. One woman said, 'I've been on a diet for two weeks, and in support of you I'm going down to your Irving Street store and buy not one but two pieces of apple pie à la mode.' " [Hoffman laughs.] "So it's mixed, and that's a risk you take when you say and do what you think is right."

Intended or not, though, Just Desserts' civic activities have helped the business. "We're very well known in San Francisco for being a socially involved company," Hoffman notes. "The causes that we get involved with are things that, by and large, are very dear to a lot of people here, and I think that's one reason our customers are a pretty loyal group." His employees are, too. They know that, as with Ben & Jerry's, the amount of butterfat in its products is not always the best measure of a company's soul.

The Just Desserts story suggests several ways that business citizens like Elliot Hoffman view their community role.

· *Whether they seek the mantle or not, business leaders are community leaders by definition, and therefore have a responsibility to the community that transcends ordinary citizenship.* Of course, as James O'Toole points out, not all community activists welcome business participation. Some distrust business intentions, even in charitable activities, and therefore fear business's disproportionate ability to shape outcomes.

• *Because business leaders know how to get things done quickly and cost-efficiently, they constitute a unique and invaluable resource for those trying to solve community problems.* While the Garden Project is not yet self-sustaining, it's designed to support itself eventually. Thanks to Hoffman's business acumen, the Project now has the potential to expand far beyond its original bounds without diluting its social mission.

• *Business leaders have far more ability than individual citizens to mobilize corps of volunteers and aggregate material donations.* Esprit, the San Francisco–based sportswear company, is one of several progressive companies that subsidizes or otherwise positively encourages, as opposed to pressures, its employees to volunteer in their local communities. In the Esprit model, employees may take up to ten paid hours per month to volunteer for the community activity of their choice. The company also schedules what it calls Labor Days approximately twice a year. On these occasions, the entire company divides into work crews ("like a huge guerrilla team," in the words of co-founder Susie Tompkins) to do community volunteer work.

• *In critical situations, such as when lives or basic human rights are at stake, business leaders have no less a responsibility than other community leaders to provide moral leadership, even at the risk of alienating customers.* Such an occasion arose in November 1992 in my state. Oregon's ballot for that election included a state-wide initiative, Measure 9, that would have mandated discrimination against homosexuals. Recruited by Jim Kelly, president of Rejuvenation Lamp & Fixture, and his brother John, forty companies based or with operations in Portland added their names and logos to a full-page ad in the city's major newspaper, *The Oregonian,* urging voters to reject the initiative. Signees besides Rejuvenation included the northwestern one-stop shopping chain Fred Meyers; the Portland Board of Realtors; the Portland Trailblazers basketball team; northwestern department store chain Meier & Frank; Hanna Andersson; the city's biggest booksellers, Powell's Books; McMenamin's Pubs & Breweries; a variety of local outfits and professionals; and the apparently fence-mending Carl's, Jr., a company once boycotted by many gays because of CEO Karl Karcher's support of homophobic candidates and ballot measures. Measure 9 lost, and the Portland area vote made the difference.

Only the hardest of hearts could mistake the community projects of a Just Desserts for a cynical publicity gambit. Still, it's worth remembering that, as I noted earlier, other such outstanding corporate citizens as The Body Shop and Stonyfield Farm Yogurt don't advertise. It's their good works and the publicity they generate, along with word-of-mouth about their superior products, that keep their names before the public. Some of the companies in the examples below are also getting commercial mileage—intentionally or otherwise—from their community involvement.

Improve the Business Climate with Community Projects.
In 1992, Cargill, the Minneapolis-based agribusiness, donated $100,000 to help the American Library Association (ALA) develop literacy projects that could involve Cargill volunteers. ALA then created a resource kit provided to all Cargill locations and nearby public libraries. The kit shows volunteers how to develop activities that encourage parents to read to their children. The payoff for Cargill, besides warm feelings from the volunteers, is a more literate work force years down the line.

Product-Related Community Involvement.
Portland, Oregon–based swimwear manufacturer Jantzen cosponsors two beach cleanups a year along the Oregon coast, an update—and environmental upgrade—of its 1926 "Clean Water" campaign to clean swimming pools.

Promoting Community Economic Development.
Ben & Jerry's Partnership program matches retail opportunities with specific social needs in communities. For instance, Partnership arranged for a Baltimore scoop shop to be owned and operated by People Encouraging People, a rehabilitation program for the psychiatrically disabled.

Caring About Community Impact

The economically stressed town of Chester, Pennsylvania, wasn't up to hearing more bad news in 1980 when the bad news came: old friend and neighbor Sun Ship, in better times the largest shipyard in the world, was pulling out. Declining for years because of withering competition from Korea and Japan, the operation was losing boatloads of money and had shrunk from a World War II high of 35,000 employees to just 4,200.

However, those 4,200 lived in Chester and most of them made pretty good wages. The sale of the operation, occasioned not only by hard times but also parent Sun Company's decision to divest all nonenergy subsidiaries, would impact the town far beyond the job losses (the new owner was scaling back the yard). Chester depended upon Sun Ship for much of its tax revenue. Several local social service agencies fed off the company's historical largesse.

Observers still argue about whether Sun might have done more to keep the shipyard operating. But as reported by radio producer and author David Freudberg, once Sun handed down its decision, many of those victimized by the closing, including laid-off employees, felt the company took extraordinary steps to ease the pain. For almost a year, Sun representatives discussed how best to end the marriage with employees, city officials, and staff of the social service agencies. Ultimately, Sun gave laid-off employees generous early retirement and severance packages, continued medical benefits, and provided job counseling; agreed to give Chester a three-year voluntary payment of up to $800,000 to compensate for lost taxes, shocking the city officials who had suggested it; donated $210,000 to the local United Way to make up for lost employee contributions; and established, through a $360,000 grant and free executive guidance, a major nonprofit organization to spur economic redevelopment in Chester.

The Sun Ship example demonstrates much more than a caring response by a company ending a long-term relationship with a community. It also implies that Sun Company felt a sense of obligation that is all too rare in company/community alliances. Clearly, an employer provides benefits to its resident communities. For instance, no matter what else can be said about its community impact, a company provides jobs.

But a business also takes from its community. For example, if the company is part of a large national chain that sells goods or services to the community, wealth is sucked out of the area in the form of profits sent to national headquarters. The chain operation will probably also do most of its purchasing outside the community, again having a less beneficial effect than might a local operator in a similar business.

As management author James O'Toole notes, companies also benefit disproportionately from the local social and economic infrastructure in their communities. For instance, companies profit from the local schools, libraries, and universities that educate and train many of their valued employees. They benefit from the local social and cultural climate that makes the community a desirable place to live and thus a recruiting asset to the company. They benefit from the local health infrastructure that treats their sick and injured employees so they can return to work.

Obviously, there is no precise way to calculate whether a company's effect on its community is ultimately beneficial or exploitive. But the work of O'Toole, Kirk Hanson, and others suggests several criteria by which that relationship might be measured:

- *Does the company provide steady employment?*
- *Does the company site and design its facilities to maximize their social benefit?*
- *Does the company provide goods and services that the community needs?*
- *Is the company improving the standard of living and quality of life of the community?*
- *Does the company pay its fair share of the tax burden?*
- *Does the company behave ethically—that is, do no harm, tell the truth (such as disclose potential toxic impacts on employees and neighborhoods), obey the law, live by the Golden Rule, and so on?*
- *If an industrial accident could cause a community disaster, is the company prepared with adequate emergency procedures and equipment?*
- *If management feels compelled to lay off employees or close a site, what does it do to mitigate the damage done to the community?*
- *Does the company encourage employees to volunteer in the community and otherwise be good citizens?*
- *Does the company contribute to the community philanthropically?*

Obviously, some of the criteria on the above list—obeying the law, disclosing toxics, preparing for disasters, and so on—hardly require further comment. But others may seem more like items on a civic wish list than behavior we can ask of a company pleading that its first obligation is to its shareholders. For example, we expect, however jadedly, that mainstream business will fight increased taxation at every opportunity, couching its protest in alarmist rhetoric about the economy, jobs, and "wasteful government." These arguments also conveniently justify increasing profits at the public's expense.

But that's "just business," according to contemporary commercial ethic, so why even discuss a higher standard? For one thing, because when businesses turn their backs on communities, they often get bitten on their behinds. As we've seen throughout these pages, socially irresponsible business behavior often reveals itself to be shortsighted fiscal behavior because the suffering wrought often envelops the offending businesses as well.

Take, for instance, the tribulations of the Wal-Mart corporation during 1993, which gave off the unmistakable odor of backfire. Wal-Mart is one of America's best large employers according to Moskowitz and Levering, and a good environmental citizen as well in the informed opinion of the Council on Economic Priorities. But many Americans don't feel very neighborly toward the corporation, despite these positives. Specifically, many small retailers accuse the company of preying on local economies by pricing its merchandise so low— below cost, if necessary—that local businesses can't compete. They point to the failure of long-established merchants in many of the small cities where the corporation has landed.

Wal-Mart counters that its presence stimulates local economies and that its stated pricing policy to "meet or beat the competition without regard to cost" was established to benefit customers and produce profits, not destroy competition. But a judge in the company's home state of Arkansas ruled otherwise in 1993, agreeing with three pharmacies in the town of Conway that the company indeed had engaged in "predatory pricing" specifically "for the purpose of injuring competitors." As of this writing, the company faced similar suits in up to twenty-two other states, according to *Business Week*. Meanwhile, Wal-Mart announced almost simultaneously with the ruling that it would not be siting stores in several northeastern communities where retailers had protested loudly that the company should take its economic stimulation elsewhere.

Wal-Mart and its defenders might well counter that the company is simply being penalized for being too successful. Without taking sides in this particular argument, let's just suggest that investing in local economies and communities has *its* business advantages, too. For instance, companies that support affordable housing near their operation may find it easier to recruit and retain a work force. Companies that support education in their local communities, through Adopt-a-School programs and other projects, should reap long-range benefits in the form of more able future employees.

In 1991, Ben & Jerry's, committed to buying its dairy ingredients from small local sources rather than purchase from large agribusinesses outside its region, took the extraordinary step of volunteering to pay the farmers a premium whenever milk prices drop below the farmers' cost of production, as they had that year. Stonyfield Farm Yogurt, similarly dedicated to the small farmers' cause, made a comparable commitment and in 1993 convinced Ben & Jerry's to join it in rewarding farmers that switch to more sustainable agricultural methods. The program doesn't seem to have curtailed either company's profits or growth—and may have advanced them through increased customer and worker loyalty. Besides, when has a community ever bemoaned a new Ben & Jerry's store opening in their midst or the local health food store stocking Stonyfield's yogurt?

A key measure of a company's commitment to its resident community is how it handles a threatened site closure. We looked mainly at the up side of the Sun Ship case earlier in this chapter. However, despite Sun Company's efforts to minimize the divestiture's impact, it took a human as well as a financial toll in Chester. Few of those laid off found jobs with wages or benefits comparable to what Sun had paid them. Some became drug abusers. Some abused alcohol. Some abused their children.

A far more severe human tragedy will likely accompany Chrysler's relocation of its headquarters from the inner-city neighborhood of Highland Park to the Auburn Hills suburb outside Detroit. Highland Park, an incorporated city within Detroit, counted on Chrysler's tax payments for half of its $16 million annual budget, and Chrysler's five thousand employees there formed the basis of the local economy. Lee Iacocca explained that the move would make the company more efficient (it has a huge new technical complex in Auburn Hills and wants its executives next door). To its great credit, the company volunteered to pay $14 million over eight years to soften the blow to

Highland Park. But the blow will be a haymaker despite the generous gift. In late 1992, with Chrysler still around, unemployment in Highland Park stood at 31 percent, and median household income had fallen to $9,805, down 25 percent over the past decade.

While Chrysler and many others head for the 'burbs, as companies have for decades, several corporations have taken the opposite tack, siting facilities in blighted areas whenever they can or otherwise helping to spur economic redevelopment. As O'Toole notes, Weyerhaeuser, Levi Strauss, Dayton-Hudson, John Deere, Honeywell, and Control Data have all pursued that community involvement strategy in recent years. For example, in several cities around the U.S., Control Data has built factories in run-down areas, providing training and jobs to minority residents and helping to revitalize health care, transportation, and affordable housing in those communities as well.

In some cases, such broad community-mindedness justifies itself in strict business terms. In other cases, the explanation is not so simple. Ben & Jerry's price supports paid to local farmers cost it $480,000 in over-market payments the last eight months of 1991 alone. Writing about the program for a Social Venture Network publication, a company spokesperson explained the initiative thus: "In announcing our intention to pay this premium, we pointed out that it was not good business to ask a supplier to provide a product to us at [a price that] threatens the viability of the supplier. . . . [The program] represents our belief that the social value of this business-to-farm relationship is of greater importance than our supposed right to buy at the cheapest possible price."

Some will call the actions of Ben & Jerry's and Stonyfield on behalf of northern Vermont farmers foolish, even irresponsible in Friedmanesque terms. Some will call the companies hopelessly idealistic. I prefer to call them simply good citizens who recognize their implied civic role and act appropriately. Being in business does not relieve the people that operate it from their ordinary obligations as citizens and implies obligations far beyond the ordinary. Because of the scale of their activities, larger companies significantly shape social outcomes whether they intend to or not, as the Sun and Chrysler examples demonstrate.

What Ben & Jerry's and Stonyfield do for local farmers is laudable for a business but to be expected, albeit gratefully, from a neighbor. If those companies had exploited the situation and bought milk below cost, prevailing business values would have justified the behavior. What sets Ben & Jerry's and Stonyfield apart time and again is their rejection of ordinary business thinking and their recognition that business is a social enterprise whether it seeks to make a difference or not.

Corporate Giving (Back)

Shareholders who agree with Milton Friedman that corporate charity steals from their potential returns should look up a study by two Dickinson College economics professors, Stephen E. Erfle and Michael J. Fratantuono. The study examined correlations between various categories of social responsibility and financial performance. Among the many factors that positively related to profitability was philanthropy. Another, by the way, was community involvement.

This certainly seems to be the case at Home Depot, one of the fastest growing, most profitable large companies in America and a charitably minded outfit of rare commitment. The company donates 1 percent of pretax profits to nonprofits, actually somewhat less than average for a major corporation (although that 1 percent amounted to $5.5 million in 1992 alone). However, the number only begins to describe the company's community spirit. When I visited Home Depot's Atlanta headquarters in early 1993, my first stop was the office of director of community affairs Suzanne Apple, who oversees the corporation's charity and volunteer efforts. It hadn't been that long since Hurricane Andrew had blasted through southern Dade County, Florida, forcing two Home Depot stores to be abandoned and completely destroying a third that had been open just five days. The incident taught her something special about the company she had joined just about a year before:

"The way this company came together—we literally dropped everything—to serve the communities that were hit hard was absolutely incredible. It sounds very trite, but I was really proud to work for this company. The hurricane hit on Monday. By Tuesday morning, we had hurricane relief teams put together that included the vice president of human resources, Don McKenna, our traffic department arranging to ship stuff to Florida, and everybody in between. Our manager of relocation was in there because she could access apartments to send our employees to. We had about a hundred employees without homes."

It's admirable but perhaps to be expected that a company would take care of its own. But Home Depot reached out far beyond its work force. "We mobilized collections here in our stores for food, clothes, water, and diapers," Apple recalled. "We also purchased truckloads of food and grills so we could cook. We sent over fifteen tractor trailers full of supplies and just pulled up to the parking lots of stores and started handing it out, to our employees, to our customers, to anybody who showed up. At each store, we mobilized our smaller trucks so that as soon as employees became stabilized they could fill up the truck with stuff and distribute it through the neighborhood. And this went on for two weeks."

Home Depot maintained its relief efforts in the southern Florida community long after the immediate crisis had passed. While other building supplies vendors were jacking up prices to exploit the sudden market (seventy-five thousand homes in southern Dade County sustained damage), Home Depot, in cooperation with Georgia Pacific, the nation's largest plywood producer, held its prices on building materials for hurricane relief. "Effectively, we donated the materials at cost," Apple noted, "because we ate the increase."

In less demanding circumstances, Home Depot's philanthropic initiatives still reveal a level of passion and involvement unusual in big companies. "Corporate giving here is not something on the eleventh floor where I read proposals and make grants," Apple said. Every Home Depot store manager has a contributions budget for the local community, and much of Apple's work involves supporting them in spending it. In fact, the company distributes about 70 percent of the philanthropic budget outside its base city. Employees have direct input into how some of the money is spent, since the company will match dollar-for-dollar any contribution an employee makes to a legitimate nonprofit, without judgment about the target.

The company's community-conscious style sometimes blurs the line between philanthropy and volunteerism. Take, for instance, the company's involvement with Habitat for Humanity in Atlanta. Relying on volunteer labor and charitable donations, Habitat builds homes in low-income neighborhoods, and finances their purchase with no-interest loans to area families; over the past several years, Home Depot has led the entire Atlanta business community in both contributions and volunteer participation.

I wanted to examine Home Depot's philanthropy through the other end of the telescope, so I visited Habitat's center in the south Atlanta neighborhood where the organization has concentrated its work. Habitat's Atlanta director, Larry Arney, gushed more about the company's generosity than Apple did.

"I've just been overwhelmed by the spirit of what they do and the way they understand our needs," Arney told me as we talked in his office in a prototypical Habitat house. "With a lot of corporate givers—and it's reasonable that they feel this way—their involvement is much more based on their needs than ours. It's like, 'I will give you this, no matter what, and you find some way to make it work.'"

Arney has been astounded by nearly every aspect of the company's participation. When Habitat invited Home Depot to place someone on the Habitat board, Andy McKenna (no relation to Don), the company's vice president of information systems, took the post and brought the full power of his department with him. After McKenna determined that Habitat's antiquated computer system hurt its fundraising-by-mail, he arranged for one of Home Depot's computer vendors to donate new computers and network hookups, had his staff help implement the system, and invited Habitat staff to a custom instructional session to train them on it. He also involved Habitat with a Home Depot promotion at a big home show that helped the organization both raise funds and publicize itself.

By 1991, Home Depot was established as a regular giver and Arney invited them to send over volunteers to help build the houses. Again, Home Depot responded with gusto, but not in the way Arney might have expected. The first volunteer crews came from corporate headquarters, since Habitat construction is usually done on Saturdays when Home Depot store employees are busy serving weekend do-it-yourselfers. They were back to help in 1992, and built three houses in 1993 (one constructed by Home Depot store employees on a special Thursday session arranged to better fit their schedules).

Arney does wish Home Depot behaved more like other corporate sponsors in one respect—glorifying their gifts. He's encouraged them to publicize their Habitat efforts, which would both draw attention to Habitat and send a message to other corporations. "It's a natural tie-in to Home Depot's business, which I think both parties can exploit more than we do," Arney told me. "But Home Depot wasn't really into it. And finally Suzanne says, 'You've just got to understand that advertising and publicity is one thing, and corporate support of things like Habitat is another, and we don't really want there to be a connection.' Essentially what she was saying was that we want to give away money to things that matter in the community but we don't particularly want recognition.' "

Home Depot's philanthropy exhibits many other qualities of a thoughtful corporate giving program, including:

Professional Oversight and Management.
Obviously, Suzanne Apple does much more than disinterestedly write checks.

Democracy.
Democratizing the giving process helps counter the skeptical way, mentioned earlier, that some community activists regard corporate philanthropy. Home Depot's policies of matching employee contributions to the charities of their choice and diffusing funds to individual store managers so they can sponsor their own projects demonstrate two strategies for democratic giving. Other approaches include involving employees in the grant-making, either through grant-review committees or directly. For instance, Levi Strauss invites employees at each worksite to join Community Involvement Teams that decide how to distribute funds to local community projects.

Noncash or Leveraged Giving.
When Home Depot sells building materials at cost to Habitat for Humanity, its gesture is worth more than a comparable amount of cash. Noncash giving also provides smaller, cash-strapped companies with a way to make important community contributions. Examples of noncash giving include not only donations of company products but also loans of managerial or technical assistance given to local community projects, or setting up work-release programs for employee volunteers to approved community activities. Earlier in this chapter, we characterized such efforts as community volunteerism, but for a cash-poor company, they cross the line into philanthropy.

Of course, many large companies employ noncash giving strategies as well. In fact, some large companies with community-based charitable giving programs lend expert assistance as a way of ensuring the success of their charitable ventures. Other benefits may accrue from noncash giving as well, such as employees learning job-related and interpersonal skills during their voluntary leave activities.

Focused Charity.

Many companies prefer to write a single check to established umbrella charities like United Way and be done with it. The major umbrella charities tend to be top-heavy in administrative costs and salaries and are inclined to give to the same nonprofits year after year, making it difficult for worthy new organizations and causes to find funding. Although Home Depot designates 10 percent of its corporate contributions for local United Ways in communities where it is also supporting affordable housing, Suzanne Apple explained to me that giving to the locals seemed the most efficient way to support the kinds of social services that help make housing projects successful. She also pointed out that the local United Ways don't necessarily replicate the problems of the national.

Patagonia's giving program provides an outstanding example of generous, focused giving. The company donates about 10 percent of its pretax profits (the legally allowable deductible limit) to environmental charities, primarily smaller, grass-roots organizations.

Although it certainly doesn't seem to be Home Depot's style, some companies have found creative ways to integrate philanthropy with business goals. In fact, William Ruckelshaus, with an apparent nod to Milton Friedman, has argued that "enlightened self-interest" is the only way a company can justify substantial gifts. At its best, this giving strategy represents an imaginative marriage of functions, without compromising the philanthropic spirit in any substantial way. Enlightened self-interest charity can take many forms.

"Social Venture Giving."

Although most giving is in some sense an investment in a better society, some companies use their giving as a sophisticated form of long-term business investment. These companies recognize that if business makes only "withdrawals" from society—material resources, human resources, energy, wealth—and does not invest in it, then it depletes itself in the long run. Obvious examples of such giving: a high-tech firm giving to a university's science and math colleges, and a publishing company supporting literacy programs (although regarding the first example, O'Toole argues that giving to a local college is simply paying for services rendered if the company depends upon employing the school's graduates).

Cause-Related Marketing.

Some companies donate some or all of the profits made from particular products to a designated charity; the charitable intent is generally advertised on the product packaging and other promotional media. For example, Stonyfield Farm Yogurt donates 5 percent of the profits of its Guava Papaya yogurt to Cultural Survival, Inc. The yogurt flavor further supports the Amazon rainforest and indigenous people who live there because the fruit in it is sustainably harvested from standing trees. Along similar lines, many popular musicians have assigned a portion of the profits from their recordings to a favorite nonprofit. Typical is David Grisman and Jerry Garcia's *Not for Kids Only,* a wonderful collection of regional folk songs for all ages, released by Grisman's label, Acoustic Disc. All song publishing proceeds go to the Carousel Fund, which assists families with children afflicted with a catastrophic illness, and proceeds from the sale of limited edition prints of Garcia's cover art support both Carousel and a music therapy clinic.

In a few cases, companies have associated not just a product but the entire enterprise with a cause. Ryka, maker of women's athletic shoes, donates 7 percent of its profits to a foundation it created to help female victims of violent crime. (Founder Sheri Poe is herself a rape victim.) Coors has adopted adult literacy as its social market, but goes way beyond the usual purchase-linked donations to push the cause. The company has used its advertising expertise to promote a toll-free Coors Literacy Hotline and related company-sponsored programs and events, and involved its employees, distributors, and retailers in grassroots outreach efforts. Through its advertising, Ashland Oil has tied its company name to support of public education, including the recognition of teachers; the program focuses on the four states where the company subsidiaries are headquartered, a social investment that should ultimately improve the quality of Ashland's work force.

The business benefits of cause-related marketing include both increased sales and high visibility. In a 1993 poll, two thirds of consumers surveyed said they preferred to buy a cause-linked product, everything else being equal. Advertising campaigns like Coors's or Ashland's that push causes push products, too. Coors's efforts also landed the company coverage on *Good Morning America* and talk shows.

CHAPTER 9

———— ⚜ ————

Principled Purchasing: Buying a Better World

THEY DON'T CONDUCT SECRET TRAININGS or even commune in cyberspace, but people applying social values to their purchasing and investing have made enough cumulative impact to turn business on its ear. As Rejuvenation Lamp & Fixture president Jim Kelly described the way customers responded to his company's social initiatives, he seemed almost overwhelmed: "There are lots of people out there who are conscious of these issues and it's making a tremendous change in industry and commerce. Definitely, consumer interest is forcing businesses to be more environmentally responsible. I think it's a wonderful part of being in business now. You can do these things you believe in and it comes back to you so easily."

As more and more consumers "buy-cott" companies they perceive as being socially responsible and boycott those they don't, ethically motivated companies are beginning to apply the same sorts of financial pressures in the supplier universe. The environmentally sensitive Home Depot, one of the nation's major lumber retailers, decided it was no longer willing to passively support unrestrained timber cutting. Environmental marketing manager Mark Eisen told me how the company had resolved the conflict between its customers' demands and the company's environmental considerations:

"It's not possible for us to sell only sustainably harvested wood because less than one percent of the wood in the world meets that criteria. What we're going to do is use Scientific Certification System's index that ranks operations based on sustained yield, ecological health, and community benefits on a one to one hundred scale. When you need as much product as we do, you may have to buy in, say, the sixties or fifties or forties. But we're going to set a level below which we won't buy. And then when this index system gets out there in the marketplace, you'll have these forest companies out there trying to improve their scores." As we have seen, Home Depot also leads its industry in introducing alternative building materials such as engineered-wood products.

Because management bothered to reflect on the social implications of its purchasing choices, Home Depot will make a significant impact on forestry practices by simply doing what it must do anyway: purchase product from wholesalers. Other companies are helping minority communities raise themselves up by their own bootstraps by conscientiously purchasing needed products and services from minority vendors. Values-driven outfits like Ben & Jerry's or Stonyfield Farm and nonprofit organizations like Cultural Survival are taking the idea of social purchasing a step further still, crafting mutually beneficial purchaser/supplier relationships that further social goals not addressed by minority purchasing.

The beauty of socially responsible purchasing begins with the amount of good a company can accomplish just by conscientiously conducting ordinary business. It is bracing to consider how few are the numbers of corporate purchasers that integrate social considerations with their day-to-day buying and how much social and environmental potential remains unfulfilled because of those oversights. The up side of this situation, of course, is the substantial pool of social capital still available to be put to work.

Purchasing from Minority- and Women-Owned Businesses

Corporate America's commitment to purchasing from minority businesses hasn't much impressed Harriet Michel, president of the Minority Supplier Development Council. During a minority sourcing workshop that I attended in Atlanta in 1993, she told us: "It's like sex among teenagers in the 1950s. Everybody's talking about it, few people are doing it, and damn fewer are doing it well. When you really peel it away, I can tell you that only about one percent of the corporations, maybe less, in this country are running significant programs."

When majority-owned companies pass over minority businesses, as they do routinely, the entire nation loses, for probably no solution to minority poverty and all its attendant problems is both more accessible and yet more frustratingly ignored. As Michel pointed out that day in Atlanta, minority businesses are a vital source of minority job creation. Successful minority businesspeople also provide something that is otherwise in short supply in many inner cities: positive role models. And their contributions to their communities only begin there. Again, Michel: "We hear about all these other glitzy donors, but it's the minority businesses that are usually giving the scholarship money, buying the tables at the dinners, supporting kids through college, and giving back to their communities in lots and lots of ways."

According to Michel, the $20 billion in goods and services that American businesses purchased from minority firms in 1992 represented less than 1 percent of all business purchasing that year. What's more, that percentage hasn't grown in twenty years. According to the latest U.S. Census data available (1987), firms owned by white males averaged gross receipts of $189,000. African-American-owned firms grossed $46,593, Hispanic firms $58,555, and Native-American firms $42,610. (The "favored" minority, Asian-Americans, averaged $93,222.)

Factors that we've examined in earlier chapters partially explain this disparity.

Good Old Boy Networks of Purchasers and Suppliers.
As with any other business decision, purchasers often select suppliers on the basis of noneconomic considerations such as personal rapport, particularly in cases where, business-wise, there is little to differentiate competing bids.

Minority Businesses' Lack of Access to Capital.
All start-up and small businesses—and most minority businesses qualify in one or both categories—have trouble getting banks to lend to them, but minority businesses face the additional obstacles of lender prejudice and lack of personal and family wealth on which to fall back. Thus, minority businesses rarely can afford the large sales forces or travel budgets to call on potential customers or deliver in-

person service the way their majority competitors can. They may need to be paid more frequently than their competitors, have limited computer capabilities, and have other idiosyncrasies that a large purchaser would rather not bother with.

Prejudice.
Michel said her organization's biggest challenge is convincing companies that minority products and services "are not only equal but in many instances better, because minority suppliers are hungrier than anybody else out there" and will work harder to prove their worth. Many purchasers also have stereotypical ideas about the types of businesses that minorities run—such as janitorial services, printing, and office supplies—and often don't even look for minority suppliers outside those categories. The stereotype isn't entirely unfounded historically, Michel acknowledged, but today "the typical minority businessperson is someone who has a college degree, very often a graduate degree, has five to twelve years in a corporation, gets pissed off, hits a glass ceiling, gets fired, gets downsized, rightsized or whatever they call it, and takes his chips and starts a business." Whatever your needs, she says, her organization can match you with a supplier.

Michel also noted an insidious fact of life in business purchasing that keeps minority firms on the sidelines, unable to get into the game. In her experience, Michel said, purchasing departments in most companies sit near the bottom of the company totem pole, always struggling to justify their contribution to the bottom line. This already pressing agenda makes it doubly hard for an organization like hers to find someone in a company who will add minority considerations to the mix. Michel had recently attended a meeting of the Center of Advanced Purchasing Studies with some sixty vice presidents of purchasing from both foreign and domestic companies. The Center asked participants to rank fifty-three items that purchasing people were concerned about, including three items of concern to minority- and women-owned businesses. The hosts revealed the results at day's end—the minority and women's items had finished last.

Clearly from the above, minority purchasing doesn't "just happen." While a surfeit of minority firms may be able to offer your company just what it's looking for, don't expect them to come knocking on your door any time soon. They don't have the reach. And while you have every reason to expect a minority firm's products or services to fit your specifications, you may have to extend yourself in other aspects of the relationship because of the economic handicaps endemic in minority companies. Compiled from the advice of various experts, here are some ways to establish a successful minority purchasing relationship.

Establish a Goal.
The goal need not be numeric, but keep in mind that minorities constitute 28 percent of the population. One major department store chain has set a goal of always buying from the minority supplier if its product is at least equal to the majority competition's. If you worry that minority purchasing will unjustly take business away from majority suppliers who have served you well, try a couple of strategies suggested by Ben Cohen, a panelist with Michel at the Atlanta workshop, and workshop participant Liz Bankowski of Ben & Jerry's. The first is to leave existing supplier relationships intact, but buy from minority suppliers when purchasing new products or services. The second is to continue your purchasing levels with existing suppliers, but as your company's needs grow, expand the purchasing with minority vendors.

Utilize Matchmaking Organizations.
The nation's premier such outfit is the National Minority Supplier Development Council (NMSDC). Companies pay dues, based on a sliding scale, to join NMSDC, which then links them to minority-owned vendors. NMSDC certifies minority (African-American, Latino, Native American, and Asian-American) ownership through its forty-five affiliated regional councils, a necessary step considering the false fronts that many majority companies have created to take advantage of government minority preference programs. As of this writing, NMSDC represents some thirty-five hundred corporate members (both large and small companies) and offers a database and referral network of nearly fifteen thousand certified minority businesses. The Council also supports minority business development through its Business Consortium Fund, Inc., supported by corporations, state governments, and foundations. When certified minority companies with a contract or purchase order in hand from a NMSDC member need working capital to fulfill it, the Fund endeavors to supply the loan. (Contact information for NMSDC and other minority business matchmakers is listed in Resources.)

Set the Tone for Your Purchasing Department.
Given that people in the purchasing department may well resist doing things differently from how they have always done them, show them that minority purchasing is important to the company by contracting for legal, consulting, architectural, and other professional services with minority firms.

Treat Your Minority Vendors with Equal Consideration.
Says Michel: "Every day in corporate America, buyers make decisions based on personal feelings, personal relationships. If the bid comes in and it's not done quite right, they send it back to the company and they say, 'Redo it. We'll give you a few more days and we'll skip the deadline.' All we're saying to the broader corporate community is do the same thing for your minority suppliers that you do for your favorite suppliers."

Don't Base Judgments on One Bad Experience.
Deeply rooted prejudices about minorities sometimes take unconscious hold even in those who consider themselves enlightened in this area. Its most common form is generalization, as in: "All minority firms are screw-ups because Amalgamated Gizmo screwed up."

As she concluded her presentation, Michel sighed that corporate America's failure to use minority vendors was especially frustrating because they're missing a good bet: "In particular, consumer-based firms are looking more and more at people of color as customers. Let's be real about what really drives this. Minority consumers consume way out of proportion to their income level and if you're fighting off global competition and trying to stay in business, you want to expand your minority niche. That's the real reason most people are trying to address the diversity issue and the minority business issue." When they read about the commitment of a Ben & Jerry's, she noted, many minorities will gravitate to their products even if they have to travel outside their area to find them. "We are so desperate as a community that anything that looks like it's resonating with us, we are going to respond. And once we respond, we are damn loyal. I don't think there are any customers as loyal as minorities in terms of brands. Heck, we're still driving Cadillacs!"

valuable when left standing than when chopped down or burned. His approach integrates concern for the material and cultural needs of the rainforest's indigenous residents with environmentalists' concern for the forest itself and the nonhuman species that it harbors.

In 1989, Clay founded Cultural Survival Enterprises (CSE) as a project of the Cultural Survival organization. CSE works with rainforest communities to develop and expand markets for nontimber products—products that can be harvested without destroying forests—from which the communities can benefit as well. Ben & Jerry's signed on to this particular mission by developing Rainforest Crunch ice cream, which uses Brazil nuts and cashews indirectly purchased through Cultural Survival.

Rainforest Crunch also sweetens philanthropic support for the rainforest cause. Ben & Jerry's buys the candy in Rainforest Crunch from the nuts' direct purchaser, Community Products, Inc., of Montpelier, Vermont. CPI in turn distributes 40 percent of profits from the candy to rainforest preservation groups and other international environmental projects.

Validating Clay's original concept, a *Business Week* piece on sustainable development noted that the value of products harvested from standing forest *each year* can reach double the one-time revenue from logging. On the basis of food production alone, forests justify themselves economically—2,750 pounds of foods annually per acre of standing forest compared to 220 pounds of meat per acre of pasture on cleared forestland.

I had my own social mission purchasing experience when I bought lumber for an addition to my home from the Rogue Institute for Ecology and Economy, an organization that in a sense is trying to do for Northwest forests what Cultural Survival is attempting with tropical forests. The Institute, established in 1990, has developed a certification process for wood harvested in a sustainable manner. My wife and I needed the extra rooms in our house but felt bad about the resources it would take to build them. We solved our ethical dilemma by helping to create a market for sustainably harvested wood and pumping some money into the Institute's important work. And though, like many of the values-driven companies covered in these pages, we weren't seeking any recognition for our efforts, we got more than our share—a mention in a public radio feature broadcast throughout southern Oregon and northernmost California and a substantial quote in an Associated Press piece run in papers across the country.

The Rogue Institute also provided the lumber—300,000 board feet worth—for the Wal-Mart eco-demonstration store in Lawrence, Kansas (see page 168). (Contact information is in Resources.)

Setting Supplier Standards

In the early 1990s, large companies like Levi Strauss and Reebok raised the ethical crossbar in mainstream corporate purchasing by requiring that their contractors and suppliers also reflect the purchaser's core values. As apparel giants, both companies do considerable business in the Third World. Each has committed to similar standards regarding human rights, wages, and labor conditions. Neither will work with vendors that utilize forced, child, or prison labor; pay wages below minimum national standards; or subject workers to unsafe or unhealthy working conditions. In addition, Levi Strauss has declared that it will not do business in countries "where there are pervasive violations of basic human rights," and Reebok's Human Rights Production Standards announce that the company will seek business partners that share its commitment to workers' rights of freedom of association, including the right to organize and bargain collectively.

A number of environmentally sensitive business citizens endeavor to hold suppliers to the same strict code of minimally impacting the environment that they enforce in their own operations. The Body Shop asks all suppliers of raw and packaging materials to describe in writing the life cycle of the item, including all suppliers involved in its production. Nova Scotia–based Seagull Pewter has its suppliers complete a questionnaire that addresses the recyclability and biodegradability of their products and packaging, and the products' toxicity. The form also asks, "Is the product made under conditions supportive to the well-being of humans?" and "What steps has your company taken to create a sustainable environment?"

CHAPTER 10

Corporate Citizenship at Home and Abroad

THE PRESENT SUBJECT —corporate citizenship—may seem like a catch-all to cover a potpourri of topics that didn't fit into previous chapters. However, the topics discussed below share at least one attribute—a fairly clear window into a company's soul. The types of products and services a company designs and markets, the messages and methods it uses to sell them with, the way it forms and conducts business relationships in foreign lands, and the manner in which it interacts in the country's political life all reveal volumes about how executives approach the most basic of ethical business decisions—whether to serve or exploit.

Advertising and Marketing

I suspect most of us tell ourselves that ads don't affect us, that we don't pay attention to them, that we know what we want and that's what we buy, period. We zone out during TV commercials or hit the mute button on the remote control, tell the telemarketers where they can stick it, and dump the junk mail, unread, in the recycling bin so it can begin life anew as some other company's wasted message.

So why then do corporations spend $130 billion dollars a year on advertising? Why do they send between 60 and 70 billion ads a year through the mails? Obviously, because it works. Despite the fact that we don't put much stock in what advertisements tell us and that many of us tune out the content altogether, something still gets through. Name identification, for one thing—we may ignore ads, but if they're at all competently produced, we'll remember *whose* ad we're ignoring. For another thing, the low effectiveness rate (say, 2 percent for a well-designed direct mail campaign) still pays for itself, particularly given the tax deductibility of advertising expenses. Finally, subliminal content impresses itself upon us despite our conscious efforts to resist it.

And that's why advertising is more pervasive and obnoxious than ever. Not only does it holler to us from the commercial blocks on radio and television and in movie theaters but increasingly is embedded in the programming itself. On NBC pro football broadcasts in 1993, announcers always found a reason to analyze the "clean, efficient natural gas quarterback ratings," a chart of passing stats sponsored by the natural gas industry. The Bruce Willis movie blockbuster *Die Hard II* included as many as nineteen paid ads, noted Deborah Baldwin in *Common Cause* magazine. In the guise of extended mentions of "sponsorships," advertising infects "noncommercial" public radio and television. It drapes museum exhibits and the buildings that house them. Like foreign bodies invading our bloodstreams, it commandeers our phone lines and post office boxes. And if a Roswell, Georgia–based outfit called Space Marketing gets its way, it will even blight the heavens in the form of orbiting signs up to three quarters of a mile long, visible to the entire western hemisphere.

While waves of ads assault our well-defended beaches, a fifth column of marketing geniuses and complicitous media outlets is working behind the lines. Increasingly, corporations are turning to public relations firms to buoy up their marketing campaigns with precisely timed talk show appearances, sponsorships and, most perniciously, video news releases (VNRs).

As business watchdog Art Kleiner noted in the *San Francisco Bay Guardian*, network and independent station takeovers in recent years have left newsrooms nationwide with barebones budgets and staffs. Hungry for good visuals and program segments, and short on resources to develop their own, they turn to downloadable VNRs on satellite news services. There the PR firms lie in wait for them with prepackaged pap, often costumed as independently reported news stories which, Kleiner writes, "just happen to also promote the agency's clients." This "soft news" approach not only furthers name recognition but gives marketers something that advertising doesn't— credibility, which explains why we can expect to see even more of this tactic in the future.

Marketing has also contaminated our public schools. During the year that I was writing this book, I ventured into my local high school and was shocked to see, in the corridor leading to the lobby, framed posters advertising junk foods. To be fair, most of each poster's space was devoted to a positive, youth-oriented message on such topics as career, racism, and voting. However, prominently displayed below the message was the name and picture of a popular, youth-oriented snack food such as Snickers bars, Pepsi, and Doritos. Along the opposite wall sat three vending machines, one that dispensed juices and two that offered some of the foods the posters advertised.

The posters were placed in the corridor, I later discovered, by Whittle Communications, which runs similar "place-based" informative advertising campaigns in veterinary and doctors' offices. Whittle later abandoned "Connections," as the school project was called, because the company had figured out a better way to push its clients' products at students. And Rogue River High went for the new vehicle, too—Channel One, a 12-minute teen-oriented daily news show that includes two minutes of commercials. Whittle makes the program available for free and fattens the deal with loans of satellite dishes, VCRs, and TVs for any school that can guarantee a captive student audience. It's an offer that many underfunded schools such as Rogue River High can't resist.

As the subtlety and ubiquity of corporate marketing grows, so does its social impact:

• *Nearly all ads push a message—excessive consumption—that is increasingly out of step with an environmentally sustainable economy.*

• *Consumerism has also eroded community-minded values in general.* Ronald K. L. Collins and Michael F. Jacobson of the Center for the Study of Commercialism suggest that the selling of endless, needless consumption has made citizens callous about their civic responsibilities and thus vulnerable to anti-tax sentiment and its exploitation by disingenuous politicians."

• *Marketing is eroding the quality of public institutions and the contributions they make to culture and to national discourse.* In this area, mainstream business bears a double responsibility. Reagan-era tax cuts, sought and thus much applauded by mainstream business lobbies, starved public TV, museums, schools, libraries, and other institutions for operating capital and made them more susceptible to financial pressure from contributing corporations. Media scholar Herbert Schiller has noted how corporate involvement in museums leads to self-censorship by curators, who get skittish about scheduling exhibits with controversial themes that would offend business sponsors. This development strips art of one of its primary functions— social consciousness–raising—and, Schiller argues, communicates a veiled substitute message, that art is socially neutral: "The art object is abstracted from its social and historical contexts and becomes merely a product in itself—lovely perhaps, but without meaning or connection."

· *Direct pressure on the media from advertisers, as well as the media's self-censorship for commercial reasons, has degraded—and in some critical cases, devastated—national debate on key issues.* As has long been recognized, newspapers and magazines that do a lucrative business in cigarette ads have generally been reluctant to editorialize on the dangers of smoking or, obviously, call for a ban on cigarette advertising. Self-censorship and more overt forms of censorship by the media also eviscerated the public health-care debate of the mid-1990s. In 1993, the Campaign for Health Security, a citizens group advocating a Canadian-style, single-payer health care system, produced an ad advocating their approach but couldn't get most of the major city network affiliates they targeted to run it. According to David Corn, writing in *The Nation,* eight out of ten stations approached refused to carry the ad; in some cases, station executives or sales reps bluntly acknowledged protecting their insurance company clients or the industry in general. Meanwhile, of course, the insurance industry was blanketing the country with ads advocating various approaches that would preserve their function—and profits.

· *Advertising aimed at children exploits their innocence, financially pressures their parents, and profoundly affects the content of child-oriented media.* The cat wriggled all the way out of the bag in the 1980s, when the Reagan-era Federal Communications Commission (FCC) relaxed nearly all regulations controlling advertising and encouraging quality programming for children. Pre-Reagan, the content of a children's show could not be used to market products, and the number of commercials per hour was limited. Once those regulations were canceled, toy manufacturers predictably swarmed into the program production business, developing new toys in concert with programs to push them. As writers Nancy Carlsson-Paige and Diane Levin reported in the periodical *Dollars and Sense,* the ten best-selling toys all were connected to programs by December 1985. Less than two years later, toy companies were producing 80 percent of all children's programs.

Program-associated children's products and other heavily advertised toys also train little Susie and Billy to be thoughtless, frivolous consumers from their earliest years. Levin and Carlsson-Paige noted that the G.I. Joe fifty-item line turns over completely every two years. The Teenage Mutant Ninja Turtles logo was affixed to more than a thousand products, licensed by over two hundred companies, in readiness for the Ninja Turtle movie release. As for Barbie, heaven forbid that Ken should ever see her in the same outfit twice.

Perhaps parents could find some redeeming social value in all this if toymakers' invasion of the production studios had a beneficial effect on kids' programing content. However, in a sample week of fall programing surveyed by Concordia College (Moorhead, Minnesota) researchers, CBS's *Teenage Mutant Ninja Turtles* was the second most violent cartoon show (123 violent acts per hour), narrowly losing out to Fox's *X-Men* (129), another toy-associated show.

· *Advertising of dangerous products adversely affects the health of the nation and contributes to excessive health spending.* An RJR Nabisco advertising campaign, featuring ultra-cool cartoon dromedary Joe Camel, seems to have almost single-handedly expanded the appeal of smoking among teenagers. According to University of California at San Diego researcher John Pierce, the percentage of people starting to smoke suddenly began to rise in 1988 after a fifteen-year slide. The increase, mostly centered in the 10-to-20-year-old age group, coincided with the introduction of the Joe Camel ads. Since Joe's debut, teen smoking has been climbing by about 1 percent a year; prior to that time, it had been dropping by a similar amount. RJR denied that the ads were aimed at youth, but the company was certainly aware that most new smokers are teens and have been since at least 1980.

Few bought the RJR disavowal. In September 1993, attorneys general of twenty-seven states asked the Federal Trade Commission

(FTC) to ban the ads, as did FTC staff in a recommendation document. Also supporting a Joe-ban was Joe Camel creator Nicholas Price, a British artist who told *Newsday* he was "mortified" at how his character was being used.

· *Some advertising promotes racial, gender, and other socially destructive stereotypes.* Actually, in regards to race anyway, many major ads now reflect an increasingly multicultural society. Although commercials still rarely feature Hispanic and Asian faces, at least in starring roles, African-Americans now play a variety of parts, including professionals and executives. This is a real change—I remember a charcoal-filtered cigarette ad of 1960s vintage that promised "only the white touches your lips." In the fairly recent present, marketers worried both about turning off southern whites by showing African-Americans in superior positions and offending African-Americans by showing them as subservient, so often chose to not show them at all.

However, by 1993 or so, racial harmony had actually become a lucrative commercial theme, particularly in ads targeting youth. Young people recognize that they live in a multicultural world and embrace it; inner-city fashions, rap music, and all things Michael Jordan dominated American youth culture of all colors in the early 1990s. A survey by New York research firm BKG Youth, Inc., revealed that only 15 percent of teenagers polled said they would "never" date a person of another race.

To advertisers and their clients, such data mean that racial harmony sells—big-time, as was evident in a Kmart ad insert in my local newspaper in December 1993. The insert's clothing section featured a sleepwear-clad family standing by their Christmas tree. In the photo, Mom is a lovely African-American, as are young brother and sis. However, Dad is Caucasian, although his kinky dark hair and swarthy complexion might lead those made uncomfortable by black-white unions to project otherwise.

Given the increased buying power of women, another trend with no end in sight, advertisers have also been busily updating gender images. But not always in politically correct fashion. To some agencies and their clients, redressing the balance simply means occasionally focusing the camera on shapely men's buns, too. Women buy beer, but I watch enough television to know that the old warhorse theme, brew-guzzling-boys-at-bikini-beach, is hardly in danger of extinction.

Marketing can also serve positive social ends. In previous chapters, we've seen how Coors and Ashland Oil have supported educational initiatives through their regular advertising and marketing mechanisms. We've noted how Stonyfield Farm and The Body Shop forgo traditional advertising and marketing, relying on their aggressive citizenship to generate attention from the public. We've examined Esprit's groundbreaking ad discouraging needless consumerism. We've observed how numerous companies, rather than avoid controversy, have risked alienating customers by advertising their sentiments on important public issues such as the Gulf War and homophobia.

In one other example, a few companies have gone beyond exploiting racial harmony as a youth marketing theme to confronting it as an issue, using their ads as the communicator. In January 1993, the chairman of Mercedes-Benz responded to attacks on minorities by German skinhead groups by writing an "open letter," run as an advertisement, attacking racial intolerance. That same month, bootmaker Timberland Company of Hampton, New Hampshire, began a five-ad campaign against racism with a print piece headlined "Give Racism the Boot." Another in the series displays a Timberland product under the message, "This boot performs best when marching against hatred." The company placed the ads not only in the U.S. but also in European countries including Germany, a major Timberland market.

We've seen throughout these pages how good corporate citizens, including conscientious marketers and advertisers, bond both employees and customers to them, often for life. Still, there's no denying that cynical marketing sometimes pays. We've seen evidence of that in this very section. But those who choose to play that way risk costly social ricochet.

For instance, two companies that targeted their unhealthy, socially destructive products at African-Americans in the early 1990s saw all their research and development blow up in their faces when society voiced its opposition. Heileman Brewing Company designed its Powermaster malt liquor, with its higher-than-usual alcohol content, to appeal to low-income, inner-city African-Americans. But the Treasury Department's Bureau of Alcohol, Tobacco and Firearms withdrew approval of the product's name because it violated a ban on power claims for malt liquors. Heileman, in turn, abandoned the product. Earlier, R. J. Reynolds Tobacco canceled market tests of its Uptown cigarettes, targeted at African-American smokers, after widespread protests from African-American community leaders.

Socially Responsible Products and Services

Determining whether or not a product is socially appropriate is one of the most ethically complicated questions the public can ask of a company, or a company can ask of itself. A quick survey of the usual suspects plus one generally applauded product reveals the ambiguity of "social responsibility" when applied to products or services.

· Despite tobacco's undeniable harm to smokers, those exposed to exhaled smoke, and the cost of health care, I think most Americans defend current smokers' right to continue the habit. Tobacco is also a sacrament in the spiritual practices of many Native Americans.

· Although alcohol abuse leads to addiction, broken homes, ruined health, highway massacres, and industrial accidents, medical research suggests that, for some, moderate alcohol consumption may have beneficial health effects.

· Some ethical purists who otherwise praise Ben & Jerry's social stance reproach the company for promoting products with a high fat and sugar content. Of course, Ben & Jerry's never suggested that its customers make a seven course meal out of Cherry Garcia and Peace Pops. But should a truly responsible ice cream company be advising customers to eat only modest amounts, and explain why?

Finally, as already emphasized in Chapter 6, environmental degradation and depletion of natural resources has made nearly every current business activity, even those of the most environmentally idealistic companies, socially suspect. But putting that consideration aside for a moment, it's still almost impossible to determine whether or not a product is socially responsible without answering further questions about use, potential abuse, and marketing, among others. Toward that end, I offer the following as a test of social responsibility that might be applied to almost any product or service.

· *Does the product or service fulfill a social need or merely promote frivolous consumerism?*

· *Is the product designed for maximum durability and re-cyclability, or will it break down, go out of fashion, or become obsolete far before its potential useful life is over?*

· *Does the company disclose all harmful or unsafe ingredients or characteristics of the product?*

· *Does the company both warn consumers of the dangers of misuse and market the product in a manner that minimizes misuses?* Obviously, the mandated warnings on the sides of cigarette packs, already weakened by tobacco lobbies, do little to mitigate the social consequences when the product is pushed at naïve or poorly educated populations or, for example, tobacco-addicted pregnant women.

· *Is the product priced fairly in relation to its actual cost and with regard to its social impact?* The hugely profitable pharmaceutical industry came under considerable criticism in the early 1990s for excessively benefiting at the expense of customers, medical patients such as elderly people on fixed incomes, and the health care economy as a whole. The industry was at pains to explain why the cost of immunization rose 1,250 percent between 1981 and 1991. Another oft-cited example involved Johnson & Johnson, ironically known for being a good corporate citizen in many respects. In 1990, the company priced a new human colon cancer treatment at $1,300, the approximate price of competing products, as soon as the FDA approved it; essentially the same substance had been used for decades to deworm sheep, selling for $14 in that version.

Critics were also asking why U.S.-made drugs cost so much more here than in Canada, which controls prices as part of its national health care system. For instance, Upjohn's Xanax sold for $47.81 in the U.S. but only about a third as much ($16.92) across the northern border.

Drug companies countered complaints by noting that their research and development costs are high, and that White House–proposed price controls would inhibit their ability to develop important new medicines. However, most of that furious, costly lab work seems to make little impact on public health. The FDA classified about 80 percent of the drugs it approved between 1985 and 1990 as "copycats," drugs only marginally different from existing products. Even *Business Week* seemed skeptical in early 1993 about the industry's defense of its pricing practices.

· *Has the company taken significant steps to minimize the product's environmental impact, both in production and in use? Is the product or service maximally energy-efficient?*

· *Is the product or service advertised and marketed truthfully?*

· *Is the product or service priced so as to be affordable to the people to whom it's marketed?*

· *Does the company provide appropriate warranties, customer service, and customer support?*

Business responsibility for its products or services doesn't end with the above-mentioned issues, most of which revolve around product creation and marketing. Sometimes problems that the company claims weren't anticipated occur from the product's use. That raises three additional questions:

· *Does the company monitor its product or service to make sure that its impacts are positive?* Tobacco companies certainly have had no shortage of clues that something was wrong with their product— R. J. Reynolds, Jr., was among the millions killed by emphysema after years of heavy smoking.

· *Does the company respond adequately when problems do turn up?* The standard, of course, remains Johnson & Johnson's behavior following the Tylenol scare. In 1982, seven people died after ingesting Extra-Strength Tylenol capsules that had been laced with cyanide. The company instituted an immediate recall, at an estimated cost of over $100 million, although it had yet to determine whether it shared in the guilt. Company executives and representatives also spoke openly with the press, let CBS's *60 Minutes* probe where it would, and initiated communication with the health care community.

Johnson & Johnson's behavior shocked a cynical public. As James O'Toole has written, "Whether it was Richard Nixon and Watergate, GM and the Corvair, or Hooker Chemical and the Love Canal, the public had grown to expect an official denial followed by stonewalling on the facts of the incident." As it turned out, of course, the company had no legal responsibility whatsoever; a psychopath had tampered with the bottles after they left the plant. But when executives committed themselves to total openness, they didn't fully know how the incident had happened, how many people might be affected, or what their legal liability might be.

· *Is the company telling the truth when it says it didn't expect the problems that occurred?* After months of denials, Dow Corning

Corporation finally admitted in February 1992 that it had known for decades that its silicone gel breast implants might leak, and that many of its own employees had expressed serious concerns about them. However, in the weeks prior to its admission, according to *Business Week*, Dow Corning was still trying to discredit one of those employees, ex-company engineer Thomas Talcott. Talcott had warned the company about the leaks for years before quitting in protest in 1976. Subsequently, he helped lawyers for implant recipients and testified to the FDA about suppressed company documents.

In its admission of fault, the company continued to insist that the leaks could not cause cancer or other life-threatening problems. Its position was less than convincing, however, given not only its previous lack of candor but also its new admission that under certain conditions, a leak could lead to "persistent tissue inflammation."

The way a company responds to a crisis involving a product or a service with unintended negative consequences not only speaks volumes about the company's mettle but also has profound financial implications. Johnson & Johnson's response to the Tylenol poisoning proved to be correct not only morally but also strategically. Within two years, Tylenol, previously the best-selling drug in the country, had recovered all of its market share.

Of course, some viewed the outcome more skeptically. Cynics decried—or applauded, depending upon perspective—the company for pulling off a marketing coup, and undoubtedly J&J executives, whatever their original motivation, were never unaware of the public relations advantages of their actions. To most of America, Johnson & Johnson had revealed itself as that rarest of icons, a mega-corporation for the people. I agree with the majority and O'Toole that "clever marketing could never have concealed a cold corporate heart." Unfortunately, the company managed to squander some of that goodwill six years later with the pricing of a certain former sheep wormer (as mentioned above).

International Human Rights Issues

When Levi Strauss and Reebok conditioned their international purchasing and contracting on respect for human rights, they established a standard far above their own government's. We can only speculate how much farther the cause of international human rights might advance if offending regimes knew that their actions would inevitably dam the flow of American dollars and trade. But, in fact, the American government, captive to corporate campaign dollars, generally capitulates in such matters whenever pushed by business lobbies with less principled members than the above-mentioned apparel companies.

For example, in the years prior to the Gulf War, the U.S.-Iraqi Business Forum, an organization of firms dealing weapons to Iraq, successfully fought, with the Reagan administration's cooperation, congressional efforts to economically punish Saddam Hussein for his chemical attacks on the Kurds. The failure to penalize Iraq paved the way for the Iraqi arms buildup that eventually led to war. The Clinton administration failed to use the negotiations over the North American Free Trade Agreement (NAFTA) and General Agreement on Tariffs and Trade (GATT) to pressure for strong labor and human rights assurances. Not coincidentally, lax human and labor rights standards in the Third World serve the interests of corporations who would take advantage of a permanent source of cheap, docile workers.

Ironically, the government's failure in the human rights area puts corporations on the hot seat with regards to pressuring for human rights guarantees, since the public necessarily must look to them for action. In fact, the growing power of multinationals, the relaxing of international trade barriers, and the increasing flight of manufacturing from industrialized nations to Third World countries all make human rights the key corporate responsibility topic of the 1990s. True, the opportunity to exploit cheap labor in unsavory environments has never been greater. However, the spotlight on companies doing so has never been brighter, as Wal-Mart discovered the week of Christmas 1992.

To the corporation's considerable embarrassment that week, the news magazine show *Dateline NBC* ran a segment showing children working in a Bangladesh factory that manufactures clothes sold in Wal-Mart stores. The company refuted the program's charges, saying that "manufacturers have certified that no illegal child labor has ever been used in manufacturing Wal-Mart merchandise," but the denial hinged on the word "illegal," since much of America saw videotape of children at work. The legal work age in Bangladesh is fourteen, but factories there commonly hire younger children.

Unconvinced by Wal-Mart's denials, the Working Assets Citizens Funds were among those in the socially responsible investing movement divesting Wal-Mart stock. Another mainstay in the movement,

Franklin Research & Development, filed a shareholder resolution requesting that the company adopt vendor responsibility standards. After months of debating the issue with Franklin, Wal-Mart drew up new policies forbidding business with vendors using child, prison, or forced labor; the policies also established standards regarding such labor issues as discrimination, wages, work hours, and workplace health and safety. Just as important, the company committed to enforce the policies through on-site inspections.

Wal-Mart's response satisfied Franklin, which withdrew the resolution, but left much of the damage to the company's public image unrepaired. The *Dateline NBC* piece was noisy national news; I read about the company's reforms in *Business Ethics* magazine, a publication that most Americans don't know exists.

The Wal-Mart incident is yet another example of both the rapidly increasing influence of the socially responsible investing/consuming movement and the very different social considerations of doing business at the century's close. As more and more companies export manufacturing and import supplies, a snarling pack of multinational watchdogs monitors their every move. And behind them waits a bevy of news magazine shows hungry for exactly the sort of content that made such a splash on *Dateline NBC*.

After all, it wasn't Franklin or Working Assets that "ratted on" Wal-Mart to NBC. It was Jeff Fielder, official of the AFL-CIO, long irate over Wal-Mart's heavy trade in imported merchandise. And if a multinational no-no gets by Fielder, there are plenty of others to catch it— social investors and consumers anxious to dissociate their money from corporate transgressions; environmentalists outraged by multinationals exporting environmental degradation; religious organizations such as Interfaith Center on Corporate Responsibility hoping to inspire companies to higher levels of world citizenship; and of course, human rights groups.

Wal-Mart executives must wish now that they had been a little more proactive about establishing vendor standards, as many of their corporate colleagues have. Besides Reebok and Levi Strauss, the list of big companies enforcing vigorous supplier policies includes Home Depot, an all-around good citizen; Phillips–Van Heusen; and Sears. Levi Strauss in particular has made a dramatic show of applying its international standards by visiting all 600 of its worldwide suppliers, canceling contracts with about 30 (as of February 1993), and getting some 120 others to make specific reforms. (Among the suppliers fired was the Mariana Islands' Tan family, who reportedly held women in guarded compounds sewing pants for up to 74 hours a week.) The company also pulled all operations from Burma (Myanmar), where the military government in charge is considered one of the world's most persistent violators of human rights.

The Burma situation, in fact, illustrates the role that corporate actions play in either propping up or helping to undermine repressive international governments. The Burmese government crushed a peaceful pro-democracy uprising in 1988, killing thousands of pro-testers and imprisoning an even greater number. Since that time, the government's stranglehold on its people has only increased, and human rights violations along with it. According to a study by Franklin Research & Development, the government economically sustains its grip through revenues generated by foreign investment and export of the country's natural resources; some 60 percent of money obtained from foreign sources goes to the army.

In 1991, U.S. companies exported $23 million worth of goods and services to Burma and imported $27 million. U.S. trade with Burma also has profound environmental implications. Rainforest wood products are one of the principle U.S. imports from Burma; some 80 percent of the world's remaining teak rainforests stand there.

Corporations such as PepsiCo, Amoco, Dean Hardwoods, and Unocal minimize or deny their role in propping up the Burmese regime, professing political neutrality or arguing that they try "to improve conditions for the local population by providing employment, medical care and other benefits" (Amoco's words, essentially the same argument used by companies choosing to stay in South Africa during apartheid). But others ask how a company can avoid being politically involved in such a place. As Levi Strauss's manager of corporate communications Sabrina Johnson told Franklin, "Under current circumstances, it is not possible to do business in [Burma] without directly supporting the military government and its pervasive violations of human rights."

Of course, human rights issues are more complicated in some countries than they are in Burma. Again, in Bangladesh children below legal age commonly work outside a weakly enforced law and provide much-needed support for their families. When Levi applied its new code of conduct there, the immediate effect would have left forty children without jobs, and their families in danger of destitution. The company solved the dilemma by committing to help educate the kids until they turn fourteen, with the suppliers agreeing to pay them regular wages until that time. But the situation still points out the ethical ambiguities of applying our standards to a far different culture overseas.

The one unfortunate consequence of investors, unions, activists, and consumers pressuring companies to behave themselves internationally is that such ambiguities can get buried in the process. That is, the company may act broadly and preemptively to avoid bad publicity at home without Levi Strauss–type concern for unfortunate side-effects abroad. Nor are all accusations accurate or fair. McDonald's found itself lumped together with other fast-food chains when it was accused of getting its burgers via cattle grazed on cleared rainforest land. Following the "perception is reality" guideline, McDonald's banned the practice in writing even though the company was apparently innocent in practice.

I sympathize with executives' frustration in such circumstances. I also bemoan the damage done to the credibility of more discerning progressive protests. But acknowledging such difficult situations is no reason to throw the baby out with the bathwater, especially when that baby is a suffering human being in a foreign factory or militarily held country. The defeat of apartheid in South Africa tells us all we need to know about the relative effects of corporate involvement and disengagement in a repressive environment. Western corporate involvement kept the South African economy strong and financially supported the government, thus helping to underwrite the status quo. But once large numbers of Western corporations began to abandon operations there, Pretoria realized that apartheid's end was nigh and involved itself proactively in dismantling the system.

The fact that most companies that left did so for financial, not ethical, reasons—because they were losing money, because they were suffering boycotts at home, because of the financial and physical risks of staying, because their stock was being dumped by principled investors—only shows how the ethical and the financial become tightly intertwined over time. Now that apartheid is history, some companies will inevitably forget these important lessons. However, just outside their doors wait plenty of shareholders, citizen organizations, union officials, and news magazine shows anxious to remind them.

Other Issues Involving International Operations

Although most Americans recognize bald social irresponsibility such as the marketing of unsafe products, the subtler social consequences of putting profits first often escape public attention, particularly when those effects are complex and occur far from our borders. However, with the ever-expanding involvement of multinationals in the Third World, such consequences are multiplying at a rate that will soon be hard for anyone to ignore.

· In Africa, Western economic aid policies, tailored to the needs of multinationals, have undercut African economic development efforts and led to widespread war and famine. Aid is predicated on recipient countries dropping self-sufficiency goals and restructuring their economies to serve Western interests—developing export crops to pay off debt to Western institutions and importing goods that the nation is unable to produce. As writer Gayle Smith, a veteran of African relief efforts, has pointed out, the above syndrome overlapped with another—a weapons-dealers–fueled Cold War competition between the U.S. and Soviet Union to arm despotic governments. The combination produced predictably disastrous results: the contemporary cycle of war and famine that has devastated Ethiopia, Somalia, Sudan, and many other African nations.

· In Mexico, as in other Third World nations, multinational influence is displacing the relatively healthy native diet with corporate-produced junk food that is not only more costly, but also far less nutritious. Under government policies favorable to multinationals, more and more prime agricultural land now grows cash crops for export and feed crops for cattle-raising, reducing the supply of traditional food staples. The trend stands to deepen the country's malnourishment problem, which already affects about half the population and leads to high infant mortality, low birth weight, and developmental dysfunctions.

· In Guatemala, cheap loans through such institutions as the Agency for International Development and the World Bank have also reinforced an agro-export development path favorable to U.S. transnational companies. According to *The Multinational Monitor,* land devoted to cotton, one of the most heavily pesticide-sprayed crops, increased by 2,140 percent from 1956 to 1980, after a CIA-backed coup in 1954. By the 1970s, levels of DDT in mother's milk and human flesh grew to the highest in the world, 185 times the limits set by the World Health Organization. Meanwhile, the intense pesticide applications have created succeeding generations of pesticide-resistant insects, causing applications to increase from eight to forty times per year over two decades' time, and pesticide runoffs, carried away by the heavy Central American rains, to contaminate Pacific Ocean fisheries and drinking-water supplies. Rates of pesticide poisoning among agricultural workers, unprotected by safety equipment, have also soared.

As dire as the above scenarios seem, some are unfolding in a way that foretells a more hopeful outcome. For one thing, the design of developed nations' assistance to undeveloped nations has been so insensitive and short-sighted that flocks of chickens are coming home to roost. In Guatemala, for instance, the spiraling need for pesticides created by nontraditional agricultural methods has increased production costs and depleted the soil, severely compromising crop yields and driving many small farmers out of business. In turn, local populations are now more aware of the need to participate in decisions regarding how their economy should be developed and their resources used. At home, as we've seen, offending multinationals face increasing exposure by citizens' groups and media, a critical consideration particularly for companies marketing consumer goods.

Other signs of hope come from the good examples set by conscientious companies doing international business. I visited one such outfit in October 1993, Shaman Pharmaceuticals, a development-stage company located in South San Francisco. As the company name implies, Shaman's entire raison d'être revolves around Third World ventures. Specifically, company "ethnobotanists" collaborate with native healers to identify tropical medicinal plants that have a history of folk use. Although it's surely the hippest pharmaceutical company going, Shaman's focus boasts a far more practical rationale. Its reliance on native expertise reduces the time and money needed to find promising compounds and get them into clinical trials, and its insistence on a history of substantial previous use reduces the probability of danger to humans.

In the hands of another company, such an approach might mean the usual exploitation of native culture and plunder of tropical resources. But Shaman professes to care as much about preserving biodiversity and forest cultures as it does its own survival, and its policies cement those priorities in place. "Part of our selection criteria is that you have to be able to sustainably harvest the plant, not create a shortage," Lisa Conte, president and CEO, explains as we sit in her office in the company's adobe-colored headquarters. "The plant we're using now [at the time, the two drugs Shaman was testing clinically came from the same plant] is a weed. It's what's called a pioneer species. When land is cleared, it's the first plant to reestablish itself. If our research turns out a billion-dollar drug, it would only require one tenth of one percent of the world's supply of this plant."

Sustainable harvesting also figures into what Shaman calls its "reciprocity guidelines," its multipronged approach to compensating native communities for their cooperation. "If a plant they show us is the one," Conte says, "we create a locally owned and managed industry for them and we teach them all about sustainable harvesting. We don't let them just pull trees for us, give us what we need, and then not repair it. We pay a premium price for the plant and give them an economic means of earning money that is a direct alternative to the incentives motivating them to destroy the rainforest.

"Our concept is that poverty is the only thing that makes them clear the rainforest. Some cattle rancher says, 'I'll give you a dollar a tree,' or whatever the amount is, and that money is a fortune, the only way they have of earning enough money to bring in medical supplies or food or build a water system or whatever. We create the same kind of economic opportunity but through a sustainable harvesting solution."

Creating a local, sustainable industry is only Shaman's mid-range form of benefiting native communities. Short-term compensation usually begins even before actual work with the community has started. Steven King, the company's vice president of ethnobotany and conservation, has pointed out that conventional pharmaceutical companies generally make rewards to native helpers contingent on successful development of a product, a process that usually takes ten to fifteen years. However, King writes, "Indigenous people typically have immediate—often urgent—needs."

"Before we even go into a community," Conte tells me, "we ask the community, 'What can we do in the short term to tell you we're for real?' In one case, we extended an existing landing strip before we ever went into the community to work. [The Quichua community in the Ecuadoran Amazon had requested this for emergency medical evacuations and other travel needs.] We've helped with water well systems, medical supplies. We've helped by creating an annual stipend for a shaman's assistant. He used to have to leave six months of the year to make money to support his family. Now, we pay him to maintain his apprenticeship as a shaman."

Like a company-wide profit-sharing plan, Shaman's long-term compensation to native peoples recognizes the contributions of all collaborators, not just the one with the hot idea, or in this case, the one who identifies the right plant. Once products come to market, Shaman will distribute a portion of the profits to all communities and countries in which they've worked. (The plan includes profits generated by products not sourced in native communities, such as products licensed from another company.) Administering the distribution will be the Healing Forest Conservancy, an independent nonprofit conservation organization created by Shaman, which will consult both a multilateral advisory board and representatives from the regions that will receive benefits.

Answering concerns that leaders of a Peruvian association of indigenous peoples expressed to King and Conte in 1993, Shaman now credits native populations as the original scientific discoverers of, and experimenters with, medicinal plants in the company's scientific and educational writings. The company meets another expressed wish by sharing the results of its research with forest communities, since Shaman might conceivably uncover a use for the plant that natives hadn't realized. The company also distributes results of its studies on sustainable management of medicinal plants with interested government ministries, nonprofits, nongovernmental organizations, and other scientists to further international conservation and reforestation efforts.

Like that of other mission-driven firms, Shaman's conservationist passion runs far deeper than a long-term business interest. Company scientists and executives have lectured everyone from elementary school audiences to members of Congress about the importance of conserving tropical forests and the various human, plant, and animal communities they house.

Obviously, Shaman's constructive approach to Third World commerce is a boon to rainforests and the people who live there. But what's it doing for Shaman? For one thing, it's bonded its work force to the company like epoxy. Says Trish Flaster, botanical sourcing manager, who has joined us in Lisa's office, "I don't think that this is just a job to most people. I can't speak for everyone who works here but I know that the people I work closest with care deeply about bio- and cultural diversity and that extends to our backyard here." I ask about turnover. Trish replies, "There's none," and she and Lisa laugh as if the notion of leaving was absurd. Lisa then reminds her of two people who had left in the last two years. That's out of a 90-person work force at the time of my visit.

Shaman's employee loyalty can't be entirely attributed to the conservation mission. Under Conte, Shaman is a generous, familial employer, offering flextime, stock ownership, free lunch provided on-site to strengthen work relationships, and frequent parties, picnics, and other social activities. Employees everywhere want their work lives to be meaningful; at Shaman, every aspect of the operation seems to have been socially considered, from its "green, green, green" (Trish's description) recycling and purchasing, to its E-mail system to reduce paper use, to its close monitoring of the compassion of its animal testing.

The company also demonstrates a subthesis of this book, that social sensitivity often signifies unusually sharp business acumen as well. In its primary current activity—identifying useful plants and getting them into clinical trial—Shaman far outstrips its competition. For example, the typical pharmaceutical company may screen thousands of plants to find one with promise; Shaman has been finding one prospect for every two tested (about 290 active extracts total as of December 1993, "perhaps the richest and most diverse product pipeline ever developed in a three-year period," according to S. G. Warburg Securities analysts). Where most companies take two to six years to get a drug to the human clinical trial stage, Shaman's first product made it in sixteen months, with another one following eight months later.

The likelihood of those products making it through to FDA approval is also tremendously high, since they've been used for thousand of years by traditional cultures. Yet don't expect another company to be cloning the Shaman concept anytime soon. For one thing, Shaman has all but locked up the supply of tropical forest ethnobotanists. For another, its sympathy for forest communities and their issues has gained it the inside track with the indigenous expertise as well.

TOWARD A SET OF INTERNATIONAL OPERATING PRINCIPLES

New Consumer is a British, charitably supported public interest research organization. Its book *The Global Consumer,* a socially responsible consumers' guide to the products of multinationals, asks the following questions about companies. The list is not a bad start for multinationals to ask themselves if they want to be a positive force in the host economy.

· Are local people involved in decisions that affect their lives?
· To what extent are communities or countries dependent on a product for their survival?
· What is done to protect workers from unsafe machinery or chemicals?
· Are basic rights denied specific groups of workers or ethnic minorities?
· To what extent do dollars gained for goods exported from the host country improve the incomes of the host's poor?
· Who decides whether food or export crops are to be grown?
· Do the local people have the opportunity to add value to their exported crops by making manufactured products?
· What is being done to ensure that fairer prices are paid for Third World products?
· Do multinationals close local factories to search for still cheaper labor?
· Does the company take into account its impact on the host community?
· Is the industry sustainable or does it destroy the means of survival?
· Can local people organize to improve their working conditions?
· How do wages and working hours compare with reasonable standards in the host country?

Participating in Politics

Until the U.S. Congress passes meaningful campaign finance reform, the interests of the American public, the planet, and the Third World will continue to be held hostage to a narrow, often avaricious corporate agenda. Not that all corporate political activity serves destructive purposes. When the Bush administration fought family leave legislation, Stride Rite loudly declared its support for the bill, pointing to the economic advantages of its own programs for working parents. When the same administration tried to undercut civil rights legislation, AT&T and a number of other majors replied, Not on my account!

Nevertheless, most corporate lobbying recognizes the interests of only one group of stakeholders, its stockholders, leaving employees, taxpayers, customers, and communities to fend for themselves in a very rigged game. Not only can business lobbies build a far bigger war chest than most any public interest group that might oppose them, but they manipulate the mass media with the club of their advertising dollars and their deployment of master spin doctors from public relations firms. By 1993, they had so influenced the public debate on entitlements and the role of government that a Democratic president was leading the charge against welfare for poor mothers while what Ralph Nader calls "aid to dependent corporations" remained largely undiscussed.

Nor is socially influential corporate lobbying confined to the political arena. In fact, some destructive campaigns come gift-wrapped to look very much like social consciousness. As reported by Monte Paulson of Detroit's *Metro Times,* the huge chemical company Imperial Chemical Industries (ICI) foots the entire expense for National Breast Cancer Awareness Month (BCAM) and has since the event's inception, conditioned on approval of all copy for BCAM posters, ads, and pamphlets. "Not surprisingly," writes Paulson, "carcinogens are *never* mentioned in BCAM's widely distributed literature" despite mounting evidence connecting breast cancer to exposure to chlorine-based chemicals, the financial backbone of chemical giants like ICI. A Canadian government environmental agency estimates that one third of the toxic chemicals dumped in the St. Lawrence River come from a Quebec-based ICI subsidiary.

Of course, lobbying and other corporate campaigns can be waged in the public interest as easily as they can against it. Other principled companies have made their mark by refusing to play the influence game. Here are a few alternative paths.

Refrain from Political Activity.
Pitney Bowes neither contributes to political action committees (PACs) nor backs political candidates.

Join Socially Sensitive Business Lobbying Organizations.
The most important of these, at the national level anyway, is the
fledgling Businesses for Social Responsibility (BSR), formed in 1992.
BSR seeks to be the public policy voice for an alternative vision of
business health, one that incorporates such long-term perspectives as
environmental responsibility and social equity. In a nutshell, BSR
promotes a sustainable economy. Members include such mainstream
companies as Stride Rite Shoes, Lotus Development, Philadelphia
Coca-Cola Bottling Company, and Reebok, in addition to such usual
suspects as Ben & Jerry's, Rhino Records, Hanna Andersson, Esprit,
Stonyfield Farm Yogurt, The Body Shop USA, Rejuvenation Lamp &
Fixture, The Calvert Group, Rodale Press, and Aveda. Typical of
BSR's orientation was its 1992 announcement of opposition to then
Vice President Dan Quayle's Council on Competitiveness. "BSR
members contend that pursuing short-term profits at the expense of
workers, consumers, or the environment is not 'pro-business,'" a BSR
piece on the Council read.

In some cities and communities, progressive-minded businesses
have also allied to represent socially responsible business values at the
local level. For example, Hanna Andersson and Rejuvenation Lamp
& Fixture belong to a local chapter of BSR that has formed in
Portland, Oregon.

Participate in Political Activity in the Public Interest.
As implied by the rise of organizations such as BSR, when values-
driven companies do participate in political campaigns, you'll often
find them on the opposite side from the mainstream business community. Contemporary business ethic may forgive companies for fighting
for their own narrow interests at the public expense or even justify it
("What's good for General Motors . . ." and all that), but public-
minded companies reject this rationale as a cop-out.

That's not to say there's a progressive business "position." "Some
things we're in favor of in terms of increased community control and
less government make us bedfellows with the far right," Stonyfield's
Gary Hirshberg told me. By the same token, Stonyfield has assisted
progressive candidates in its conservative home state of New Hampshire, backed Planned Parenthood and the pro-choice movement in
general, was a signee to the *New York Times* ad protesting the Gulf
War, and by nearly any measure is one of the most social-minded
companies in the country. As discussed in Chapter 4, some otherwise

progressive companies oppose unionization of their work force, but those numbers too include some of the most generous, caring employers in America.

In fact, many of the more compassionately run companies are led by fiercely independent thinkers who won't be bound by either business or progressive orthodoxies. But it's not hard to guess why rebels like Ben Cohen or Anita Roddick dominate the territory of responsible business. After all, it's still a rebellious notion that business concerns, ethical or strategic, can't be separated from human or planetary ones.

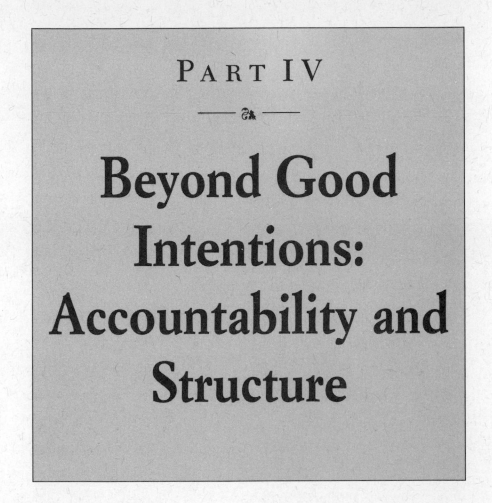

PART IV

Beyond Good
Intentions:
Accountability and
Structure

CHAPTER 11

Leadership by Example: Setting the Tone and Following Through

YOU CAN PICK OUT IN A MINUTE those companies led by principled people, because employees love to invoke their names. When I visited Home Depot's Atlanta headquarters, manager of environmental marketing Mark Eisen made it clear that it was the public-spirited goals of "Bernie and Arthur" (company founders Chairman Bernie Marcus and President Arthur Blank, whom everybody at headquarters seem to call, affectionately, by their first names) that freed him to push the envelope on the company's environmental citizenship. At NationsBank's Atlanta offices, the name of CEO Hugh McColl came up over and over when I spoke to employees and to vice president of corporate personnel Edith Banta about the company's work/family programs. Clearly, it was McColl's unequivocal support for the initiative that gave both employees and those administering the program the confidence to use the generous policies exactly as written.

That managers and employees should feel free to simply follow policy may seem like a given. However, at many companies, social policies come shrouded in double messages. Gretchen Fields, now human resources manager at the exceptionally family-friendly Hanna

Andersson, told me about the problems of being a working mother at a previous employer: "The bank had a policy whereby you could use sick-leave days for child emergencies. But I was told by my supervisor never to call in saying that I was staying home for a sick child."

At values-driven companies such as Hanna Andersson, which by virtue of their smaller size tend to be more intimate outfits anyway, the tone set by company leaders absolutely defines the company. In fact, when you spend time with Hanna's Gun Denhart, as well as Rejuvenation Lamp & Fixture's Jim Kelly, Just Desserts' Elliot Hoffman, Shaman Pharmaceuticals' Lisa Conte, Stonyfield Farm Yogurt's Gary Hirshberg, Emerald Valley Kitchen's Mel Bankoff, and Deja Shoe's Julie Lewis and Bruce McGregor, you understand just what a values-driven company really is—a commercial extension of a values-driven person.

Nevertheless, while a company's social stance inevitably originates in the executive suite, executives themselves aren't always the best judges of how the company is doing in regard to its stated mission, as the best leaders know. The employees near the bottom of the chain of command may see compromises and outright violations that executives overlook, or even perpetuate. Outside observers may notice the same.

Nor is executive modeling, even when exemplary, usually sufficient to perpetuate a company's social goals. Without structure, social initiatives often dissipate into so much wishful thinking. The topics covered below, assessing ethical performance and institutionalizing ethical standards, reveal the difference between a few good intentions and serious social business.

Social, Environmental, and Ethical Audits—Measuring Company Conscience

"We've learned that a social assessment is an essential part of being a socially responsible company. It's the only way to answer the question of how are we doing. Most importantly, it allows us to integrate the social mission into our agenda."

The author of those remarks isn't an executive of some mainstream company newly thinking about the social implications of its operation. It's Liz Bankowski of Ben & Jerry's, the epitome of socially responsible business in most aspects of its affairs, speaking to the Social

Venture Network at a 1993 conference in Atlanta. Ben & Jerry's social accomplishments get loads of attention. What is less known about the company is its courage in examining the gaps between its ideals and actualities, and its willingness to share those failings with the world.

Since 1988, the company has compiled what it calls a social performance report and published the results in its annual report to shareholders. But not as an exercise in self-flagellation—as Bankowski indicated. A company can hardly claim to be socially concerned, much less "responsible," if it isn't willing to ask itself the hard questions that reveal the truth behind its rhetoric.

The term most often used to describe a formal social assessment is "audit." Although social audit goals vary both with the party performing the assessment and the company examined, audits fall into three rough categories.

Environmental Audits

This grouping includes such subgroups as energy audits, which measure energy efficiency and, in more discerning cases, the energy use embedded in the company's products and services; waste audits, which measure the company's contributions to the solid-waste stream; product audits, which we mentioned in Chapter 7 by their other name, life-cycle analyses; and comprehensive environmental audits, which examine the company's total environmental performance.

Environmental audits differ in intent as well as type. According to some surveys, as many as 90 percent of large companies conduct environmental audits, but some of these are strictly legalistic, measuring only compliance with existing laws and regulations. In other cases, executives use audits to make an initial appraisal before instituting environmental upgrades. At the far end are those who employ the audit process to move their companies toward not just environmental excellence but sustainability.

As in most areas of environmental responsibility, European nations have forged way ahead of the U.S. in seeing both the ecological and competitive benefits of environmental auditing. According to Joel Makower, the European Community seems to be moving toward a voluntary, and ultimately mandatory, "internal environmental protection system" based on formal audits, reporting of findings, follow-up reforms, and environmental certification of products and plants.

The most forward-looking approach to auditing is that taken by the Elmwood Institute; then again, when it comes to protecting the environment, the future is already here. Elmwood, an ecological think tank in Berkeley, California, founded by well-known physicist and author Fritjof Capra, stresses the "deep ecology" approach to corporate environmental behavior. In essence, Elmwood promotes a conceptual shift in business from dominating nature to partnering with her. Obviously, Elmwood also hopes to nudge the audit process past the goal of compliance with politically compromised rules and regulatory guidelines. Executives serious about their companies' environmental citizenship as well as concerned that their investments in environmental upgrades have long-term viability should carefully consider Elmwood's perspective. (See Resources.)

Social Audits.
Although some public relations–minded companies publish "social reports" highlighting select good deeds, the art of true social auditing remains in an infant state today. However, values-driven outfits like Ben & Jerry's are doing their best to articulate and advance the process. Bankowski shared much of what the company had learned at the SVN conference, including why they like the term "social performance report" better than "audit":

> We find traditional financial audits to be increasingly inaccessible. They do not illuminate, they do not educate, and most importantly they lead us to devalue that which we cannot measure. Essentially what we are measuring in a social performance report are value-based decisions and choices that we make every day in the course of doing business. Much of this is quantifiable and should be measured to establish baselines and progress—workplace benefits, amount of energy used per unit of production, percentage of materials recycled, percentage of waste reduced, diversity of the organization including vendors and other business partners, pay equity, percent of profits given back to the community, and in our case tons of ice cream given away. Quantifiable data, and there is more.
>
> But some value-based decisions are not quantifiable. Things like a plant-siting decision where there are conflicting social and environmental issues. The quality of the relationships with our neighbors. Two years of an unsuccessful effort to source peaches from black family farmers who are losing their farms at more alarming rates than even white family farmers.
>
> It's also hard to measure that which is experiential, the soul of the organization. We can count the numbers of opportunities and ways that

we have created access to the social mission for everyone who works at Ben & Jerry's but we cannot begin to assess the impact, the transformation in thinking.

Ben & Jerry's 1993 report evaluated social performance in five broad areas: employees, ecology, customers, community, and openness of the system. Another improvement in the report process concerns the reliance on an objective auditor. For the company's first three reports, staff compiled the data and an outside party reviewed them and reported findings to the shareholders. For example, Control Data Corporation founder William C. Norris, a leading thinker on the social role of business, reviewed the 1989 report. Now the company hires the outside expert—in 1992 Milton Moskowitz, in 1993 Paul Hawken—to conduct the entire analysis.

Despite Ben & Jerry's efforts on behalf of social reporting, its leaders relinquish all proprietary interest in the process. Again, Bankowski: "Our major advice to all of you is don't wait for somebody else to figure it out and don't wait for a perfect tool. I would pass on the same advice I get from a farmer in Vermont when it comes time to pick strawberries. He tells me, 'Just put your bucket down where you are and start there.' "

Ethics Audits.
As Frank Navran puts it, values are what you say you believe, ethics are how you actually behave, and ethics audits measure the difference. A much narrower and less lofty focus than social responsibility, ethical consistency counts at any company that wants to maximize its quality, customer satisfaction, and employee performance. The audit also reveals how deeply employees have absorbed the company culture and how well management has communicated that culture to the work force.

Perhaps most important, an ethics audit can diagnose the cause of thorny problems. If employees think management cares more about production than safety or playing by the rules, their actions may lead to expensive, embarrassing, and sometimes dangerous regulatory violations. When employees are angry because management gives double messages on integrity or puts too much pressure on them to produce, they may quietly punish the organization by sabotaging its efforts.

In fact, ethical gaps can cause just as much trouble even when sabotage isn't the intent. Navran tells the story of a corporate client frustrated by customer service representatives cutting off callers in midsentence, which the reps blamed on problems in the phone system, and incorrect customer billings. Convinced the problems were electronic, management spent considerable time and money trying to track down the gremlin in their computer system before an audit performed by Navran Associates located it in the company culture.

Essentially, employees resented that a company that professed to value excellent customer service was pressuring them to meet what they felt were hopeless sales and calls-answered quotas. As follow-up interviews revealed, reps who fell behind had been hanging up on customers as soon as the calls were logged, and charging sales to callers who didn't buy anything. (By the time the company corrected the billing, the employee would have met the monthly quota.) Without the audit, management might never have learned how its overly aggressive approach had undermined its purpose.

An ethical audit can reveal a wealth of useful data to executives committed to quality and excellence. How aware are employees of the company's standards and policies? How do employees perceive the congruency of management behavior with stated company standards? How do employees feel about the ethics of the company they work for (and about themselves for working there)? Before employees can care about their contribution, they must care about their employer.

Popular auditing tools and processes, among several others, include the "Integrity Audit," a computer-scored multiple choice questionnaire developed by the Center for Ethics, Responsibilities, and Values at the College of St. Catherine (St. Paul); the "Values and Vulnerabilities Assessment," created by the Ethics Resource Center (Washington, D.C.) and driven by information gathered anonymously in interviews and focus groups; and Navran Associates' "Ethics Quick Test," which like the ERC test measures a company's ethical congruence. (See Resources for contact information.)

In the same way a psychotherapy patient can undermine the goals of therapy by concealing uncomfortable information from the therapist, a company can subvert the value of an audit by doing a quick fix-up in time for its self-examination. Experts recommend that the audit be seen as a movie of a work-in-progress, not a snapshot of a pretty moment in time.

Still, hanging one's dirty laundry out for all the world to see can lead to some uncomfortable moments, as Ben & Jerry's leaders discovered when *Newsweek* writer Carolyn Friday pounced all over the failings uncovered by Paul Hawken's review of the company. Buried near the end of the July 1993 magazine story was Hawken's finding that "an overwhelming number of employees are happy with the company and their work" (Friday's words), but she had conveyed quite the opposite impression by putting the controversial elements up front. What the writer neglected to mention altogether was management's courage and resolve.

Writing about the audit later, Hawken asserted, "I can attest that their status as the leading social pioneer in commerce is safe for at least another year. They are an outstanding company. Are there flaws? Of course. Welcome to planet Earth. But the people at Ben & Jerry's are relaxed and unflinching in their willingness to look at, discuss, and deal with problems."

Reasons besides courage and commitment will be compelling more and more companies to audit their operations in the future.

· Groups like the Council on Economic Priorities, the Interfaith Center on Corporate Responsibility, and various social investment services conduct their own social "audits" of leading American companies and publish the results. Increasing numbers of citizens consult this information before making purchase and investment decisions.

· Particularly in the environmental arena, companies doing international business are increasingly having to meet much tougher standards than ours to market their products in environmentally progressive nations in the EC. Eventually, they may have to submit to a mandatory international audit just to certify their products.

· Government regulators look favorably on companies that institutionalize ethical safeguards, of which audits are an example, and forthrightly disclose violations. For instance, Makower notes Justice Department guidelines that emphasize the importance of voluntary disclosure, cooperation, compliance programs, and remedial behavior in determining whether the department will press charges for environmental violations. Navran points out that a "good faith ethics management program and cooperation with authorities" can cause fines for ethical violations to be lowered by as much as 80 percent. As of this writing, the maximum fine for ethical violations is $290 million.

Beyond Auditing—Institutionalizing Ethics and Social Responsibility

Obviously, auditing can't prevent all ethics problems, even when management follows up the audit by spot-fixing problems. In effect, an audit is to company health what a physical exam is to personal health. A physical exam doesn't prevent the onset of diseases. At best, it may identify a few conditions in the pre-crisis stage. Preventing problems means adopting healthful habits—that is, *structuring* prevention. The same goes for the leaders of companies, who must institutionalize ethics and social responsibility to ensure a top-notch social performance, not to mention impress federal enforcement authorities.

Institutionalizing social performance begins with declaring the company's intentions, priorities, values, and standards to the work force, and ultimately the world, through a well-articulated company credo. Most companies of some size and durability have one. Then again, most hotel rooms have a Bible in the dresser drawer, so there's clearly more to drafting an effective credo than writing a few lofty thoughts down on paper. Here's what the experts recommend.

Invite Input from All Levels of the Work Force.
Credos written primarily by CEOs tend to be impractical, because CEOs are often unaware of the full spectrum of day-to-day ethical dilemmas faced by middle management and lower-level employees. Credos drafted by attorneys may fail the inspirational and aspirational test, focusing on narrow, legalistic concerns and written in cold or negative language. A credo written with the full participation of the work force can be an exciting exercise in workplace democracy and helps ensure ownership of the encoded principles.

Distribute the Credo to All Employees.
The Ethics Research Center, with clients including Standard Oil of Ohio and Chase Manhattan Bank, surveyed a large number of corporate executives and found that only a few had circulated their codes below a certain level of management or even posted them in a common area of the workplace.

*Acknowledge a Responsibility Broader than Simply Playing
by the Rules.*
Many executives as well as economists like Milton Friedman would
fight me on this one. By and large, however, industrial polluters play
by the rules. So do tobacco companies. Of course, their money and
power helps shape the rules in the first place.

The mission statement of a company that recognizes its social
responsibilities will, at minimum, acknowledge that it represents the
interests of all its stakeholders, not just its shareholders. For example,
Seventh Generation's statement declares: "Our stakeholders include
customers, employees, shareholders, vendors, directors, advisors, and
everyone else who is affected by our existence." Values-driven companies such as the many we've met in these pages also state their
commitment to using their company as a vehicle to better society. In
their statement of "caring capitalism," Ben & Jerry's promises to
"operate the company in a way that actively recognizes the central
role that business plays in the structure of society by initiating innovative ways to improve the quality of life of a broad community—local,
national, and international," a promise they continue to keep.

Beyond adopting an individual company credo, companies now have
the opportunity to publicly declare their support of shared community interests regarding the environment, fairness to employees with
HIV/AIDS, recycling, and other vital social issues. Various public-
interest organizations have drafted sets of issue-specific business principles and sought corporate signatories. Recall, for example, our
discussion of the Citizen's Commission on AIDS, its "Ten Principles
for AIDS in the Workplace," and its over six hundred corporate
signees.

In the environmental arena, the International Chamber of Commerce (ICC) sponsors a sixteen-point "Business Charter for Sustainable Development," and it too had gathered over six hundred
corporate endorsements internationally as of this writing, including
Allied Signal, Eastman Kodak, Apple, Dow Chemical, Du Pont, Union
Carbide, Merck, and Procter & Gamble. In this country, the Coalition
for Environmentally Responsible Economies (CERES), founded by
Joan Bavaria of social investment advisor Franklin Research & Investment, has drawn up a set of environmental business standards called
the CERES Principles (formerly the Valdez Principles). In early 1993,

petroleum giant Sun Company became the first Fortune 500 company to sign on, joining a roster of usual suspects such as Patagonia. Sun's commitment signals an effort by oil-related companies to clean up their image post-Valdez (incident, not Principles). We can hope it also signals a march of American companies, many of which have been pressed by shareholder resolutions to join CERES, toward greater public accountability.

Since talk *is* cheap, the real work and investment of institutionalizing social performance begins after the credo is drafted and the chosen set of principles signed. Ethics management concerns all business leaders, whether they aspire to social responsibility or not, so let's look first at basic ethical management structures before considering the larger social frameworks of more values-driven companies. A soup-to-nuts discussion of ethical corporate structures—Navran calls his system Total Ethics Management (TEM)—is beyond the scope of this section, but important considerations include the following.

Involving Top Management in Regular Ethics Oversight: No company can ensure ethical performance if its leaders don't take regular and sincere interest in values and compliance—with internal and legal standards—issues. In Navran's model, the ombudsperson chairs an executive ethics committee on which sit the president; the chief executive, chief financial, and chief operating officers; and all functional and regional vice presidents.

Establishing Alternative Reporting Routes for Ethics Violations: We visited this idea in Chapter 5 in connection with workplace democracy. Essentially, line employees must have some way of reporting ethical or safety problems to upper management without going through their supervisor in case the supervisor is the problem. In many companies, an ethics ombudsperson serves this function. In any case, Navran and other ethics experts stress that some reporting route always be accessible to employees, that it be a safe route, and that the route lead ultimately to the executive suite. Ombudspersons often serve other roles as well, such as receiving and investigating complaints by public agencies or officials, or private citizens; interpreting rules for questioning employees; and providing guidance to employees facing ethical dilemmas.

Guaranteeing Employees That Whistle-Blowing Will Not Be Punished: Says Navran, "At one of my client companies right now, we're calling the ombudsman's office 'the office of the safe haven.'"

Rewarding Ethical Behavior: Navran points out that both positively recognizing ethical performance and decisively sanctioning ethics violations communicate to the work force that the company stands behind its values statements.

Regularly Measuring Ethics Performance and Making the Indicated Corrections: Audits are one such measuring tool. Navran advises his clients that "ethics effectiveness should be treated as just another success indicator."

Companies with proactive social missions tend to be smaller, less formally structured outfits. The lack of structure can be an advantage in maintaining the sense of social calling but can also lead to embarrassing oversights in the same area. Ben & Jerry's was well into its transition from founder to professional management when it invited Liz Bankowski, a veteran liberal political aide and campaigner, to join its board. "I would frequently ask [the board] why we didn't staff our social mission," Bankowski told us at the above-mentioned Atlanta conference, recalling her first meetings. "We were certainly staffing our quality mission and our financial mission. And the response to that was the company made me director of social mission development, a position that had not previously existed, and left it to me to define the job."

As it turned out, the company had outgrown its social design but it took an outsider to notice it and do something about it. "My job is to facilitate the handoff of the social mission from the founders and the visionaries to the entire organization. As you know, Ben & Jerry's is now a national company with over $130 million in sales, and unfortunately we can no longer rely on simply personal interactions to communicate our social mission and our values. We know we need to create systems that institute social responsibility in our day-to-day business practices."

At Stonyfield Farm Yogurt, employees at all levels can join the Social Vision Team, an informal committee whose charge, according to a company document, is "to fulfill, communicate, and enhance the company's mission to be environmentally and socially responsible." CEO Gary Hirshberg's yearly lunches with each employee also serve as a forum for employees to reach company leadership with social, safety, and quality concerns and suggestions. Hirshberg credits much of the company's phenomenal growth to ideas generated in those meetings: "We're now over a hundred people. I don't know what we'll do when we're over three hundred people. I'll just be obese, I guess."

Particularly at smaller companies, styles of structuring the social vision will vary as widely as the personal styles of their founders. But it matters less how companies carry through on their values than that they do carry through. Although talk is cheap, hypocrisy is expensive.

POSTSCRIPT

—— 🐝 ——

IN PREVIOUS CHAPTERS, we've seen example after example of companies that break all the contemporary rules of business regarding social commitments and yet either don't suffer for their pledges or thrive in large part because of them.

We've observed the mysterious mathematics of companies like Stonyfield Farm Yogurt and Cin-Made Corporation, reminiscent of the enterprising Milo Minderbinder in the novel *Catch-22*, who would buy eggs at three cents, sell them for two, and turn a profit.

We've noted companies like Southwire and The Robbins Company that turned around their slumping fortunes not by slashing their work force to ribbons, with all its consequent individual and social fallout, but by taking advantage of the embedded financial advantages in eco-friendly strategies such as pollution control, waste and packaging reduction, and especially, energy efficiency.

We've noticed how companies like Rejuvenation Lamp & Fixture and Just Desserts, along with Stonyfield Farm, Ben & Jerry's, The Body Shop, Patagonia, and many others take gutsy stands on community issues only to bond their customers and employees to them even more tightly.

We've also questioned the usual defense offered by Fortune 500 executives that they are constrained socially by the interests of their stockholders. Of course, these same executives rarely mention the growing percentage of shareholders that press them to take socially responsible stands such as committing to public environmental audits, signing on to the CERES Principles, ending animal testing, curtailing business in repressive regimes, and so forth. We've noticed too that Dayton-Hudson addressed its responsibility to shareholders by polling them on a social issue, rather than deciding for them that they cared only for profits.

We've seen as well how Wall Street analysts didn't mind that Shaman Pharmaceuticals builds partnerships with indigenous peoples instead of exploiting their knowledge and labor, and conserves biodiversity instead of packaging and selling it. Shaman's initial public offering in early 1993 attracted so much interest that the company had to expand the number of shares from 2.5 to 3 million.

We've considered the impact that business could have on the environmental crisis and the plight of minorities just by doing what's in its own long-term interest, angling to capture future markets in environmentally appropriate technology and hiring and promoting more multicultural employees. In fact, as regards the environment, we've seen that while our corporations continue to view the world through the lens of the quarterly report, forward-looking governments in Japan and the European Community are, through progressive environmental policies, positioning their domestic companies to dominate the environmental markets that will themselves dominate the future economy. We've examined other strategies such as minority and environmental purchasing that may not produce direct financial gains but do pay off socially with no apparent financial cost.

Indeed, we've focused on the pragmatic advantages of socially responsible practices because I don't think they are widely recognized and because I agree with Gary Hirshberg that if these practices can't justify themselves financially, then they have no prominent part to play in future commerce.

But there's another incentive that drives the socially responsible business leaders I know, an incentive that operates irrespective of dollars and cents issues. As the social stakes grow higher in coming decades, I suspect this motivation will begin to manifest itself more widely in mainstream business circles as well. It has to do with the fact that most people who head corporations also head families. Hirshberg speaks for dozens of people who contributed to this project when he says: "I have three young children. I feel that I've got to stand up for a better world individually, as a leader within my own company, and as an inspiration to other companies. This is how I sleep at night."

Resources

— 🐝 —

AUDITING: ENVIRONMENTAL AND ETHICAL

Environmental

Green Audit, Inc.
1220 Broadway
New York, NY 10001
Tel. 212/594-0479

Ethics

"Integrity Audit"
Center for Ethics, Responsibilities, and Values
College of St. Catherine
2004 Randolph Ave.
St. Paul, MN 55105
Tel. 612/690-6646

"Values and Vulnerabilities Assessment"
Ethics Resource Center
600 New Hampshire Ave., NW
Washington, DC 20037
Tel. 202/333-3419

"Ethics Quick Test"
See Navran Associates under General/Management Consulting *below.*

BENEFITS

Helen Mills
The Mills Group

10600 Arrowhead Dr., Ste. 190
Fairfax, VA 22030
Tel. 703/352-8248
Employee benefits consulting and brokerage firm with expertise in socially responsible programs.

BUSINESS DEVELOPMENT

National Partnership for Social Enterprises
6 Brigade Hill Rd.
Morristown, NJ 07960
Tel. 201/540-1900
Finds partners for and helps build businesses that address social problems.

CHARITABLE GIVING

Council of Federations
8608 McHenry St., Ste. 1000
Vienna, VA 22180
Tel. 703/222-3861
Cooperative representative of hundreds of local, national, and international charities, united to assist employers in broadening their workplace giving campaigns. Through this organization, employers can gain access to such federations as Earth Share, a federation of environmental charities; International Service Agencies, the agencies of which provide relief and long-term development solutions for deprivation in world crises and impoverished nations; and National/United Service Agencies, serving a wide range of human care issues.

Gifts in Kind America
700 North Fairfax St., Ste. 300
Alexandria, VA 22314
Tel. 703/836-2121
Assists companies in donating products and services to the nonprofit sector.

DIVERSE HIRING AND PROMOTING

American Association of Retired People (AARP)
Joan Kelly, Business Partnerships

601 E St., NW
Washington, DC 20049
Offers a number of free publications and services regarding hiring and working with older workers.

Harbridge House
1 International Pl.
Boston, MA 02110
Tel. 617/478-3600
Diversity consultant.

Institute of Women's Policy Research
1400 20th St., NW, Ste. 104
Washington, DC 20036
Tel. 202/785-5100
Nonprofit research organization. Excellent source of research regarding women's and family-related work issues.

INTER-RACE
600 21st Ave. S., Box 212
Augsburg College
Minneapolis, MN 55454
Tel. 612/339-0820
Provides research, curricula, training, and consultation to promote interracial interaction, including work interactions.

The National Association of Female Executives
127 W. 24th St.
New York, NY 10011
Tel. 212/645-0770

See also Executive Search *below.*

EMPLOYEE OWNERSHIP

National Center for Employee Ownership
2201 Broadway, Ste. 807
Oakland, CA 94612-3024
Tel. 415/272-9461

ENVIRONMENTAL

Cin-Made Corp.
1780 Dreman Ave.
Cincinnati, OH 45223
Tel. 513/681-3600
Makes recycled custom paper-based containers.

East-West Development Foundation
55 Temple Pl.
Boston, MA 02111
Tel. 617/542-1234
Exports donated, intact computer equipment to Russia and Eastern Europe.

Energy Investment, Inc.
286 Congress St., 2nd Fl.
Boston, MA 02110
Tel. 617/482-8228
Specializes in financing and developing energy conservation projects for major industrial and commercial endeavors. Interfaces with demand-side management utility programs.

European-American Chamber of Commerce
Tel. 202/347-9292
For information on the European Commission's eco-label.

The Forest Partnership, Inc.
PO Box 426, 431 Pine St.
Burlington, VT 05402-0426
Tel. 802/865-1111
Promotes sustainable forestry.

The Green Business Letter
Tilden Press, Inc.
1526 Connecticut Ave., NW
Washington, DC 20036
Tel. 800/955-GREEN
Helps companies make environmentally appropriate decisions. Edited by Joel Makower.

Hexacomb, Inc.
75 Tristate
Lincolnshire, IL 60069
Tel. 708/317-1991
Produces paper honeycomb, a recyclable alternative to wood, corrugated cardboard, and plastic foam.

Highland Energy Group
885 Arapaho Ave.
Boulder, CO 80302
Tel. 303/786-9310
Designs energy-saving programs.

William McDonough Architects
116 E. 27th St.
New York, NY 10016
Tel. 212/481-1111
One of the world's leading architects and a specialist in environmental and energy efficient design. Designed the Wal-Mart "eco-store."

Moulded Fibre Technology, Inc.
82 Scott Dr.
Westbrook, ME 04092
Tel. 207/772-5535
Produces cushion packaging from 100 percent post-consumer recycled materials.

National Office Paper Recycling Project
U.S. Conference of Mayors
1620 I St., NW
Washington, DC 20006
Tel. 202/223-3089

Pacific Materials Exchange and National Materials Exchange Network
Tel. 509/325-0507 Information
    800/858-6625 Network access number (for modems)
PME is a regional materials exchange. The Network is a PME-created data service linking all U.S. waste exchanges and several in Canada.

Partnership for Plastics Progress
1275 K St., NW, Ste. 400
Washington, DC 20005
Tel. 800/243-5790
    202/371-5319

Rocky Mountain Institute
1739 Snowmass Creek Rd.
Old Snowmass, CO 81654
Tel. 303/927-3851
Amory Lovin's organization.

The Rogue Institute for Ecology and Economy
PO Box 3213
Ashland, OR 97520
Tel. 503/482-2307
Promotes sustainable forestry and has limited ability to supply sustainably harvested lumber.

Solid Waste Information Clearinghouse Hotline
Solid Waste Association of America
PO Box 7219
Silver Spring, MD 20910
Tel. 800/677-9424
Advice includes assistance with outmoded computer equipment.

Environmental Business Consultants

The Elmwood Institute
PO Box 5765
Berkeley, CA 94705
Tel. 510/845-4595

Seventh Generation
Colchester, VT 05446-1672
Tel. 802/655-6777

William Shireman
California Futures
601 Crocker Road

Sacramento, CA 95864
Tel. 916/482-5200

EXECUTIVE SEARCH

Isaacson, Miller, Inc.
334 Boylston St., Ste. 500
Boston, MA 02116-3805
Tel. 617/262-6500
Specializes in serving socially responsible companies and organizations, and in recruiting women and minorities.

GENERAL

Organizations

The Business Enterprise Trust
204 Junipero Serra Blvd.
Stanford, CA 94305
Tel. 415/321-5100
Promotes business responsibility and produces educational and video materials.

Businesses for Social Responsibility (BSR)
1850 M St.
Washington, DC 20036
Tel. 202/872-5206
A national trade association for socially responsible businesses, large and small.

Council on Economic Priorities
30 Irving Pl.
New York, NY 10003
Tel. 212/420-1133
Promotes and researches corporate responsibility.

Franklin Research & Development Co.
711 Atlantic Ave., 5th Fl.
Boston, MA 02111
Tel. 617/423-6655

Helps develop social criteria for investors, among other services for ethical investing movement.

New England Business Association for Social Responsibility
(NEBASR)
524 Boston Post Rd.
Wayland, MA 01778
Tel. 617/890-4542
A major regional trade association for socially responsible businesses.

Social Venture Network (SVN)
1388 Sutter St., Ste. 1010
San Francisco, CA 94109
Tel. 415/771-4308
A network of successful entrepreneurs, investors, executives, and intellectuals promoting just, sustainable business activity. Membership limited to applicants of some substance—e.g., businesses with at least $5 million in annual sales.

Management Counsulting
Susan Davis
Capital Missions Co.
2400 E. Main St., Ste. 103
St. Charles, IL 60174
Tel. 708/876-1101
Specializes in social venture capital and marketing.

Frank Navran
Navran Associates
3037 Wembley Ridge
Atlanta, GA 30340-4716
Tel. 800/635-9540
Specializes in business ethics, a subset of social responsibility.

Robert Rosen
Healthy Companies
1420 16th St., NW
Washington, DC 20036
Tel. 202/234-9288

Brings a strong behavioral sciences and teaching background to work-place issues.

HIV/AIDS

American Red Cross
(Contact your local chapter.)
Presents basic education programs for managers and employees.

Centers for Disease Control
Tel. 800/458-5231
Publishes a comprehensive guide, Business Responds to AIDS.

\Citizens Commission on AIDS for New York City and Northern New
Jersey
121 Ave. of the Americas, 6th Fl.
New York, NY 10013
Tel. 212/925-5290

National AIDS Clearinghouse
Tel. 800/458-5231: Monday–Friday, 9A.M.–7P.M.
    800/243-7012: TDD for the hearing-impaired
Provides information to employers on national, state, and local re-sources regarding HIV/AIDS in the workplace. Reference specialists help employers identify videos, posters, brochures, guidelines, and other educational materials suitable for the workplace. Most such materials are free of charge. Refers employers to low- or no-cost HIV/ AIDS program providers in local communities.

National Leadership Coalition on AIDS
1150 17th St., NW
Washington, DC 20036
Tel. 202/429-0930
Provides information, specific workplace strategies, civic support, and leadership.

HUMAN RIGHTS

"Thinking Globally: Franklin's Insight Study of International Corpo-rate Responsibility"

Franklin Research & Development
See General *above.*
Study of how human rights standards affect corporations, how companies can influence specific human rights issues, and related social investment information.

MINORITY AND OTHER SOCIAL PURCHASING

Cultural Survival, Inc.
215 First St.
Cambridge, MA 02142
Tel. 617/621-3818
Markets tropical forest commodities in North America and Europe to create value for standing forest and preserve indigenous cultures.

National Minority Supplier Development Council, Inc.
15 W. 39th St., 9th Fl.
New York, NY 10018
Tel. 212/944-2430
The country's largest organization building mutually beneficial relationships between purchasers and minority-owned vendor businesses.

Red Pages: Businesses Across Indian America
LaCourse Communications Corp.
PO Box 431
Toppenish, WA 98948-0431
Directory of Native-American businesses.

Tribal Assets Management
One Monument Way
PO Box 4834
Portland, ME 04101
Tel. 207/772-1765
Represents Native American vendors.

MARKETING

Constance Best
Best & Co.
PO Box One

Yorkville, CA 95494
Tel. 707/895-3616
Management and marketing services on consultant basis for socially responsible companies with innovative products and services.

Cone Communications, Inc.
90 Canal St.
Boston, MA 02114
Tel. 617/227-2111
Specialist in cause-related efforts.

Co-op America
1850 M St., NW
Washington, DC 20036
Tel. 202/872-5307
Links consumer members and socially responsible businesses through a catalog and annual directory.

OFFICE SUPPLIES AND SERVICES

Conservatree Paper Co.
10 Lombard St.
San Francisco, CA 94111
Tel. 415/433-1068
Distributes recycled printing and writing papers.

Working Assets Credit Card Services
Tel. 800/522-7759

Working Assets Long-Distance Telephone Service
Tel. 800/788-8588

Working Assets Travel Service
Tel. 800/332-3637

PRINCIPLES

Coalition for Environmentally Reponsible Economies (CERES)
711 Atlantic Ave., 5th Fl.
Boston, MA 02111
Tel. 617/451-0927

Ten Principles for the Workplace
Citizens Commission on AIDS
See HIV/AIDS *above.*

Mobro Principles
c/o Conservatree
See Office Supplies *above.*

SEXUAL HARASSMENT

9to5, National Association of Working Women
614 Superior Ave., NW
Cleveland, OH 44113
Tel. 216/566-9308

WORK/FAMILY ISSUES

Boston University Center on Work and Family
1 University Rd.
Boston, MA 02115
Tel. 617/353-7225

Families and Work Institute
330 Seventh Ave.
New York, NY 10001
Tel. 212/465-2044

The Partnership Group
840 West Main St.
Lansdale, PA 19446
Tel. 800/847-5437

Work/Family Directions
930 Commonwealth Ave. W.
Boston, MA 02215
Tel. 617/278-4000

Work Options Group
1810 30th St., Ste. G
Boulder, CO 80301
Tel. 303/440-0293
Advises on dependent care, including consortium formation for small companies.

Corson, Ben, John Downey, et al., and Council on Economic Priorities. *Shopping for a Better World.* New York: Council on Economic Priorities, 1990.

Domini, Amy, and Peter Kinder. *Ethical Investing.* New York: Addison-Wesley, 1986.

Donaldson, John. *Key Issues in Business Ethics.* London: Academic Press, 1989.

The Earthworks Group. *50 Simple Things Your Business Can Do to Save the Earth.* Berkeley, CA: Earth Works Press, 1991.

Faludi, Susan. *Backlash: The Undeclared War Against American Women.* New York: Anchor Books, 1991.

Freudberg, David. *The Corporate Conscience: Money, Power, and Responsible Business.* New York: Amacom, 1986.

Garfield, Charles. *Second to None: How the Smartest Companies Put People First.* Homewood, IL: Business One Irwin, 1992.

Glouchevitch, Philip. *Juggernaut: The German Way of Business: Why It Is Transforming Europe—and the World.* New York: Simon & Schuster, 1992.

Goldsmith, Edward, Nicholas Hildyard, et al. *Imperiled Planet.* Cambridge, MA: MIT Press, 1990.

Gore, Al. *Earth in the Balance: Ecoology and the Human Spirit.* Boston: Houghton Mifflin, 1992.

Green, Mark, ed., for the Citizens Transition Project. *Changing America: Blueprints for the New Administration.* New York: Newmarket Press, 1992.

Hanson, Kirk, Bob Rosen, and Milton Moskowitz. "Best Practices." Presented at the Social Venture Network Spring Conference, April 4, 1993, Lake Lanier Islands, GA.

Hanson, Kirk, and Eric Weaver, eds. *Social Venture Network Best Practices Source Book.* (Unpublished; compiled by Social Venture Network for its members, 1993.)

Hawken, Paul. *Growing a Business.* New York: Fireside, 1987.

Heilbroner, Robert L., and Lester C. Thurow. *Economics Explained.* New York: Simon & Schuster, 1987.

Judd, Elizabeth. *Investing with a Social Conscience.* New York: Pharos Books, 1990.

Selected Bibliography

— ❧ —

In addition to interviews and visits to companies, the present work is based on hundreds of source materials including newspaper articles, magazine articles, in-house company documents, books, academic journal articles, research reports, speeches, and television and radio broadcasts. The following are some of the most important of those sources, including periodicals consulted on an ongoing basis.

BOOKS

Alperson, Myra, Alice Tepper Marlin, et al. *The Better World Investment Guide.* New York: Prentice-Hall, 1991.

Bankowski, Liz. "Ben & Jerry's Social Audit." Presented at the Social Venture Network Spring Conference, April 2, 1993, Lake Lanier Islands, GA.

Bartlett, Donald L., and James B. Steele. *America: What Went Wrong?* Kansas City, MO: Andrews and McMeel, 1992.

Birnbach, Lisa. *Going to Work: A Unique Guided Tour Through Corporate America.* New York: Villard Books, 1988.

Booth, Helen, and Kenneth Bertsch. *The MacBride Principles and U.S. Companies in Northern Ireland.* Washington, DC: Investor Responsibility Research Center, 1989.

Brown, Lester. *Building a Sustainable Society.* New York: W. W. Norton, 1981.

Brown, Lester, et al. *State of the World 1989.* New York: W. W. Norton, 1989.

Brown, Lester R., et al. *State of the World 1992.* New York: W. W. Norton, 1992.

Cohen, Gary, and John O'Conner, eds. *Fighting Toxics.* Washington, DC: Island Press, 1990.

Lappé, Frances Moore, and Joseph Collins; *Food First*. Boston: Houghton Mifflin, 1977.

Levering, Robert, and Milton Moskowitz. *The 100 Best Companies to Work For in America*. New York: Currency, 1993.

Lydenberg, Steven, Alice Tepper Marlin, Sean O'Brien Strub, and Council on Economic Priorities. *Rating America's Corporate Conscience*. New York: Addison-Wesley, 1986.

Makower, Joel. *The E Factor: The Bottom Line Approach to Environmentally Responsible Business*. New York: Times Books, 1993.

Meadows, Donella, Dennis Meadows, and Jorgen Randers. *Beyond the Limits: Confronting Global Collapse, Envisioning a Sustainable Future*. Post Mills, VT: Chelsea Green, 1992.

Meeker-Lowry, Susan. *Economics as if the Earth Really Mattered*. Philadelphia: New Society, 1988.

Michel, Harriet, Ben Cohen, and Rebecca Adamson. "Minority Sourcing: How to Purchase Products and Services That Can Strengthen the Community." Presented at the Social Venture Network Spring Conference, April 2, 1993, Lake Lanier Islands, GA.

Morgan, Hal, and Kerry Tucker. *Companies That Care: The Most Family-Friendly Companies in America—What They Offer, and How They Got That Way*. New York: Fireside, 1991.

Nader, Ralph. "Keynote Address on Corporate Responsibility." Presented at the Social Venture Network Spring Conference, April 3, 1993, Lake Lanier Islands, GA.

Navran, Frank, *The 1993 Desktop Guide to Total Ethics Management*. Atlanta: Navran Associates, 1992.

Oelhaf, Robert C. *Organic Agriculture*. Montclair, NJ: Allanheld, Osmun, 1978.

O'Toole, James. *Vanguard Management: Redesigning the Corporate Future*. Garden City, NY: Doubleday, 1985.

Plotkin, Mark, and Lisa Famolare. *Sustainable Harvest and Marketing of Rain Forest Products*. Washington, DC: Island Press, 1992.

Ray, Michael, and Alan Rinzler, eds. *The New Paradigm in Business*. New York: Jeremy P. Tarcher/Perigee, 1993.

Reiss, Bob. *The Road to Extrema*. New York: Summit Books, 1992.

Resnick, Idrian, Laurie McDonald, Margarite Kyen, and Thad Jackson. "Corporate Responsibility." Panel Discussion at the Social Venture Network Spring Conference, April 3, 1993, Lake Lanier Islands, GA.

Roddick, Anita, Adele Simmons, Karen Nussbaum, and Marie Wilson. "Women in Power." Presented at the Social Venture Network Spring Conference, April 2, 1993, Lake Lanier Islands, GA.

Rosen, Robert H. *The Healthy Company: Eight Strategies to Develop People, Productivity, and Profits.* Los Angeles: Jeremy P. Tarcher, 1991.

Schaeffer, John, ed. *Alternative Energy Sourcebook.* Ukiah, CA: Real Goods Trading Corporation, 1992.

Shames, Laurence. *The Hunger for More: Searching for Values in an Age of Greed.* New York: Times Books, 1989.

Smith, Hedrick. *The Power Game.* New York: Random House, 1988.

Stack, Jack. "The Great Game of Business." Presented at the Social Venture Network Spring Conference, April 3, 1993, Lake Lanier Islands, GA.

Tepper Marlin, Alice, Joan Claybrook, John Richard, Lindywe Mabuze, and Ralph Nader. "When Big Companies Do Bad Things." Presented at the Social Venture Network Spring Conference, April 4, 1993, Lake Lanier Islands, GA.

Wilkins, Alan L. *Developing Corporate Character: How to Successfully Change an Organization Without Destroying It.* San Francisco: Jossey-Bass, 1989.

PERIODICALS

I drew from the following publications not on an occasional basis but consistently, because of their dependable elucidation of business issues.

Business & Society Review
Management Reports, Inc.
25-13 Old Kings Highway N., Ste. 107
Darien, CT 06820
Superior coverage of social issues related to commerce from widely disparate points of view.

Business Ethics
52 S. 10th St., Ste. 110
Minneapolis, MN 55403
Tel. 612/962-4700
Covers both ethical and social issues with consistent style and insight.

Business Week
McGraw-Hill Publishing Co.
PO Box 421
Hightstown, NJ 08520-9493
Tel. 800/635-1200
Although mainstream corporate in its point of view, not regressive or Tory in its editorial stance, particularly regarding social issues affecting, or affected by, business. Some of its writers are quite progressive. Excellent features on social topics.

In Business
419 State Ave.
Emmaus, PA 18049
Tel. 215/967-4136
Covers business opportunities and developments related to environmental issues.

Inc.
PO Box 54129
Boulder, CO 80322-4129
Tel. 800/234-0999
Focuses on smaller companies. Frequently covers topics related to business responsibility and profiles responsible companies.

The Multinational Monitor
PO Box 19405
Washington, DC 20036
Tel. 202/387-8030
Its writers tend to be antibusiness in their orientation. Then again, they monitor corporate behavior at its worst, in particular its offenses off-shore.

The Nation
PO Box 10791
Des Moines, IA 50347-0791
Tel. 800/333-8536
*Irritating because of its knee-jerk mistrust of all for-profit intention,
this publication is nevertheless required reading for anyone wanting
to understand the political/corporate interface. And it is certainly no
more prejudiced in its way than the mainstream and business presses
are in theirs.*

The Utne Reader
1624 Harmon Pl.
Minneapolis, MN 55403
Tel. 612/338-5040
*Culls outstanding articles from the alternative press. Good coverage
of business and work issues. Although most writers take a progressive
stance, publication gives considerable space to opposing points of
view, making it consistently provocative reading.*

Index

—— ❧ ——

About the Author

———— ❧ ————

Alan Reder's first book, *Investing from the Heart: The Guide to Socially Responsible Investing and Money Management* (co-written with Jack A. Brill; Crown, 1992), was a selection of both Book-of-the-Month Club and Fortune Book Club, and is now a standard reference on the subject. His work has appeared in numerous major periodicals and in the anthology *Being a Father* (John Muir, 1990). Reder lives in Rogue River, Oregon, with his wife, Hyiah, and their daughter, Ariel.